Andrew T. Cummings

Myth and Mythology

Tales from the Ancient World

Astrolog Publishing House

Cover Design: Na'ama Yaffe

P. O. Box 1123, Hod Hasharon 45111, Israel
Tel: 972-9-7412044
Fax: 972-9-7442714

ISBN 965-494-188-0

Published by
Astrolog Publishing House 2004

For Contents (and Index) see page 300

Gods of Greece and Rome

Foreword

We tend to mention the Greek and Roman gods together in one breathe, since in many cases they are identical or parallel to one another. The myths of the Greek gods have become united with those of their Roman counterparts. In order to make sense of the significance of this hodgepodge, this book will give attention to two interesting points of view, neither of which takes the myths at face value. We will keep these two views foremost as we examine the subject of the Greek-Roman deities through the eyes of ancient writers and poets such as the Greek Hesiod and Homer, and the Roman Ovid and Virgil.

The first point of view is the ethno-historical, based on the theory that the Greek pantheon and the Roman pantheon were each never fully conceived, but were gradually formed during the pre-classical period. This view is marked by the belief that the gods were conceived of during the time of the wandering of the ancient tribes, and that while intermingling with one another these groups also mixed the images of their gods, causing the amalgamations which we recognize today.

Robert Graves, the renowned mythology researcher, holds that the so called wars of the gods were but analogies to the battles between certain groups and tribes, each being represented in the myths by its local gods. According to this opinion, myths of marriage between gods and goddesses and/or victory of one god over another, are actually representations of the exchange of power between the different tribes, describing both the struggles and the cooperation between them. Sometimes, in order to appease a losing tribe or to bring about harmony, the god of one tribe would "marry" the female counterpart of the opposing tribe.

The second fascinating view (which does not negate the previously mentioned ethno-historical view) is purported by Jean Shimoda Bolen. This is a Jungian theory which is based on the tradition of archetypes. According to this view, each of the gods is an archetype of a particular human attribute, and taken together, these archetypes make up the whole of the collection of human qualities. Each god offers in his character and his facets a particular aspect of humanity. A deeper look at the values and qualities of the gods allows us to discover within them familiar human images and sometimes, our very selves.

Classical mythology played a vital role in the molding of the Western world. Numerous names and terms were borrowed and adapted from mythological figures and are found in the differing areas of science – astrology, botany, zoology, and more. Countless ancient myths have permeated the arts, providing rich fodder for writers, poets, painters, sculptors, and musicians. The true secret to the myths' popularity is not found it the fact that the stories are interesting, which they surely are, but more so in our ability to personally connect to them, and to subjectively understand them.

In this book, I describe the characters and the story behind each of the many gods as they appear in the ancient prose. You the reader, however, are invited to read with a free imagination, to see them as human figures, as so human-like they are! Alternatively you may want to see them as representative of the cosmic forces which surround the universe, or to contemplate the perceptions of those who lived thousands of years before our time.

Creation

Chaos

In his essay, Theogony, the famous poet Hesiod describes the creation of the world, beginning with "Chaos was the very first that came to be." The chain of events took place such that Chaos existed alone at the start, with no hint as to its creator or how it came to be. From Chaos – the void, the emptiness, the space dividing earth and heavens – sprang Arabus (God of primordial darkness) and Nyx (Goddess of the blackness of night).

Nyx

One of the earliest Greek deities, Nyx is described as dressed in black garments studded with stars. Mating with Erebus, Nyx gave birth to Aether, God of light, air and the upper stratosphere – that airy substance, clear and glowing, as opposed to the lower air layers found closer to the earth. Hemera, the day god, also sprang from Nyx. All of the subsequent gods were offspring of Nyx. Nyx's many direct descendants other than Aether and Hemera were birthed without benefit of coupling. They embodied the negative attributes and influences that could befall humankind:

Eris: Jealousy
Nemesis: Revenge
Morose: Inescapable fate
Ker: Bad Luck, Unnatural Death
Hypnos: Sleep
Thanatos: Death
Oiyzis: Distress
Momos: Shame

The **Hesperides,** also children of Nyx, were the beings that guarded the golden apples. While amongst themselves the Hesperides were pleasant enough, legend holds that their golden apples are what brought about the Trojan war.

Nyx also brought forth the **Moïras,** (Three Fates), and the **Kerrs** (inescapable destiny), as well as **Philotas** (desires of the flesh, aging, and friendship), and Apate (deceit).

Eros/Cupid

In Theogony, Hesiod describes Eros as Love, the third being, coming after Chaos and Gaia. According to Hesiod, Eros is a most beautiful god to behold and has the ability to control the hearts and bodies not only of mortals, but also of the other gods. Eros has only to aim his desire at a "victim" and he relieves the man or god of the burden of his intelligence and common sense, awakening him to the powerful force of love within. Hesiod sees in Eros a cosmic power that exists above and beyond that of the gods. Without the power of love, no creature would ever be born.

In later periods, Eros was considered the son of Aphrodite, goddess of beauty and love, and of Ares, the god of war. Some also hold that Eros was the offspring of Aphrodite and Hermes, the messenger god. In these myths, Eros is wild and mischievous and has the curious ability to split himself into many smaller love gods. Eros carries a bow and shoots his arrows at the hearts of his targets who then find themselves instantly in the grip of feelings of love so powerful they are helpless in the face of them. Eros symbolizes mighty love, and love at first sight, both so strong they cannot be denied. Victims of Eros' arrow lose normal use of their minds and other senses and are at the mercy of love alone.

The Roman counterpart to Eros is Cupid, described as a winged infant who carries a bow and arrows.

Erebus

Primeval darkness. Erebus embodies the dark out of which sprang Chaos. As a result of its coupling with Nyx, the light of day, the night-time, and the ether were born. Erebus is often identified with the underworld.

Tartarus

The Tartarus was one of the first beings to be created out of matings between Chaos, Gaia (Earth), and Eros (Love). Tartarus was the great abyss of oblivion which covered the earth, surrounded by gated walls made of metal. On the depths of Tartarus the monstrous sons of Uranus, Cyclopes and Hecatoncheires were revealed and the Titans were trapped after the Olympian gods took control. The Hecatoncheires were the guardians of the Tartarus and prevented the Titans from returning to power.

Titans

The Titans, also known as the "elderly gods" represented the awesome power of the forces of nature. Huge and mighty, they could never be compared to human beings, as were the gods of Olympia. The cult of these offspring of heaven and earth reigned for many generations, until it was replaced by the cult of the Olympian gods. The Titans then began to appear in most of the myths as the fathers of the Olympian gods. Although quite numerous, only a few of the Titans actually appear in the mythology.

The following are the Titans, in the order they appear in Hesiod's *Theogony*.

Gaia, Ge

The name Gaia means "Earth". Gaia, offspring of Chaos, was a mother-goddess. Gaia gave birth to the sky, Uranus, who later became her husband. In addition, Gaia produced the mountains, the sea (Pontus), and twelve of the Titans: Oceanus, Iapetus, Hyperion, Coeus, Crius, Thea, Rhea, Themis, Mnemosyne, Phoebe, Tethys, and Kronos. She also produced the Cyclopes and the Hecatoncheires, each of whom had fifty heads and one hundred hands. Gaia's husband, Uranus, quickly buried the atrocious and frightening Hecatoncheires deep within the earth. This angered Gaia who sought revenge against Uranus by encouraging their son Kronos to castrate their father using a sickle-shaped blade. From the blood of Uranus, Gaia created Gigantes, Erinyes, and the Dryads. Gaia then mated with the sea, Pontus, and brought forth Nereus, Phorkys, and Keto and Eurybia.

When Zeus, the son of Kronos, engaged in war against the Titans, Gaia sent aid to her sons after Zeus succeeded in overcoming them. The battle between Zeus and the gods was difficult and protracted, and in the end Gaia was forced to accept the change in situation: Zeus was now the Father of the Gods.

In *Theogony,* Hesiod describes the battle between the Olympian gods (at whose head stood Zeus) and the Titans. The victory of Zeus gave him dominion over of all humankind. This story apparently describes the overthrow of the ancient feminine system of religious rule and its replacement with a patriarchy at whose center was the worship of the "Great Mother".

Objects of art and ritual items, as well as ancient myths, teach us that the ancient European and Neolithic religions were based on a "mother-goddess" that took various names and descriptions, most of which were related to fertility and the earth. Male gods did not exist at all in ancient Europe in fact, and the great goddess, the Mother, was the immortal and eternal mistress of all.

There was no concept of fatherhood in early religious thought. The great female deity took lovers for enjoyment, and not for the purpose of having children. The men feared, admired, and obeyed the matriarch. The fireplace, which was tended to by the mother, be it in a cabin or a prehistoric cave, was the earliest human social center, and motherhood was the earliest prehistoric mystery. In early times, it was not known that a man was needed to fertilize the female for procreation. Often it was believed that the touch of a plant, the swallowing of a certain potion, or other such event brought about a pregnancy. Among the lovers of the great deity was chosen one who would be sacrificed at the end of the year for purposes of dedicating the New Year. This sacrifice could be carried out in actuality, or representatively by fashioning a doll in the man's image which was subsequently ceremoniously thrown from a high cliff or burned.

The removing of Gaia from religious worship symbolized the end of the mother deity and the move to a male god who commanded in her stead.

Uranus

The name Uranus means "heavens" or "sky". According to Hesiod's Theogony, the fact that Uranus was the son of Gaia did not in fact make him her inferior. Rather, he was her equal, and when he matured he became her theological mate.

Uranus was the father of the Titans, the Cyclopes, and the Hecatoncheires (the fifty-headed, one hundred-handed giants whom he later threw to the depths of Tartarus). Right from the start, Uranus despised his own children. He hid them in the bowels of the earth, and took pride in the act of doing so. Gaia, his wife, was filled with rage at this betrayal, and called upon her children to revenge their father. She fashioned a blade in the shape of a sickle and bade them castrate him. Of all of the offspring, Kronos alone found the courage within his heart to bring harm to his father. He hid in the shadows when at the dark of night Uranus came to Gaia, and finding an opportune moment, he sprang, cutting off Uranus' genitals with one swipe of the sickle.

From the blood of the mutilated Uranus, Gaia formed the Erinyes, the Gigantes, and the Nymphs. According to the myths, Kronos threw his father's severed organs into the sea, and out of the foam rose the goddess Aphrodite.

Robert Graves, in his book *The Greek Myths*, holds that the patriarchal legend of Uranus was officially received under the auspices of Olympian religion. He further explains that Uranus attained his stand as the First Father by means of identification with the god Varuna – one of the three gods of the male trilogy.

It bears pointing out that the Greek form of the name Uranus comes from the male counterpart of UR-ANA, which means Queen of the Mountains, Queen of Summer, Queen of the Wind, or Queen of the dancers of the Wild. This was the goddess in her orgiastic element.

Pontos

Gaia gave birth to Pontos, "the fruitless and raging sea", as Hesiod puts it "without benefit of the sweetness of a union of love". (Theogony, 131-132) Later Gaia coupled with Pontos and gave birth to, among others, Nereus, Phorkys, and Keto.

Oceanus

Oceanus was the god of the mighty river which was said to encircle the earth. The son of Gaia and Uranus, Oceanus was husband to Thetis, who gave birth to three thousand water gods, of which Styx was the most well-known. Thetis also begat daughters who resembled nymphs, and whose names described characteristics of flowing water, such as Elektra (the shining).

"And Thetis bore for Oceanus the winding rivers, the Nile and the Alpheus.... She also brought forth a holy company of daughters, who together with Apollo were charged by Zeus to watch over the young men as they matured…" (*Theogony 3336-370*)

Iapetus

Son of Gaia and Uranus, Iapetus fathered Atlas, who carried the earth on his shoulders, and Prometheus, savior of humankind. These two sons were the only Titans not banished with the arrival of Zeus, though they were taken down somewhat in rank.

Hyperion

Son of Gaia and Uranus, Hyperion's name meant "supreme, upward movement". Hyperion's mating with his sister Thea brought about the birth of Helios – the sun, Selena – the moon, and Eos, goddess of the dawn.

Homer mentions Hyperion several times in close identification with Helios.

Thea

Daughter of Gaia and Uranus, Thea was mother of Helios (sun), Selena (moon), and Eos (dawn). "Thea mated with Hyperion and bore the great Helios, the clear Selena and the Eos that shines upon all who walk upon the earth…." (Theogony 371-374)

Rhea

Daughter of Gaia and Uranus, Rhea was both sister and wife to Kronos, with whom she begat six Olympian gods: Hestia, Demeter, Hera, Hades, Poseiden, and Zeus. Rhea rescued her son Zeus from being swallowed up by his father, Kronos, and then helped him cause Kronos to regurgitate the rest of Zeus' siblings. The image of Rhea is parallel to that of the great mother, and usually identified with the goddess of the earth.

Themis

The name Themis means "justice". A daughter of Gaia and Uranus, Themis was the wife of Zeus. She symbolized law and order. Her coupling with Zeus begat six daughters, all of whom were of great importance in mythology. These belonged to two groups: The first was responsible for the laws of man, and for justice, peace, and order. The second was fate.

Themis was the strength of the famous Oracle of Delphi, before it became the temple of Apollo. After the great flood, Deucalion and Pyrrha turned to Themis, who warned Zeus against a relationship with Thetis (mother of Achilles, not Thetis the Titan).

Mnemosyne

Daughter of Gaia and Uranus, Mnemosyne was the goddess of memory and mother of the Muses. Hesiod tells us that Mnemosyne lay with Zeus for nine nights, and a year later the nine Muses were born.

Kronos/Saturn

Kronos, or the Latin Saturn, was the most important of the Titans. He was the youngest god born to Uranus and Gaia, the sky and the earth, and he ruled all the Titans until his son Zeus dethroned him and took over his sovereignty. According to legend, Gaia encouraged Kronos to castrate his father, Uranus, using a sickle blade. The castration was Gaia's revenge against Uranus for burying their hundred-handed, fifty-headed children, the Hecatoncheires – Cottus, Briareus, and Gyes, who were shocking and frightening in their appearance. The castration won Kronos rule over the entire world. However, Gaia and Uranus warned him that he, Kronos, would suffer a fate similar to that of his father. One of his sons would surely topple him from his dominion.

In an attempt to escape this prophecy, Kronos swallowed up his children, one after the other. After the birth of his sixth son, however, Rhea tricked him. When Kronos asked to be handed the infant so that he could swallow him, she wrapped a stone in a diaper and gave it to Kronos instead of the child. The baby, Zeus, she kept hidden in a cave. Later, with the help of Rhea, Zeus made Kronos regurgitate all of the children, including the diaper-wrapped stone.

The Olympian gods united under the scepter of Zeus and went to war against Kronos and the rest of the Titans. After a long and exhaustive battle the Olympians were victorious and banished the Titans.

According to the Roman version of this myth, after Jupiter (the Roman name for Zeus) trounced Saturn, the latter ran off to

Italy carrying the dove of peace, and heralding in a period of prosperity, peace and happiness.

Hesiod calls Kronos the "youngest, most wily and terrible of Gaia's children" and says that he "hated his bright father". *(Theogony 137-138)*

Kronos was worshipped in several localities, and a yearly festival in his honor was held – the Festival of Kronia. The fact that this festival took place strengthens the notion that Kronos was in fact parallel to the Roman god Saturn, who was originally, apparently, the god of sowing of seeds. The date of the festival was the seventeenth of December, just after the autumn sowing season. This was the biggest festival of the agricultural year and bore characteristics of the agricultural society which predated the Greek/Roman deities.

In astrology, Saturn is believed to control the fates of humans.

Cyclopes

These awesome giants were the children of Gaia and Uranus. The job of these one-eyed creatures was to provide thunder and lightening to Zeus, the father of the gods. Hesiod describes them in Theogony 140-146: "Brontes, Steropes, and Arges... imparted to Zeus his thunder and made the thunderbolt: They were godlike in all manners, but each had one eye only, set in the middle of the forehead. Thus they were called Cyclopes (round-eyed), after the one orb-shaped eye. They were strong, mighty, and crafty."

In *The Odyssey*, Odysseus meets a Cyclopes which is characterized as an evil human-eating being that does not respect its visitors. When Odysseus and his entourage arrived after a brutal sea voyage, the Cyclopes trapped them in a cave. The giant placed a huge boulder in the opening to the cave, eliminating all chance of escape. Odysseus and his people watched in horror as the Cyclopes began to kill his captives one by one by butting their heads together, and then consumed them for his meals.

Odysseus conceived a clever plan; he caused the giant to become drunk and pass out. While the Cyclopes slept, Odysseus used flame to sharpen a huge wooden stick, and gouged out the eye of the one-eyed monster. Odysseus and his men then tied three deer together, and tied themselves underneath the deer's bellies. The now blind giant felt the back of each beast as it exited the cave in the morning, but it did not occur to him to feel their stomachs as well. Thus Odysseus and his people were able to escape to their boat which was anchored off the coast of the Cyclopes' island.

In another Cyclopes story, the famous doctor Asclepius, son of Apollo, discovered a way to bring the dead back to life. This greatly worried Zeus, who reacted to the discovery by murdering Asclepius. This in turn enraged Apollo, who immediately killed several of the Cyclopes who had provided Zeus with his thunder and lightening. Zeus vowed that Apollo would pay dearly for this, and would have thrown him into the depths of Tartarus, were it not for the intervention of Leto, Apollo's mother. Leto's efforts resulted in a much lighter punishment for her son by which Apollo was forced into slavery to King Admetus for the period of one year for his crime of killing Zeus' beloved Cyclopes.

Hecatoncheires

Cottus, Briareus, and Gyes, three of the sons of Gaia and Uranus, were giants most shocking in their deformities, having one hundred arms and hands and fifty heads each. Their own father as so repulsed by their appearance that he threw them into the Tartarus immediately upon their birth, thus incurring the wrath and revenge of Gaia.

When Zeus replaced his father Kronos as the king of the gods, he set free the three Hecatoncheires, and in return for their liberty they helped Zeus in his fight against the Titans. Once victory was had, the Hecatoncheires returned to Tartarus, but this time as guards, making sure that the Titans could find no escape from the depths of the earth.

One of the Hecatoncheires, Briareus, saved Zeus from being caught by rebels when Hera tried to lead an uprising of gods against him.

Gigantes

Uranus bled as a result of his castration by Kronos, and from his blood Gaia brought into being some huge offspring, the Gigantes. The Gigantes were fierce-looking and their legs were scaly snakes. When the Gigantes attacked Olympus, they piled mountains one on top of the other, causing grave danger to Zeus and the gods of Olympus.

The prophecy of the Oracle said that only a mortal man could be of assistance in such a situation. Gaia, who was aware of the prophecy, searched for a blade of grass which could make the Gigantes invincible. Alas, however, Zeus had forbidden the sun and moon to provide light, forcing Gaia to feel about in the darkness and to fail in her quest.

With the help of Hercules, the gods succeeded in the end in forcing the Gigantes to yield to them.

Thetis

Daughter of Gaia and Uranus, Thetis was the goddess of the sea. Oceanus was her brother and husband. Thetis provided Hera shelter when Zeus did battle with Kronos over the rule of the world.

Nereus

The mating of Gaia (earth) and Pontus (sea) brought about the birth of Nereus, the "Old Man of the Sea". According to Hesiod, Nereus was honest and good-hearted and had the ability to foresee the future. Despite his friendly nature, however, he was not willing to part easily with his knowledge and prophecies. When Hercules wanted Nereus to show him the way to the Garden of Hesperides, he was forced to try to trap Nereus, a feat made difficult by Nereus' ability to change his shape over and over again and to turn himself into various different strange beings.

Phorkys

A sea god, Phorkys was a son of Gaia (earth) and Pontus (sea). Phorkys fathered many sea monsters as a result of mating with his sister, Keto. Among these were the Gorgon and the Graia.

Keto

Daughter of Gaia and Pontus, Keto was the sister of Phorkys and Nereus. She mated with her brother Phorkys and gave birth to numerous sea monsters.

Twelve Gods of Olympus

The twelve Olympians were the most exalted of all the gods. (They inherited this position from the Titans). They were called Olympians after their home on Mount Olympus.

Zeus (Jupiter) - King of the gods, head of the family.

Poseidon (Neptune) – Zeus's brother, ruler of the sea.

Hades (Pluto) – Zeus's second brother, ruler of the underworld, the land of the dead.

Hestia (Vesta) – Goddess of the hearth-fire, sister to Zeus, Poseidon, and Hades. Hestia later gave up her place on Olympus to the wine- god, Dionysus.

Hera (Juno) – Wife of Zeus.

Ares (Mars) – God of war. Son of Zeus and Hera.

Athena (Minerva) – Daughter of Zeus, goddess of battle and wisdom.

Apollo – Son of Zeus, god of light, prophecy, art, and music.

Aphrodite (Venus) – Daughter of Zeus, goddess of love, fertility, and beauty.

Hermes (Mercury) – Son of Zeus, messenger of the gods, and god of commerce.

Artemis (Diana) – Daughter of Zeus, goddess of war.

Hephaestus (Vulcan) – Son of Hera, sometimes also called the son of Zeus. God of fire and the manufacture of metal.

An additional goddess, **Demeter,** was thought to reside on Olympus, goddess of agriculture. She left Olympus and swore never to return after her daughter Persephone was kidnapped by Hades, the god of the underworld.

Olympus

It is assumed that Olympus, home of the Olympian gods, was the highest mountain peak in Greece, which is located in Thessaly, in the northeast of the country.

In the Illiad, the most ancient Greek poem, it is hinted that Olympus was a mysterious place located somewhere above all the mountains of the world. There is some contradiction in the Illiad concerning the location of Olympus. On the one hand it is a real and actual mountain, and on the other hand it is a mysterious place not of this world. In one instance it is said that Zeus speaks to the gods "from the highest peak of Olympus", which seems to man it is an actual mountain, given to true parameters like "height". However, later Zeus says that he could hang the land and the sea in such a way that they would swing from under Olympus. It would not be possible to hang the land from a mountain, since the mountain would be part of the land itself!

If it was not land, however, it was not sky either. The three brother ruling gods divided dominion over the world among themselves. Zeus was lord of the skies, Hades was lord of the underworld and the land of the dead, and Poseidon was lord of the sea. Olympus was common to the three, as it did not exist within any of these domains.

The entrance to Olympus was by way of a large gate of clouds, guarded by the four seasons of the year.

The gods resided on the mountain itself. They were nourished by ambrosia and nectar, and were serenaded by music from Apollo's harp.

According to Homer, Olympus was a place of peace, joy, and complete utter contentment. There was no wind, and neither rain nor snow disturbed the tranquility. A firmament of lovely clouds surrounded the mount from all sides, and rays of the sun shone brightly on the summit.

Zeus/Jupiter

Zeus was the King of the mythological Greek gods. In other words, he was the Supreme Deity.

Zeus was the sixth and youngest son of his Titan parents, Kronos and Rhea. Zeus's paternal grandparents, Uranus and Gaia, had warned their son Kronos to expect a similar fate to the one Uranus had suffered at Kronos' own hands. They prophesied that Kronos would one day be overthrown by his son, just as he had castrated and toppled his father Uranus.

Kronos tried to sidestep this fate by cleverly taking care to destroy each and every one of his children as they were born. As each child emerged into the world, Kronos opened his mouth and devoured it. However, just as his Mother Gaia had taken her revenge on her husband for his treatment of their children, so Rhea plotted to foil Kronos.

Gaia and Uranus advised Rhea to go into hiding on the island of Crete when she was about to give birth to Zeus. This Rhea did, and after its birth she concealed the child in a cave guarded by servants who made sure that Kronos never heard the infant's cries. Each time the baby made a sound, they raised a noisy ruckus which could drown out even the loudest wails.

The child Zeus was cared for faithfully by the capable hands (or hooves) of Amalthia. According to some myths, Amalthia was a nymph, while according to others she was a goat. Whether nymph or goat, it is agreed that Amalthia possessed a horn of wonders, from which she drew an endless supply of marvelous gifts.

Kronos, of course, demanded that Rhea give him the child so that he may swallow him up as he had the other five children born to them. Rhea obediently handed Kronos a bundle wrapped in a diaper, which Kronos gulped down. Within the bundle was no child however, but a stone. Thus Rhea manipulated her husband into thinking he had indeed consumed the last of their offspring.

Some stories claim that the stone was so bothersome to Kronos' digestive system that he was forced to accept some strong medicine from Rhea which made him vomit. According to this account, when he vomited, up came the stone, and with it all five of the previous children as well, all of which later became Olympian gods. Other versions of this myth claim that it was Zeus himself who forced his father to regurgitate his siblings, and that the last to come out was the stone wrapped in a diaper. In any event, Zeus took over his father's sovereignty, and stood the stone at Delphi.

Zeus had to undergo a fierce battle in order to deprive his father of his rule. His brothers the Hecatoncheires, giants who were able to throw three hundred stones at once, and the Cyclopes, who brought their mighty strength to bear, provided aid and support.

At the end of the battle, Zeus tossed his father and the rest of the Titans into the Tartarus (that deep cavernous nothingness guarded by walls and metal gates which was created directly after Chaos, Gaia, and Eros). There the Hecatoncheires, the same one hundred handed giants that had been prisoners of the Tartarus themselves, stood guard.

The period preceding the reign of Zeus as the one and only king of the gods was called the Titan period. This can be thought of as a period of transition - from a belief in gods which represent the forces of nature (The Titans) to a belief in the power of the king of the gods himself (Zeus).

Even after he succeeded in toppling and capturing the Titans, Zeus's battles were not over. It still remained for him to fight against the Gigantes, sons of the earth, and Typhon, the hundred-headed monster.

After the banishing of the Titans, there remained to Zeus two formidable competitors – his brothers Hades and Poseidon. The three were able to come to a peaceful agreement as to the rule of the world. The brothers drew lots in order to decide the dividing up of territory. Thus it was decided that Poseidon would rule the sea, Hades would rule the underworld and the domain of the dead, and Zeus would have the supreme rule as god of the heavens.

Many are the descriptions of the might and power of Zeus in the stories of Hesiod and Homer. He ruled the sky and the rain, using the thunder and lightening as his weapons.

Time and again in stories of the Greek heroes, the question is asked: Did destiny itself come under the authority of Zeus in his capacity as supreme ruler? The answer would seem to be yes, since it was the destiny of Zeus, as the youngest son, to take over from his father and become the king of the gods. The tradition of power passing in such a manner had survived from the matriarchal period. Moreover, Zeus was the savior of his siblings and ended the rule of the evil Uranus.

Yet, in the *Illiad*, Homer mentions several times that there existed a mysterious and unfathomable force, a power from which there is nowhere to hide and no possibility of escape – a power more mighty than the gods, and that power was: Destiny.

In Homer's poems we hear the voice of Hera, Zeus's wife, asking him angrily whether he feels himself capable of saving a man whose fate is to be sentenced to death. Since destiny here seems to be more powerful than Zeus, Hera's question definitely makes us wonder, and moves us closer to Graves' interpretation, according to which Zeus is flesh and blood, a representation of the patriarchal king, the masculine ruler.

Destiny would certainly seem to have been stronger than Zeus when he was his family members were able to lead him passively without his prior knowledge – and when the jealous Hera tried to instigate an uprising against him.

Many of the legends about the king of the gods have as their subject his many and complicated love affairs and marriages.

Zeus's first wife was Metis, the wisest of all the gods. During this marriage, Gaia and Uranus again interfered in the course of events by revealing one of their all-knowing prophecies. This time they predicted that yet another child would be born who would grab power from its father and take over the rule of gods and men. He was to be none other than the second offspring of Metis.

Zeus did not wait to be told of a second pregnancy to take charge of the situation and divert disaster. When Metis was expecting for the first time, he swallowed her up, taking her wisdom as his own and using it to predict good and bad outcomes. The female child that Metis had carried when she was swallowed was born. Athena emerged through the head of Zeus.

Zeus's second wife was Themis, daughter of the Titans Gaia and Uranus. Themis was the goddess of justice, law and order. She bore Zeus the three Horae (guardians of the law), and the three Moirae (the Three Fates), goddesses of destiny.

Subsequently, Zeus took Eurynome, one of the daughters of Oceanus, as his third wife, and she bore him three lovely daughters, the Graces.

As his fourth wife Zeus chose his sister Demeter, daughter of Rhea and Kronos, goddess of crops and harvest. This union resulted in the birth of Persephone, the daughter who was later kidnapped by Hades.

The fifth wife of Zeus, according to Hesiod, was Mnemosyne, goddess of memory. Mnemosyne was a Titan, born from Zeus's grandparents, Gaia and Uranus. Zeus and Mnemosyne celebrated a "wedding night" which lasted nine days and nights, and resulted in the birth of the nine Muses.

Next, Zeus married Leto, daughter of the Titan Coeus. Leto gave birth to Apollo and Artemis. Although Hesiod and others state that Hera was Zeus's last wife, there are legends according to which a jealous Hera interfered in this marriage and tried to prevent Leto from giving birth to her children. In the fact of Hera's threats, the islands and continents were all afraid to give Leto a safe place for birthing. Only the rocky and unstable island of Delos would allow her refuge.

The next in line was Maia, one of the seven daughters of Atlas and the nymph Pleione. Hermes was born of Zeus's union with Maia.

Now came the turn of the most famous of the wives of Zeus – the one who tried with all her might to remain the one and only, and to rule the universe at her husband's side or in his stead – Hera. Hera is considered the third of Zeus's official wives. The first offspring from their marriage was Ares - the god of war. Next was Hebe, goddess of youth, who served the gods of Olympus their drinks of nectar, and Ilithyia, goddess of childbirth. Hera did not hesitate to use Ilithyia against her father's lovers, whether they were voluntary partners or had been taken by Zeus by force, when they were about to give birth to Zeus's children.

Athena, the goddess of wisdom, was born, as we mentioned, through the head of Zeus. According to some of the myths, Hera was greatly incensed by this unusual type of birth, and got back at Zeus by giving birth to Phaistos without benefit of a father.

Zeus may have been the almighty father of the gods, but Hera tried to challenge him in his status as single ruler. Hera forged a relationship with Zeus's brother Poseidon, and with his daughter Athena, and together they plotted to trap Zeus and take him down from his throne. Thetis was able to thwart this plan by sending the hundred-handed giant Briareus to defend Zeus. The traitors were frightened by Briareus and gave up their quest immediately. Zeus punished Hera, but he gave in when she begged for mercy and promised that this had been the last time that she would act against him, either openly or behind his back. Zeus's compassionate and humane behavior is worthy of note in this instance!

Most of the myths about Zeus characterize him with decidedly human attributes. He is shown to have had great passion and desire for females, and followed those impulses regularly, while taking pains to hide his adventures from his wife, whom he suspects is causing mischief of her own. The picture we glean from the stories is one of an almighty ruler, king of the gods, who has trouble containing his passions and who quakes in fear of his wife's wrath! He seems a human-like being indeed.

Researchers of many disciplines have found this presentation of the king of gods to be most fascinating. Perhaps the most interesting of the approaches to the subject is that of Jean Shimoda Bolen who points out the many common human characteristics among the mythical figures. According to Bolen, Zeus was the embodiment of the purely male human archetype (as opposed to other gods whose make-ups were more androgynous).

Zeus was fatherly in that he took charge and was infinitely dominant over his clan. He was tough, both physically and mentally, and had a generous and open heart. While he usually maintained a calm demeanor, his wrath when aroused was formidable, accompanied by claps of thunder and bolts of lightening. Zeus's maleness was expressed in the arena of sex as well, and he found it nearly impossible to resist the wiles of a beautiful woman whose charms could tie him with magic ropes. Zeus did not settle for mere desire from a distance! He would get what he wanted – even if it meant forgetting in the heat of the moment that a price would need to be paid later. One thing only was the all-powerful male afraid of – the jealous rage of his wife. Zeus went to any lengths to hide his sexual adventures from Hera so as not to suffer her jealousy, and indeed he himself usually managed to remain unscathed. The miserable victims of his desire, on the other hand, often paid dearly and tragically for Zeus's sins against Hera.

Zeus saw no conflict between his passion for other women on the one hand and his natural strong aspirations to honesty and justice on the other.

When the Greek army was amassed at the gates of Troy, the Greeks were told, "Zeus will never come to the aid of liars and hypocrites." Edith Hamilton, in her book *Mythology,* tells us that there are scholars who explained this bold contradiction by stating the fact that Zeus, as he was described in the various myths, was not only one entity, but he was actually an amalgamation of several gods, each having different and contradictory, perhaps, aspects of character.

It goes without saying that the tree and the animal which came to be dedicated to Zeus were of the strongest and most revered species of creature and vegetation. The mighty oak was the tree of Zeus. Priests believed they could read messages from Zeus into the whisperings of the wind through its branches and leaves. The animal of Zeus was the soaring eagle, king of the mighty fowl.

The Roman counterpart to Zeus was Jupiter, king of the Roman gods. Jupiter was "Optimus Maximus", the best and greatest of them all. Like Zeus, Jupiter ruled by the use of lightening, thunder, and weather. Justice, contracts and vows came under his jurisdiction. The many nicknames he was called spoke of his various qualities: Jupiter Lucetius – Light of the heavens. Jupiter Fulgur - Ruler by lightening. Jupiter Tonans – Ruler by thunder. Jupiter Pluvius – Sender of rain. Jupiter Stator

– Stops by staring. (Halts the fleeing army and defends Rome against danger.)

As an oath, it was customary to swear on holy stones in the name of Jupiter Lapis (stone). The Roman Plebian Games were held in honor of Jupiter. Although the Romans did not look favorably upon the less positive human characteristics of the gods, they attributed to Jupiter the tendency to chase woman and a jealous wife similar to the Greek Hera.

Poseidon/Neptune

Poseidon, bother of Zeus and Hades and son of Kronos and Rhea, was thought of as the second in line among the gods of Olympus. He was the god of water, rivers, seas, and springs. It is possible that his name meant "owner of the earth". After all, the water is the force that fertilizes the land.

The god of the sea was particularly important to the Greeks since much of their livelihood depended on the sea, and they needed its benevolence and calm on a day to day basis.

Poseidon, like the rest of the Olympian gods, lived on Mount Olympus, but he also had a wonderful palace under the sea. Most depictions of Poseidon show him holding a pitchfork which he did not hesitate to make use of to strike down or terrify whatever or whomever he wished to punish or upset.

Poseidon's official wife was Amphitrite, granddaughter of Oceanus the Titan, and daughter of Nereus and Doris. Amphitrite lived with Poseidon in the undersea palace and gave birth there to Triton, Trumpeter of the Sea. Triton's upper body was that of a man, and his lower body was fishlike.

The nymph Thoosa bore Poseidon his giant son Cyclop Polyphemus. Eurial, daughter of Minos, gave birth to his son Orion. Poseidon's coupling with Medusa Gorgon brought about the birth of the winged horse, Pegasus. Demeter, when pursued by Poseidon, turned herself into horse to avoid his advances, but to no avail. Their mating produced a horse offspring, Arion.

Amymone, daughter of Danaus, while searching for a source of water, was pursued by Satir. Poseidon came to her rescue by tossing his pitchfork at Satir. Amymone had to pay for this favor, however, by submitting to sexual relations with Poseidon, which resulted in the birth of Nauplius. Poseidon did, however, gift Amymone with the source of water she had been looking for. Nauplius fell victim to a plot and was stoned at the gates of Troy. When the Greeks would not agree to appease Nauplius, Poseidon seduced their women.

Poseidon mated with many women – goddess, mortals, and nymphs, and produced numerous children, some of whom were particularly large and strong. One of his well-known sons was Polyphemus, the famous Cyclopes mentioned in the *Odyssey* who trapped Odysseus and eleven of his crew in his. After Odysseus blinded Polyphemus and escaped the island, the Cyclopes begged his father Poseidon to avenge his blindness, and Poseidon indeed did all he could to prevent Odysseus from returning safely home.

Poseidon's greatest revenge was by way of the sea. When the Greeks were sailing on their way home, victorious, Poseidon lit smoke signals on a mountain top, causing the Greek ships to shatter on the rocks.

One of Poseidon's sons, Halirrhothius, was killed by the enraged father of a woman he attempted to rape. Poseidon tried the father in front of a panel of twelve gods, but was unable to bring witnesses to bear on his behalf.

Like Zeus's wife Hera, Amphitrite suffered from bouts of jealousy over her husband's many betrayals. Here too, the main victims of the fallout from the affairs of the god were his lovers themselves. In one instance, for example, Amphitrite turned Poseidon's hapless lover into a sea monster.

Poseidon's possessed a mighty strength. He controlled the angry sea as well as the calm waters, and decided when and where earthquakes would take place. As he sailed the sea in his golden sea-chariot, its wake would quiet the sea as he passed. When Poseidon was angry, he would pierce the waters with his pitchfork, causing the waves to rise and swell, until fierce and powerful storms rocked the land and sea.

The Greeks, who as we have said were sea farers and owners of fleets of ships, admired and feared Poseidon. Their successes at sea, as well as their safe return to the shores of home, were dependant on the moods and whims of the god.

Similarly to Zeus, Poseidon was able to change into many forms. He used this talent rarely, however, and when he did, he usually took the form of a horse. The horse is thus one of the better known symbols of Poseidon, along with fish and dolphins. Legend has it that the horse was given to mankind by Poseidon. The bull is also connected to the image of Poseidon, as it is to other gods as well.

Neptune was the Roman god parallel to the Greek Poseidon. Neptune was at first the god of water, springs, and rivers, but after he became identified with Poseidon, he too became the god of the seas. Every year on the twenty-third of July, the Neptune festival took place in his honor. Because of the special connection between the horse and Poseidon, Neptune too was depicted with this animal, and in Rome he was considered the god of horse-racing.

Hades/Pluto

Hades was the brother of Zeus and Poseidon. After the three brothers removed their father, Kronos, from his throne, Hades was assigned the rule of the underworld, the land of the dead

The name Hades means "invisible". Alternately he was called Pluto (the rich) and the "good counselor". Those who prayed for success and riches would call the god by the name Pluto.

Hades' job was punishment of criminals and god of the dead, but he was not death itself. Death was called Tanatus by the Greeks, and Orkus by the Romans.

Hades lived in the underworld, which itself was sometimes called Hades. He only infrequently visited the other gods who resided on Olympus, as he was an unwanted figure among them. Hades was thought of as merciless and fearsome, and reminded men and gods of the death itself, and of what came afterward. However, he was not evil, and usually behaved in a just manner.

The myths describe Hades as a cold character. "Strong Hades, pitiless in heart, dwells under the earth…." (Hesiod, *Theogony 453)*. His underworld palace stood in a moldy place and was full of splendiferous echoing halls. The palace was guarded by Hades' dog, Cerberus, who watched over the gates of the underworld as well. Cerberus had fifty heads, ate live meat, and had a voice of copper. Cerberus would wag his tail and wiggle his ears in welcome when anyone entered the palace. Should they try to exit, however, he would prevent them from approaching the door. If they persisted, Cerberus simply gobbled them up.

Hades' wife was Persephone, the beautiful daughter of Demeter, goddess of the harvest. Since the pleasant young lady would not agree voluntarily to come down the underworld in order to live at the side of the god of the dead, Hades was forced to kidnap her. In the end, Persephone's mother rescued her from the realm of the dead and brought her back up to Olympus, but since Persephone had tasted a few kernels of pomegranate from the food of the dead, she was forced to return and to sojourn with Hades for a few months out of each year.

Hesiod, in his essay "Shield of Heracles", tells that Hades owned a hat which made anyone who donned it invisible. Hesiod calls it the "dread cap of Hades which had the awful gloom of night".

The symbols of Hades are the horn of plenty and the scepter. The horn of plenty is associated with Pluto, the Roman king of the underworld, with whom Hades came to be identified. Pluto was also called the god of riches, and controlled, from a secret hiding place, the provision of precious metals from deep within the earth. This is the origin of the symbol the horn of plenty. The scepter was carried by Hades in his capacity of king of the realm of the dead.

Hestia/Vesta

Eldest daughter of Rhea and Kronos, Hestia was the Greek goddess of the hearth. The hearth fire was of central and vital importance to household life in ancient times, and tending to the flame was an ongoing and critical task. Hestia, through her connection to the hearth, became known as the goddess of family life in general, of hospitality, and of all that was associated with a peaceful, happy, and easy day to day existence.

Hestia was worshipped on a daily basis. At the beginning and end of each meal, a sacrifice was made to the goddess. When a child was born, it was customary to carry him round and round the hearth while blessing Hestia and asking her blessing of the child.

The worship of the household goddess was private and public alike. Each village had a communal fireplace which was dedicated to Hestia and which burned unceasingly. When a new town was established, the inhabitants took live coals from a neighboring public hearth in order to light their own eternal fire.

Hestia was a female archetype and was thought of as an elderly crone, possessed of inner peace who through her wisdom, kept calm and warmth in the family. Hestia never appeared sexual in any way.

Hestia is identified with the Roman goddess Vesta, goddess of the family, dating from the period when religion was a family, rather than a political affair in Rome. As the king's power increased, so did the king's hearth become important to the people as a whole.

The Roman worship of Vesta took place in a round building, and her priestesses were six vestal virgins, each of whom served the goddess for thirty years. At the end of this period, they were allowed to marry. The Greek goddess Hestia was also thought of as an "eternal virgin", and there is no mention in the mythology of a mating between either of the goddesses and any man or god. The vestal priestesses would light the fire by rubbing two pieces of wood together, and they were charged with keeping the fires burning continuously. If the fire should go out, the hapless virgins were flogged as punishment. They did, however, enjoy quite a bit of respect and independence. They were free from the authority of the fathers, but bound by the strict rules of the Pontifex. The Pontifex of each temple was appointed by Pontifex Maximus, head of the priesthood, who was appointed by a committee of three other Pontifexes and the high priest of the country. The virgins were forbidden to draw water from the usual sources. They were allowed to pump only from the well of the nymph, Juturna, which was in the Atrium Vestae, where the virgins resided, near the Roman Forum.

Any violation of the vows of chastity taken by the vestal virgins (any intimate contact with a man) was punished swiftly and cruelly. The offending vestal was buried alive or thrown from a cliff to her death. At least three vestals are known to have perished in this terrifying manner.

In Roman religion, Vesta is sometimes identified with Telus, goddess of the earth, known also as Tera Mater (Mother Earth) who was also associated with Gaia.

Heracles/Hercules

Heracles was one of the most notorious of the Greek heroes. Half god, half human, he received his name from the tough tests Hera forced upon him and his ability to take them on with ease. Thus his name meant: "Glory of Hera".

Heracles' mother was Queen Alkmena, wife of Amphitryon, and his father was Zeus, king of the gods. Zeus became infatuated with the queen, but had trouble convincing the righteous woman to spend a night of love with him. Undeterred, Zeus disguised himself as her husband Amphitryon, and succeeded in mating with her. Zeus had high hopes for the son that would result form this escapade, and in order to assure himself that the offspring would inherit his enormous strength and power, he caused the night spent with Alkmena to last three times the normal length of night.

Of course, Zeus tried to hide his affair with Alkmena from his jealous wife, Hera, and only on the day that Heracles was to be born did he announce to the gods: "The child about to come into the world will be a king!"

Realizing the significance her husband's declaration, Hera called upon her daughter Ilithyia, goddess of childbirth, to intervene, and the birth of Alkmena's infant was delayed. In the meantime, the birth of Heracles' cousin, Eurystheus, was induced, causing him to be the next child born, and only afterwards did Heracles emerge from his mother's womb. Eurystheus was of weak character and did not have the makings of a king, but Zeus was forced to make good on his declaration and to crown him. Zeus made peace with the fact that Heracles would not be king, but nothing could prevent him from becoming a great hero!

Although it was clear right form the start that Heracles possessed a special heroism, he was forced again and again to prove himself against horrible obstacles put in his path by Hera. While still an infant in the cradle, Hera set two cobras upon him in an effort to murder him, but the little Heracles, thinking it was a game, strangled them using the super-human strength of his hands. When Alkmena came to check on the baby she was terrified to find the two giant dead serpents in his bed, and Heracles merrily playing with their bodies.

The young Heracles was educated by the musician Linus who tried to teach him to sing and play instruments. Heracles lacked discipline in learning, however, and caused Linus many frustrations. Linus tried to rein in his difficult student using tough rules and restrictions which only served to anger his youthful but powerful pupil. Heracles became so enraged by his teacher's methods that he raised a chair, and with it struck a fatal blow to Linus' head. Heracles was tried for the murder of his instructor, but was acquitted on the finding that he had acted in self-defense.

Amphitryon, acting as the adoptive father of his wife's offspring, lived in fear of being on the receiving end of his charge's temper. He decided to put some distance between them before the worst had a chance to occur. Amphitryon sent Heracles to live in a small village, where he was to tend a flock of sheep. There Heracles met a shepherd who taught him to shoot a bow and arrow.

When Heracles was eighteen, he killed with his powerful bare hands, a lion that had hurt many members of his flock. For fifty days he hunted the lion, during which period he spent the nights at the palace of King Thespius. The king wished the hero to produce grandchildren for him, so each evening when Heracles returned to the palace to sleep, a princess was waiting in his bed. Unbeknownst to Heracles, he slept each night with a different princess – as the king had fifty daughters - and each of the princesses bore Heracles a son.

After he did in the lion, Heracles skinned it and donned its hide. Thus dressed, he happened to meet some messengers who had been sent by the King of the Minyans to collect fifty heads of cattle as tax from the people of Thebes. Heracles severed the noses, ears, and hands of the tax collectors and sent them to their king in lieu of the tax. Needless to say, this event caused a war between the Minyans and Thebes, with Heracles leading the way to victory for Thebes. As prize for his victory, the king of Thebes presented Heracles with his daughter Magra. Magra gave birth to three sons, but Hera would not stand by and allow their happiness. This time she intervened in the most dreadful manner. She caused Heracles to suffer a bout of insanity during which he killed his own babies by throwing them into fire. When the insanity subsided, Heracles was horrified by what he had done. He went to the Delphi Oracle to seek advice on how to atone for his sins.

The oracle told him to exile himself from Thebes and to put himself in servitude to Eurystheus, King of Mycenae for a period of twelve years during which he would perform twelve different labors.

First, Eurystheus ordered Heracles to kill the Nemean Lion, a beast that had been terrorizing the countryside, and to bring back its skin. The lion proved difficult to kill, and Heracles' arrows simply bounced off its impenetrable skin. Heracles trapped the lion in its lair and blocked up one of the entrances. Entering from the other, Heracles confronted the mighty animal and wrestled it to its death, snapping its neck with his brute strength.

Heracles' other tasks for Eurystheus:

2. Killing the hydra – a dreadful many-headed water serpent from the Lerna swamp.

3. Hunting the lightening quick Ceryneian Deer, which no man had been able to overtake before.

4. Catching the wild Erymanthian Boar and bringing him back alive.

5. Cleaning the filthy, dung-filled stables of Augeas. Heracles managed to clean the long-neglected stables by diverting the course of two rivers to help him.

6. Destruction of the Stymphalian Birds that stalked the carcasses of the dead and sometimes even killed human beings as prey.

7. Capturing alive the Cretan Bull which breathed fire from its nostrils.

8. Capture of the man-eating horses of Diomedes. (After which Heracles fed the horses their master.)

9. Capturing the girdle of the Amazon Queen Hyppolita for the daughter of Eurystheus.

10. Robbing the cattle of the giant Geryon.

Eurystheus decided since Heracles' cousin had helped him in the battle with the hydra, and since Augeas had paid him for the stable clean-up, that these two tasks would not count! Therefore he further ordered him to bring back the terrible many-headed guard dog, Cerberus, and the golden apples of Hesperides.

In the process of carrying out all of these assignments, Heracles traversed the entire world and had many other heroic adventures. When he finished, Hercules was granted his freedom. He returned to Thebes and tried to resume life with his wife Magra, but he was after when he had done to their children, this was not to be. Hercules gave up his claim to Magra allowing her to cohabit with his cousin Julius, while he courted Iole, daughter of the king of Oechalia.

Iole's father promised his daughter's hand to whoever would beat him and his sons in an archery competition. Heracles won the contest, but the king was still reluctant to give his daughter in marriage to someone who had lost his mind and destroyed his own three infants. He claimed there was no assurance that events would not repeat themselves, and as it turned out the king was right to suspect Heracles of instability, since shortly afterward

Heracles suffered another attack of insanity and killed one of Iole's brothers.

Heracles was acquitted of this murder as well, but when he came down with a serious illness, he understood that his guilt was still causing him to suffer. Again, he went to the Delphi Oracle, hoping for a consultation, but the priestess refused to see him. This refusal incensed Heracles, and he angrily broke into the temple, uprooted the tripod of the oracle, and declared that he would set up an oracle of his own on the site. Apollo, of course, did not take the desecration of the oracle quietly, and he fought with Heracles, demanding he return the tripod to its former condition. The battle was a hard one, and ended only when Zeus took it upon himself to come between the adversaries by sending a bolt of lightening. The gods sat in judgment of the deeds of Heracles and decided that he must be enslaved for three years as punishment.

Hermes acting as intermediary in this matter, found someone who would purchase the slave Heracles – Omphale, Queen of Lydia. While in service to the queen, Heracles had many adventures and committed various acts of heroism, but he was also required to occupy himself frequently with tasks considered feminine and beneath his dignity, such as knitting and yarn spinning. When he was released from servitude, he took part in various fierce battles with former enemies and even staged some robberies across the length of Greece. He plundered cities and took their maidens who subsequently gave birth to many more of his children.

Of all the women whom Heracles lusted after, Deianira was to cause him the most trouble. He fell in love with her, but was forced to do battle with the river Achelous in order to win her. Heracles was triumphant over the river, but he feared it would rise up again in jealousy. Achelous was not his only rival for the attentions of Deianira. Nessus, the Centaur, also did everything in his power to win get her. In their scuffle, Heracles' arrow injured Nessus, and as he lay dying of his wound, Nessus called out to Deianira, promising her that if she would dip Heracles' garment in the blood of the Centaur, Heracles' love would become so strong that he could never betray her with another woman. Deianira gathered a vile of Nessus' blood, and saved it for an opportune time.

Heracles continued on to Oechalia, in order to claim what he felt the King still owed him - his daughter Iole. That Heracles should still wish to attain the princess angered the jealous Deianira, and she deemed it time to make use of the blood of Nessus. She dipped Heracles shirt into the blood of the Centaur in hopes that his love for her would grow so strong that he would forget about the maiden from Oechalia. Heracles donned the shirt, and his chest began to absorb the poison. Realizing that something was amiss, he tried quickly to tear the garment from his body, and in so doing he tore at his skin as well. The poison caused Heracles to be gravely ill, and he did not believe he could recover. Heracles ordered the building of his funeral pyre and directed his aids to burn him alive. They refused to carry out these orders, but a passing shepherd was found who agreed to take on the task. As payment, Heracles gave him his bow and arrows. The wooden planks began to go up in flames, when suddenly bolts of lightening appeared and claps of mighty thunder were heard – brought about by the father of the gods, Zeus himself. Heracles recovered from the effects of the poison, and Zeus carried his son up to Olympus where he managed to forge a peace between Heracles and Hera. Heracles then married Hebe.

The Greeks were not the only ones who admired Heracles. The Romans called him Hercules and paid homage to his tremendous power and strength. In Rome an altar to Hercules was erected to which people would turn for help in times of trouble.

Hera/Juno

Hera, the patroness of marriage, was a daughter of Kronos and Rhea, and twin sister to Zeus, who was also her husband. Some claim that Hera was born on the island of Samos, and others say her birthplace was Argos. Hera was raised by the Titans, Tatis and Oceanus. After dethroning their father, Zeus searched out Hera, and when he located her he courted her, albeit unsuccessfully, for quite a while. In the end, Zeus masqueraded as a cuckoo bird, following Hera until she took pity on the poor creature and cradled him to her chest. At that moment Zeus returned to his own form, and the embarrassed Hera agreed to marry him. According to some myths the pair's "wedding night" lasted three hundred years.

The Greek meaning of the name Hera is "lady". The mythological researcher Robert Graves points out the possibility however, that its meaning comes from the word "shields" or "protects". Hesiod called her "the white-limbed Hera", perhaps due to her ability to renew her virginity by bathing yearly in the Spring of Canathus, near Argos.

Hera was the mother of, Hephaestus, Ilithyia, Hebe, and the twin gods Ares and Eris. Several of these children were conceived and born in what were considered virgin births. For example, Hephaestus was born without a father as revenge against Zeus for having birthed Athena with no mother. Ares and Eris were born as a result of Hera's contact with a certain type of plant, and there are accounts that Hebe resulted from her mother's touching lettuce.

In Rome, Hera was associated with the goddess Juno, goddess of women, and protector of home, marriage, and childbirth. The sixth month of the calendar is named for her. Whether as Hera or as Juno, the main occupation of this goddess was the constant struggle to maintain herself as mate to her husband, king of the gods, in the face of his many and varied extra-marital sexual and romantic adventures. Her jealousy was fierce, and her considerable anger was usually directed at the same poor miserable girls that Zeus had victimized.

Hera's wrath was mighty, and the punishments she inflicted on the women and girls were harsh. For example, Io, one of Zeus's lovers, found herself turned into a calf with the voice of a child, and to further add to Io's misery, Hera sent a fly to buzz around her unceasingly until it drove the girl mad.

Hera was particularly intent on causing sorrow to Heracles, Zeus's son from an affair with Alkmena, and she tried various methods of clashing with him. She often used her daughter Ilithyia, goddess of childbirth, in attempts to bring sorrow and hardship to the lovers of Zeus by delaying or preventing the births of their offspring by him.

Hera even made an attempt to rouse the gods in a revolution against her husband. Zeus punished her for this deed by tying her in golden chains and hanging her between the earth and the sky. Her son Hephaestus also meted out a punishment to Hera, as payment for her attempt to throw him out when he was born. She may have done this because he was born with lame legs. Other mythologists claim that Hephaestus did not believe that he was the product of a virginal pregnancy and punished her for the lie. He tied her to a chair and tortured her while she swore that he indeed had no father.

Hera raised and cared for several monstrous characters, all of which fought the various heroes of the day on one occasion or another. Among these creatures were Tifon - a huge dragon-like monster, the Lion of Nemea, and the water Hydra.

During the long and drawn out Trojan War, Hera took the side of the fighters against the Troy. According to Homer, Hera chose this side because Paris, Prince of Troy, did not award her the golden apple destined for the loveliest among women.

Historically, Hera was considered a Para-Hellenistic goddess that the Greek conquerors adopted and attached to their religious cult as the wife of the father of the gods. She was originally worshipped at Argos. A festival called Heria was held in her honor and included a military parade, sacrifices, and sporting events.

As an archetype, Hera was considered the "housewife", the faithful mate that would do all she could to protect her marriage and one whose jealousy was so fierce that it could bring about various "monstrous" results, such as anger, revenge, and intrigue.

Ares/Mars

Son of Hera, Ares was the god of war. According to Homer, he was also the son of Zeus, but certain sources maintain that his was an asexual conception resulting from Hera's contact with a flower. Ares' name is often mentioned as synonymous with war or murder, just as the name of his twin sister Eris is connected with jealousy.

Ares is usually described as a trouble-maker and an arguer who enjoyed the chaos and cruelty of battle. He tended not to have loyalty to any particular city or group, but preferred to identify with whomever was most brutal, whomever killed in the cruelest manner and was the strongest. His sister Eris, goddess of jealousy, worked alongside him, instigating competition and rivalry. Eris complicated relations and sowed seeds of envy and trouble between people, encouraging them to go to war. Ares' retinue also included his companion, Enyo, a war goddess who embodied the tumult of wild battle.

The gods of Olympus were not great admirers of Ares. Only three gods were willing to be associated with him – His sister Eris, Hades (who welcomed the victims of war to his realm in the underworld) and Aphrodite, the goddess of beauty, who with a strange sort of attraction, turned Ares into her lover.

Although he was the god of war, Ares was not considered one of the heroes of Olympus. In fact, Athena was more skilled than he was in the secrets of war, and twice beat him soundly in battle. Two giants managed to capture him and kept him in a jar for thirteen months – he had come dangerously close to death by the time he was rescued by Hermes. Heracles threatened Ares so that he could make him run from Olympus in fright.

Ares' great love was Aphrodite, who according to some of the myths was actually the wife of Hephaestus. All the gods of Olympus witnessed the betrayed husband catching Ares and Aphrodite in the act, and they were all quite amused by the sight. This event was a favorite among artists and has often been described in detail.

Aphrodite and Ares never married, but they produced three children: Phobos (God of threat and panic), Deimos (God of Fear), and Harmony, whose nature was completely opposed to the violence and anger that characterized her brothers and father.

Ares appeared as the accused party in a murder trial that took place on Olympus. Poseidon, king of the sea, accused Ares of murdering his son, Halirrhothius. Ares claimed that Halirrhothius had tried to rape his daughter and that he killed him in order to protect her honor. Since Ares and his daughter were the only witnesses to the event, and since his daughter completely backed up his story, Ares was acquitted by the court.

Despite his rather despicable character, Ares was widely worshipped in Athens, Thebes, Thessaly, and Italy. In some of these places it was mostly the women who took part in the cult of Ares. Certain sources maintain that at first, Ares was considered the god of growth!

In some places dogs were sacrificed on

the altar of Ares, who was sometimes called Enyalios, after a god of the Bronze Age who was identical in many ways to Ares.

The Roman counterpart to Ares was Mars. Since Mars was a war-god, he became connected to Ares over time, and thus some of the legends of Ares were borrowed by the Romans and attributed to Mars. The month of Mars was named for him, and on the early Roman calendar it was considered the first month of the year.

The Romans believed that the good luck shield called Ankila, was brought down from heaven by Mars. The Ankila and its eleven copies were kept in the home of the high priest of Rome.

Mars' priests, the SA'LII, would dance with their shields on the altar in honor of their god. The many sacrifices to Mars included the "October" horses which were customarily sacrificed after the horse races.

The temple of Mars stood outside the city, in a place called Mars Field, across from which was an army training camp. At one time, a five - year atonement for everyone's sins was held at the temple.

The wolf and the woodpecker were the animals consecrated in the name of Mars.

Athena/Minerva

Athena was born in a unique manner – she emerged from the head of her father, Zeus, after he swallowed her mother, Metis, the wisest of all the gods.

According to a prophecy handed down by the great Titans, Gaia and Uranus, Zeus's second offspring would topple his sovereignty over all men and gods. Zeus "outdid" this prophecy when without even waiting for Metis to deliver their first child, he made sure there would not be a second, be swallowing Metis whole during her first pregnancy. By taking Metis into his body Zeus acquired all of her wisdom and her ability to foresee the future. The destruction of Metis did not harm her unborn child,

Athena, who popped out of Zeus's head. Athena was born already a fully grown adult, armed with a golden weapon and with the call of battle on her lips.

As the daughter of Zeus, Athena was allowed to use his shield and to activate flashes of lightening.

According to another account, Athena's father was Palas, a giant in the form of winged goat. This story holds that Palas tried to rape Athena, and not only was unsuccessful, but lost his life in the skirmish, after which Athena skinned his body and donned his hide as a coat.

Some scholars claim that Athena was originally an Eastern, para-Hellenistic goddess. Today she is known chiefly as the Greek goddess of wisdom, and in later writings she appears as the embodiment of intelligence and purity. Her Greek origins are as the goddess of war in the earliest accounts, such as Homer's *Illiad*, where she is described as quite a cruel war goddess indeed.

In other sources she appears not as a warlike character at all, but as one who offers protection from war. She is even said to have been the patroness of cultural and city life.

Together with Hephaestus, Athena was the benevolent protector of craftsmen and farmers. Poseidon, god of the sea, provided humans with powerful and raging horses, while Athena, as goddess of culture, gave them bridles and the ability to train the horses. She taught the women handicrafts such as knitting and spinning, and instructed carpenters in the art of ship-building.

The Temple of Athena was called the Parthenon, after her nickname, Parthenus, meaning virgin, or maiden. Other names for Athena included Palas, meaning vital youth, and Glapukis, which meant "owl eyes".

Though Athena was the goddess of wisdom and was usually portrayed as pure and having good judgment, she showed aspects of character that strengthen the theory that the gods' personalities were "borrowed" from those of human beings. Athena was given to periodic episodes of great anger which usually occurred when others "crossed the line", such as when her temple was desecrated. When one of Athena's priestesses, Auge, daughter of the king of Tagia, hid the fact that she'd had an affair with Heracles and had born him a child in the Temple of Athena, Athena raged with anger and handed down a dire collective punishment: draught and plague in all the land!

The olive tree was consecrated to Athena after an argument with Poseidon over control of Attica and the city of Athens. The two staged a contest on the Acropolis. Poseidon struck his trident into the ground and a salt spring poured forth. Athena then speared the earth with her weapon, and a beautiful olive tree took root and flowered on the spot. A panel of judges declared Athena the winner, and she was given her beloved city Athens and the area of Attica.

The owl, a symbol of intelligence and wisdom even in ancient times, was Athena's sacred animal.

In Rome, Athena's counterpart was Minerva, goddess of craftsmanship and the arts, whose worship took place on the capital hill together with that of Jupiter and Juno. Since Minerva was identified closely with the Greek Athena, goddess of war, Minerva in time became the same, and her cult overlapped with that of Mars.

Apollo

Apollo was one of the first Greek gods. He was a god of many talents, and was associated with many aspects of human life. He was considered the god of light and his name was synonymous at times with the sun itself. He was the god of intelligence, art, and music, and he symbolized the energy and vitality of youth. It was Apollo who invented and taught humans the medical sciences.

Apollo was the son of Leto and Zeus, and brother of Artemis, goddess of hunting. He was independent and freedom-loving and extremely brave. It was said that he never lied and was always faithful to the truth. His oracle at Delphi was the destination for truth-seekers from far and wide.

Hesiod wrote about Apollo, "For it is through the Muses and far-shooting Apollo that there are singers and harpers upon the earth" *(Theogony, 94)*. Hesiod stressed that Apollo was a sharpshooter with perfect aim even from a distance, thus he was called "far-shooting". "Phoebus Apollo, the lord who shoots form afar, although strong and heroic he is, shall abhor war." *(Shield of Heracles, 100)*

The worship of Apollo took place mainly in the city of Delphi, which attracted many pilgrims, and which in those days was considered the center of the world. Those who came to Delphi saw Apollo as a mediator between the gods and humans. They believed that through his oracle the gods sent messages to man as to what was to happen in their futures.

Apollo's birthplace was the island of Delos, and thus he was sometimes called the "Deli god". Themis nourished the child Apollo on nectar and ambrosia, and he developed quickly. As a toddler, Apollo already began demanding a bow and a quiver of arrows. Hephaestus granted these readily, and Apollo hurriedly went after his mother's enemy – a monstrous python snake on Mount Parnassus. The child Apollo's arrow found its mark, and the gravely injured python slithered to the oracle of Delphi to ask for asylum. Apollo followed him there, and disregarding the holiness of the place, he put the python to death on holy ground of the temple. The oracle complained to Zeus about this desecration, and Apollo was ordered to go to return to Delphi and purify himself. The free-thinking and independent Apollo disregarded Zeus's orders however, and chose to go to Crete for the purification.

Apollo's prophetic ability was a gift from Pan, a god with legs of a goat, whom Apollo rescued. He later forced the oracle at Delphi, Pythia, to become his priestess.

Robert Graves holds that these apparent contradictions can be explained by understanding the differences between the various groups or tribes who held Apollo at the center of their religion.

After Apollo was given the gift of prophecy and made Pythia his priestess, he had another conflict with Zeus, and as usual the lucky god came out clean. Leto, his mother, arrived in Delphi when she heard that Apollo was there, and took part in a private ceremony. While she was thus occupied, Titius, one of Zeus's sons, tried to rape her. Apollo and Artemis heard Leto's screams and killed Titius with their arrows. Zeus understood Apollo's motive for the killing, and in fact punished the soul of Titius by throwing him into the Tartarus where he was to be tortured for eternity.

The next time that Apollo experienced the anger of Zeus, however, he barely escaped the death sentence. When Apollo's son, the famous doctor Asclepius, discovered a means of restoring the dead to life, Zeus was extremely unnerved by the matter. Hades, too, as could be expected, was upset by the discovery as it could mean no more newcomers to his underworld. Zeus killed the brilliant physician, and Apollo, in his grief and anger, avenged the death of his son by killing Zeus's favorite Cyclopes, maker of his lightening and thunder. This time Zeus's anger knew no bounds. Leto begged for mercy to be shown her son, but even though she was perhaps Zeus's greatest love, Apollo resisted her protests and was about to find his end in the great and horrible Tartarus. Leto did not cease to beg, however, and when she promised in the name of her son that never again would he do anything to grieve the great father of the gods, Zeus agreed to exchange the original punishment for a year of servitude during which Apollo was to shepherd the huge flocks of King Admetus. Leto advised Apollo to fulfill this punishment gratefully. He did so, and during his servitude he provided Admetus, Zeus's friend, many other favors as well.

Not all of Apollo's deeds would be called "righteous" in the eyes of modern man. He had a fanatical need to be the best musician among men and gods and to be the god of musical wonders. This often brought about the needless deaths of innocent creatures whose only crime was that they too possessed the musical gift. The Satir Marsias was one of these. Athena had fashioned for herself a double flute, which she played brilliantly and beautifully. However, it happened that she noticed Hera and Aphrodite giggling at her as she played. Embarrassed, she ran to the forest and looked at her reflection in the great river. She realized that her face was swollen and blue from the effort of playing and that she indeed looked quite ridiculous. Angry, she threw the flute away, cursing it and anyone that might ever play on it again. Marsias, passing by later and innocently found the flute. Putting it to his lips, he effortlessly made sweet and beautiful music – the lovely tones had remained in the "memory" of the instrument. The wonderful melodies wafted back to the city for all to hear, and Marsias was delighted. As he walked through the countryside, the people of the villages came out to hear his instrument and followed along behind him. They began to declare that even Apollo did not play as well.

The naïve Marsias did not realize the warning in those words, and he innocently continued to play the flute. When Apollo heard what was happening, he was furious, and he challenged Marsias to a musical contest that would be judged by the Muses. The competition went on an on -Apollo and Marsias both played so well that the Muses were hard put to declare a winner. So Apollo proposed adding another element to the contest. The competitors would have to sing while playing, and they would play their instruments backwards! It goes without saying that a harp, which is what Apollo played, can be strummed backwards, and it is no trick to sing along while doing so. The player of a flute, however, cannot accompany himself with singing, and neither can he easily play backwards. Thus, Apollo "won" the competition. Apollo then punished Marsias in a way that mars his reputation for justice and fairness. He tossed him into the air, and nailed him to an oak tree.

Graves interprets this incident as symbolic of the taking over of the harp from the flute as the instrument of choice in ancient Greece, and as the basis for Apollo's additional title, "god of music".

This was not to be the only competition between harp and flute which involved Apollo. The second contest was with none other than Pan, after which the famous Pan Flute is named. The judge this time was King Midas, who declared that he preferred the flute to the harp. This decision was so abhorred by Apollo that he turned the king's ears into mule ears as a result! Apollo explained that in his opinion only a mule could prefer the playing of the pan flute to that of the heavenly harp.

Apollo was a confirmed bachelor who never married even a single goddess or mortal, though he certainly did not lack for love affairs with members of both sexes.

Among Apollo's many lovers are counted Pathia, who bore Doris, the Muse Thalia, mother of the Corybantes, and Koronis, mother of his son Asclepius, the great physician. He also coupled with the Muse Calliope, who bore Orpheus, the admired musician and poet.

One of the most famous love stories of Apollo is that of his relationship with Daphne, the mountain nymph, daughter of the god of the River Paneus. She was Apollo's first love, and he courted her for a long time without success. Daphne loved hunting and the freedom of her life in the forest. She did not want to marry and lose her independence. When Apollo happened to lay eyes on her during a walk in the forest, he fell deeply in love at first sight and began to pursue her untiringly. He actually chased her on foot, and frightened, Daphne tried to run away. When he almost had her in his clutches, Daphne saw her father's river shining in an opening between the trees, and she shouted for his help. Instantly, Daphne turned into a tree, and Apollo had no choice but to the leaves of the mighty plant. Since then, the leaves of Daphne (bay laurel) became one of the symbols of Apollo.

Apollo's love of the handsome youth, Hyacinth, ended in disaster. At first, Apollo's only competitor for the attentions of the young man was the mortal poet Thamiris. When Apollo heard Thamiris boast that he could sing better than the Muses, he made sure to tell the Muses about this particular conceit which resulted in Thamiris being punished by the Muses. They took away his voice, his vision, and his ability to play the harp. Getting rid of competition from Thamiris did not clear the way for Apollo to take up with Hyacinth, however. Zephyr, the east wind, was also taken with Hyacinth's charms, and was jealous that he seemed to be falling for Apollo. Zephyr waited for an opportunity to strike, and he found it when Apollo gave Hyacinth a lesson in discus throwing. The east wind gusted and blew the discus from its course, causing it to hit Hyacinth on the top of his head, killing him on the spot. From the blood of the dead youth sprouted the flowering hyacinth plant.

During the ancient Roman and Greek period, music, song, philosophy, astronomy, mathematics, medicine, and science all came under Apollo's umbrella of authority. He taught medicine to mortals, and at the same time had the power to wipe out ailments before they claimed victims.

The seven-stringed harp is the symbol most often associated with Apollo. Later, the seven strings came to represent the seven movements in Greek grammar, thought to have mystical significance and therapeutic qualities.

As the patron of song, Apollo became the leader of the nine Muses, and was sometimes called Musagetes. He was also sometimes dubbed Smintheus, (god of mice), and Sauroktonos (killer of lizards).

The aphorism "know thyself" is attributed to Apollo as well as the admonition "moderation in all things" (which he demanded of Zeus when he "exaggerated" in his response to Apollo's sins).

Graves equates Apollo with the child Horus, explaining that Apollo identified with the sun, and by association, the moon.

The bay laurel tree, the crow, and the dolphin were all consecrated to Apollo.

Aphrodite/Venus

Aphrodite was the Greek goddess of love, beauty, and fertility. According to Homer, she was the daughter of Zeus and Dione, but many others have claimed that she sprang from the sea foam, and thus her name, which is a form of the Greek word for "foam".

Aphrodite was said to be the loveliest of the goddesses. She married Hephaestus, but betrayed him with Ares, god of war. It was said that Aphrodite was able to cause the emotion of love to leap in the hearts of men and gods alike. She also had the ability to cause sexual arousal, thus the origin of the word "aphrodisiac".

In the story of the Trojan War, Aphrodite won the golden apple which was given by Paris to the fairest of the goddesses. In order to insure that she would win over her rivals for the title, Hera and Athena, Aphrodite promised to deliver the love of Helena in return for the apple.

Because of their grace and beauty, the dove and the sparrow were consecrated to Aphrodite, as well as the sweet smelling myrtle tree.

Venus was the Aphrodite's roman counterpart. The name Venus comes from the words for "charm" and "beauty". Venice was originally the goddess who assured a good harvest. Apparently, the significance of her name is what caused her to become associated with the Greek Aphrodite.

Hermes/Mercury

Hermes' parents were Zeus and Maia, daughter of Atlas. Hermes was the messenger of the gods, and accompanied the dead on their journey to the underworld. He was also the god of commerce and communication, traveling, and good luck. His personality, like the metal that bore his Latin name, was slippery, and had many interchangeable and conflicting facets. Merchants respected him, but thieves admired him as well, although he was protector of homes and village squares. He was father of Pan, god of the shepherds, but he himself was known to steal cattle and sheep! Hermes was the patron of speechmaking, yet the orators feared him, since he was known for ruining their orations!

Hermes wore winged sandals which allowed him to perform his duties as messenger to the other gods as swiftly as possible. He was manipulative, resourceful, and inventive. On the day he was born he invented an instrument for himself which resembled a harp, and fashioned it from the shell of a turtle. For the strings, Hermes stole a calf from his brother Apollo's flock, and used the animal's intestines. His well-known manipulativeness was already developed as is evident by the way he hid the fact of this theft of the calf. At night, Hermes pulled the calf into a cave, making it look as if the calf was facing in the opposite direction; that is, facing the exit of the cave. That same night, Hermes fashioned himself a stove to roast the meat in order to enjoy the stolen loot. Afterwards, he returned to his cradle and lay in it in perfect innocence. When Apollo came to his brother's cradle he found him deep in the sleep of the just. When questioned, Hermes lied without so much as a bat of the eyelids, and even swore that he was not involved in any affair concerning the flock of Apollo…

Hermes lied to his father, king of the gods, as well. Zeus smiled forgivingly at his son's escapades, but asked him to replace the animal he'd stolen from his brother. Apollo requested the harp-like instrument instead, and with that the debt was paid.

Hermes set about making himself a new instrument, a flute this time, and this instrument too was attractive to Apollo who asked that it be given to him in return for a magic golden bed. On this bed, Hermes would fall into a deep slumber during which he dreamed of accompanying the dead into the underworld. The golden bed came to be one of the symbols of the god.

Other symbols of Hermes include the winged sandals, messenger cap, and piles of money.

Hermes was originally a phallic para-Hellenistic god. His statue, the head of a man atop an erect phallus, was set up at intersections and crossroads for the protection of travelers, merchants, and even thieves.

Over time, Hermes also came to be known also as a patron of literature, music, and sport.

Mercury was the parallel Roman god to Hermes. Mercury was the god of commerce, and stories about him are based on those about Hermes, but with different symbols. His cult took hold during the period of the Caesars. The festival of Mercury was a commercial fair which took place on the fifteenth of May, the day his temple was dedicated.

Artemis/Diana

Artemis was the daughter of Zeus and Leto, and the twin sister of Apollo, and she was one of the three virgin goddesses of Olympus. Artemis ruled the realm of hunting and hunters, as well as the hills, the forests, and the wild animals.

In depictions of Artemis she is usually surrounded by numerous friendly beasts, and was nicknamed the "governess of the wild animals".

There are apparent contradictions in her character. Artemis was said to be protector of young people, but on the other hand, it is told that she would not allow the Greek fleet to set sail until they had sacrificed a young virgin to her! When a woman died a quick death, without suffering, it was said that Artemis had been merciful and had killed her with her silver arrows. She also helped women as they labored in childbirth. On the other hand, there are stories in which Artemis is characterized as brutal, vengeful, and cruel. According to legend, it was customary in the land of Tauris to make human sacrifices in Artemis' honor. At the temple of Artemis in Sparta her cruelty was evident as well in the practice of whipping children until blood was drawn in order to "test their courage" and to "toughen them up".

Artemis' twin brother Apollo was the god of the sun, and Artemis was therefore thought to be the moon. In Greek, the word for moon is Selena, and in Latin – Luna.

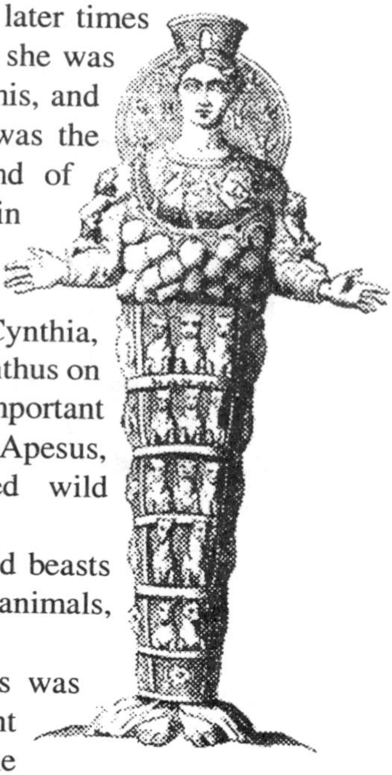

Artemis came to be associated in later times with the "triple goddess". In the sky she was Selena, on the ground she was Artemis, and in the underworld, Hecate. Hecate was the dark goddess of the crossroads, and of places which were thought to contain ill-winds, or bad spirits, such as graveyards.

Artemis was sometimes called Cynthia, after the place of her birth, Mount Cynthus on the island of Delos. The most important center for the worship of Artemis was Apesus, where worshippers often sacrificed wild animals, goats, and birds.

As the goddess of hunting, the wild beasts of the forest were her sacred animals, especially the deer.

The roman counterpart to Artemis was the goddess Diana, a very ancient character indeed. Diana was seen as the goddess of women, and those who worshipped her would use artifacts which symbolized femininity. These could be items, such as stones, shaped like the female genitalia, or images of mothers and infants. Often parades would be staged, with women carrying torches as they marched to the temple at Arikia. The fact that Diana was identified with Artemis stems from the fact that even though she was the goddess of growth and fertility, she was thought of also as the goddess of the forests, and from here it was a short leap to hunting. Like Artemis, Diana was associated with the moon, and called Luna.

Diana's priest was traditionally an escaped slave who became a priest by killing his predecessor, and knew that it was inevitable that he too should die at the hands of the next escaped slave to take his place.

Vulcan/Hephaestus

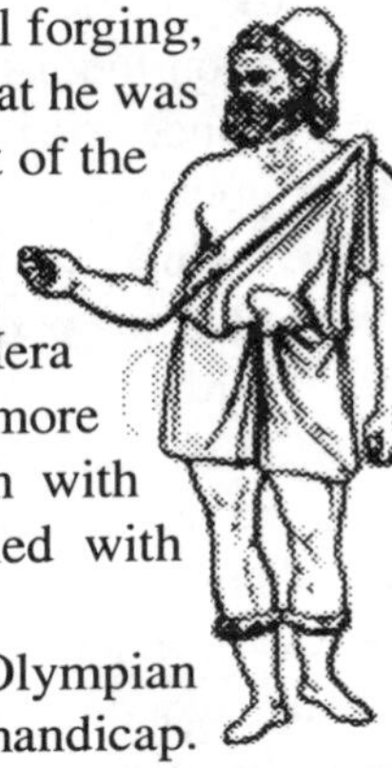

Son of Hera, Hephaestus was the god of metal forging, of craftsmanship, and of fire. Some believe that he was fathered by Zeus, but most according to most of the myths, he was born of a virgin conception, as Hera's revenge against Zeus for birthing Athena (Metis' daughter) unnaturally. " ...Hera bore Hephaestus, who is skilled in crafts more than all the sons of Heaven, without union with Zeus, for she was very angry and quarreled with him..." (Hesiod, Theogony 926-929)

Hephaestus was different from the other Olympian gods in that he had a definite physical handicap. Hesiod calls him "The famous lame one", and Homer adds to his name "The praised limping one". Hephaestus' limitations are mentioned time and again in the mythology, alongside his many notable abilities and talents.

At his birth, seeing that Hephaestus was lame, his mother Hera despised him for his imperfections and his disability, and rejected him, tossing him down from the heavens in disgust. The infant Hephaestus was rescued by Thetis and Eurynome, who snatched him from the sea and raised him. Later, Hera brought him back to Olympus, and there he remained, receiving great praise and glory for his talented handiwork and as a blacksmith.

Homer provides another, somewhat different account, according to which it was Zeus who rejected the youngster when he broke both of his legs in a fall. In still another version, it was Dionysus who returned Hephaestus to Olympus.

The gods who possessed more perfect physical forms were quick to tease and ridicule the one among them who was different. Although somehow Hephaestus managed to marry none other than the goddess most known for beauty and grace, her later betrayal of him with Ares simply gave the other gods more fuel for their humiliating diatribes against Hephaestus.

Obedius tells us that the sun, as a god, was the first to witness the perverse behavior of Ares and Venus, and that he passed on the information to Hephaestus. Upon hearing the report, dropped the metal that he had been in his hand, and set to work fashioning bronze chains so delicate and fine that they were invisible to the naked eye. These special chains were made to be responsive to every tiny movement and touch. Hephaestus strung these around the bed he shared with Aphrodite, where she carried out her illicit affair. When his wife and her lover lay together on the bed, they soon found themselves trapped in the invisible web of chains. Hephaestus then into the room through the ivory doors and called the other gods to witness what was going on. The gods were greatly amused. Most of them prayed that they too would one day be in the embarrassing situation in which Ares now found himself. The gods enjoyed the hilarity and laughed out loud, and the affair was the subject of much merry-making among them for quite some time.

Of course, Venus made sure to punish the sun for being a gossip. She made him fall in love with a mortal woman, the ones who suffered from this most being the human beings who were deeply frightened when the sun changed its course and its rays while in love.

Another version, agreed upon by Homer and Hesiod, tells that Hephaestus married Aglia, who, like Aphrodite, was known for her outstanding beauty. This archetype – marriage between the least attractive of males and the most attractive of females, is a fascinating one, and has been the subject of many works of art through the ages.

Hephaestus had ties to the island of Lemnos, where he was said to have fallen and broking his legs, causing Zeus to eject him from Olympus. These ties have to do with the physical characteristics of Lemnos. Lemnos was a volcanic island, given to frequent eruptions. Hephaestus' occupation as a blacksmith involved the forging of metal with fire resembled the volcanic eruptions and their melting lava being brought forth. In the tradition of the archetypes, we can see a resemblance between the boiling raging mountain and the anger percolating in the belly of the abandoned, lame, unwanted, and humiliated child who only desires to be respected and appreciated. The child grew up to mold his metals into works of beauty, just as the mountain molded its lava. Hephaestus' work was said to have surpassed any known to mortal or immortal man.

It was Hephaestus who made the shields and helmets for the heroes of Olympus, and his works were not only strong and attractive, but they were possessed of great natural powers. He made for Zeus, out of earthenware, a statue of a virgin – Pandora, who brought the mortals a holocaust of deadly disease and suffering. On the other hand, Hephaestus taught humans many different crafts. He built castles for the gods, and for Helios, the sun, he made a beautiful chariot.

It is possible that the origins of Hephaestus and Vulcan trace all the way back to before the days of Roman mythology. The Romans tied him to the wild and uncontrollable volcanic fires, and they worshipped him mostly in centers outside the cities. The festival Vulcania was celebrated in his honor every August 23rd, during which a special priest would make sacrifices to the god.

Hephaestus' identification with violent erupting mountains notwithstanding, he was known as one of the "good gods". He hated quarrels and valued peace. He was the patron of the blacksmiths, who played an important role in the culture of the city. He was even the god of the ceremony during which children came of age as members of society.

Hephaestus was sometimes described as inebriated, a point which strengthens the archetype he represents. His relationship to Dionysus, the god of wine, is apparent in an archeological find dating from around the year 425 BC in which Hephaestus, appearing to be drunk, is sitting on a donkey, while the animal is tied to Dionysus. Around them are crowded the entourage of the wine god.

Other than when he caught his wife in her betrayal with the god of war, there are few stories about Hephaestus which involve any intrigue whatever. The only event which shows him any sort of compromising light is when he took revenge on his mother when she refused to disclose the identity of his father, insisting that he was the product of a virgin conception. As we have said, according to most of the myths, Hephaestus had no father. Hephaestus refused to believe his mother, Hera, and fashioned her a mechanical chair which, when she sat on it, grabbed hold of her and did not free her until she swore on the holy river Styx that she was telling the truth. Still, there are sources which believe that Hera bore Hephaestus as a result on an adulterous relationship.

The archetype of Hephaestus is quite human, as his disability and his occupations made him resemble the mortals more than the gods. Hephaestus was a "working god", a manufacturer of useful goods who labored with his hands. He was a fatherless child, rejected and abandoned, who bore being made fun because of lameness. When he manages to attract a lovely mate, she turns on him blatantly, and he more ridiculed than ever. In addition, he takes no revenge on them, but rises above them by excelling in his craft, using the energy of the churning and erupting anger within him to turn out works of beauty rather than hate.

Dionysus/Bacchus

Dionysus was the god of wine, fertility and growth. He was also the god of physical and spiritual intoxication. According to the most widespread legend, Dionysus' mother was Semele (moon), daughter of Cadmus, King of Thebes. Zeus disguised himself as a mortal in order to mate with her. This illicit affair was discovered by Hera, the jealous wife of Zeus, when Semele was already expecting his child. Hera was incensed and angered, and hatched a plot to take her revenge, as was her wont, on the woman, rather than on Zeus. She dressed as Semele's elderly nurse, and under the guise of offering "advice" to the younger woman, she urged her to force her lover to reveal his true identity. "How else will you know that your child's father is not a monster?" she reasoned. Hera's words were convincing to Semele, and she indeed began to nag Zeus to tell her who he really was. When he refused, Semele banned him from her bed, which pleased Hera greatly, but angered Zeus to such an extent that he ordered huge bolts of lightening to come down from the heavens and kill Semele while his child was still gestating within her.

The wise Apollo stepped in to save the six month fetus which would be Dionysus as it fell from its mother's lifeless body and sewed it into his thigh. There he kept Dionysus safe until he was ready to be born, three months later. Thus, Dionysus is often referred to as "the twice born".

Hera would not make peace with the existence of this illegitimate son of her husband. In one account, she ordered the Titans to kill him, and they did catch him and dismember him, and even cooked his parts for good measure, eating all but his heart. The blood that was spilled in the process caused pomegranate trees to grow in every spot it touched. Rhea then took the heart and from it managed to regenerate Dionysus' and bring him back to life. In another version of this myth, when the Titans tried to catch him and kill him, he foiled them by growing a horn in the middle of his forehead and snakes from his head instead of hair.

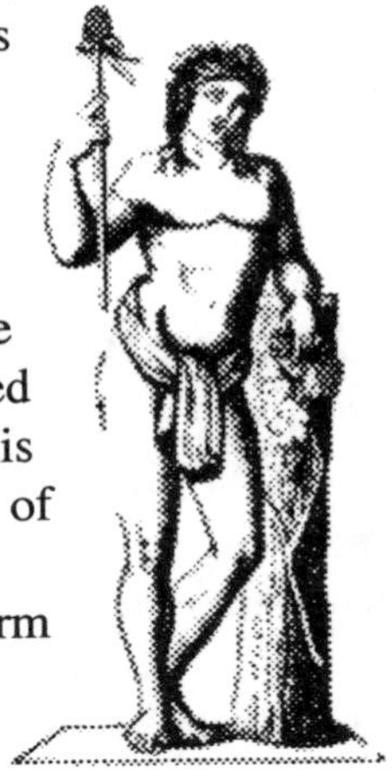

Dionysus had the skill of changing his form and of disguising himself readily. He often appeared as a lion, goat, or bull. He used this talent to escape the fury his father's wife. Hera's anger toward Dionysus never abated, and she used madness in one form or another as a weapon against him, whether directly or indirectly. Zeus, in an effort to protect the boy from Hera, sent him to the wife of the king of Athamas, who dressed him as a girl and hid him among the women of her city. When Hera got wind of this she punished the conspirators severely, causing attacks of insanity which made the king believe his son was a deer, and kill him.

Dionysus transformed himself again, this time with the help of Hermes, Zeus's messenger, who turned him into a wild ox and put him on Mount Nisa with nymphs to guard and care for him. It was on Nisa that Dionysus invented wine.

Even when he matured, his talent for disguises and changing form could not keep him safe from Hera's wrath. He escaped into a life of wandering, along with a strange entourage of gods and mortals that behaved in an outrageous manner much of the time. Among his companions were the Satyrs, -creatures that were half man and half goat, known for their profligacy and their lustfulness. He also traveled with the Maenads - wild eternally young nymphs who carried swords and whooped and shouted with abandon. The Maenads would romp about the forests small animals and even human children, and eating them alive. Everywhere this merry band traveled, Dionysus brought the wine. The cult of Dionysus was marked by a certain ecstasy. It included wild drunken orgies, a lot of wine, and perhaps even the use of other inebriating substances

On a respite from his travels, Dionysus visited Rhea, his grandmother, who acquitted him of all wrong-doing while under the influence of wine. He then continued his wanderings, bringing wine and crazed behavior with him to every destination. Anyone who opposed Dionysus came down with an attack of insanity or inebriation which would cause him to lose him mind temporarily.

One of these was the king of Argos, whom Dionysus punished by making the women of Argus swallow their young. The king watched in horror as the women began to gobble down their children, and he hurriedly apologized to Dionysus, and even erected a temple in his honor.

The cult of Dionysus spread from Greece to the entire known world. Legend has it that he was known in Egypt, Turkey, and India. He was infamous for the fact that anyone who dared to oppose him went insane!

Finally, Dionysus was received on Mount Olympus, as one of the twelve Olympian gods. He sat at Zeus's right hand. Hestia, goddess of the hearth fires and the family, gave up her place for him, voluntarily, as she knew that she was welcomed in any city in the land. As soon as he attained Olympian status, Dionysus went to Tartarus to release his mother, Semele. He accomplished this by bribing Persephone, the wife of Hades, king of the underworld, with the myrtle. Once his mother was freed, her name was changed to protect her form the jealousy of the other spirits left behind. Zeus gave Semele a place to dwell on Olympus, and Hera, in spite of her anger, rage and jealousy, never hurt her again.

Dionysus married Ariadne, daughter of Minos, and former lover of Theseus, who had deserted her. At their wedding Dionysus presented Ariadne with a gem-studded crown, and later when she preceded him in death, he threw the crown up to the heavens where the gems became stars in the skies.

Many festivals took place in honor of Dionysus, the most famous of which is the Dionysia. Participants in the festivals carried statues of Dionysus and phallic figures, as well as other representations of the male genitalia. Plays were put on which some say were the precursors of modern-day comedies and tragedies.

Dionysus was also known by the name Bacchus, which may

have its origins in the Greek word for "foolishness". The wine god held an important position in European religion, usually under the name Zagreus. Later cults of Dionysus stressed his repeated return to life after having been destroyed. The name Zagreus means "came back to life". Some of his followers were so fanatical and extreme that they committed acts of murder in the name of the worship of the god. The Roman Senate counteracted this by making it illegal to participate in the cult of Dionysus.

The symbols of Dionysus are: The grape vine, the pomegranate, the fig, and the ivy.

Demeter/Ceres

The generous goddess of the crops and harvest, fertility and growth, Demeter was "Mother Earth", daughter of Kronos and Rhea.

Just as Dionysus had been an earthbound god before he rose to Olympus, Demeter was tied to the human realm and did not dwell on the mount. She was known as a good-hearted goddess, and very rarely used her power to punish humankind, with one notable exception. Erysichthon, the son of a notoriously crude and unsavory man, raided a pear and apple orchard that had been dedicated to Demeter. He brought twenty young cohorts with him, and they uprooted numerous trees in an effort to gather wood to build themselves a place of amusement. Even when Demeter transformed herself into an elderly woman and beseeched the youth to remember the holiness of the place and to cease and desist, Erysichthon and his friends continued their desecration of the grove. Demeter would not let this go unpunished, and she sentenced the youth to a cruel form of starvation. Erysichthon ate and ate, but no matter how much he consumed his hunger only grew and he became ever weaker and more emaciated.

Demeter never married. She had a daughter, Persephone, with

her brother, Zeus, and a son, Plutus, the god of wealth, with the Titan, Iasion. Iasion fell in love with Demeter at the wedding party of Cadamus and Harmony (daughter of Ares and Aphrodite), and drunk on wine, she went out with him to a field and conceived the child. When they returned, Zeus discovered their deed by observing the mud and grass stains on their garments, and was furious that Iasion would dare even to come near Demeter. He let the Titan have it with a cruel blast of lightening and thunder which killed him on the spot.

Demeter had a sunny disposition, but the happy goddess lost her joy forever when her daughter Persephone was abducted by Hades, lord of the underworld. For seven days and nights Demeter searched for the girl, during which there was an incident which included, by some accounts an attempt by Poseidon to rape her. She continued her desperate search for her daughter, taking neither rest nor nourishment, until on the tenth day she at last took refuge with King Celeus and his wife Metaneira. They were unaware that Demeter was a goddess, and offered her a post as nanny for their new infant son. Demeter wanted to reward them for their kindness by making the child immortal. She fed him ambrosia and held him over an open flame each day to make him strong. When the queen, still unaware of Demeter's powers and origin, discovered the strange way in which she her son was being nurtured, she became enraged and put a stop to it. Demeter then decided to reveal her true identity and she ordered that a temple be built in her honor, and that festivities be held to worship her.

Hades had fallen in love with Persephone, and asked Zeus for her hand in marriage. Zeus did not want any unpleasant disagreements with his brother Hades, nor did he wish to displease his sister Demeter, so he diplomatically decline to grant permission, but neither did he deny it! Hades became frustrated by Zeus's indecision and saw in this an excuse to abduct Persephone, and did so. He waited until Persephone was merrily picking flowers in a field to kidnap her and carry her off. When Demeter heard that her daughter had been taken by the king of the underworld, she suffered deep grief. She asked Hecate to assist her in her search, and together they went to Helios, the all-seeing sun. When Helios affirmed that Persephone had indeed been stolen by Hades, Demeter's mourning was so deep that she wandered the earth inconsolably, and wherever she passed she forbade the trees to blossom and give fruit until her daughter was restored to her. Zeus wanted to remedy the situation, but he was embarrassed to approach Demeter himself, so he sent Iris, goddess of the rainbow. After Iris he sent a delegation of Olympian gods carrying all manner of gifts, beseeching Demeter to cease her wanderings and to allow the fruit to grow once again. Her wanderings were causing destruction and suffering to the entire human race. But Demeter would not agree to come to Olympus, and swore that the earth would remain barren until her daughter was returned.

Demeter received a message which said that her daughter could be given back to her, under one condition – that during Persephone's stay in the underworld she had not tasted any of the food of the deceased.

Persephone declared that she had indeed refused to taste the food, and thus Hermes was able to return her to the land of the living in his chariot. But as he was about to escort her out of the underworld, one of the gardeners of Hades shouted out that he would swear that he had witnessed Persephone take a pomegranate from its branch and eat seven seeds from the fruit. Demeter punished the gardener by pushing him into a large pit which she sealed closed with a boulder. Yet, because of the seven grains of pomegranate she had consumed, Persephone was to be required to live ever after in the land of the dead. Demeter was so upset and angered by this that she still refused to allow the earth to blossom and give fruit.

Zeus, looking for a solution, turned to their mother, Rhea, asking her to affect a compromise. Rhea suggested that for nine months out of each year Persephone be allowed to stay with her mother on the earth's surface, and for three months of the year she would return to her uncle Hades in the underworld. Hecate was charged with carrying out this agreement and making sure that Persephone would indeed serve the required time each year in the land of the dead.

Some scholars have seen in Persephone/Demeter/ Hecate the "triple goddess". (Virgin/Mature woman/ Crone) This famous triple goddess was the goddess of fertility during the earliest periods, whose cult had several variations in Europe and the Balkans. Some see the connection between the male gods and the triple female gods as a sign of relation between the cult of the original three males – Zeus, Poseidon, and Hades, with their three wives (Zeus – Hera, Zeus/Poseidon – Demeter, Hades – Kore). By way of these connections to the goddesses, the male gods associated themselves with the most important cult aside from that of fire – the cult of agriculture.

According to myth, it was Demeter who taught humans the science of agriculture, and provided them with the various seeds and grains. Demeter's center of worship was Eleusinia, near Athens. The rites of the Eleusinian mysteries were highly secret. The participants in the cult were said to deserve long life and a blessed after-life.

The gentle character of Demeter had quite a few contradictions. She is identified on the one hand with the ultimate in motherhood and on the other hand with eternal "bachelorhood". She is the patroness of growth while at the same time causing draught and desolation. Though she gave mankind seeds and the agricultural skills to make them grow, she put a stop to these processes when what was dearest to her, her daughter, was taken from her. Life and death, too, were tied to Demeter's name. Her Titan lover was murdered by Zeus, and in Athens the dead were called "Demetrioi".

The Roman goddess Ceres was all but identical to Demeter, as she too was tied to the land. A festival in her honor took place every April 19th.

The Secondary Gods

In addition to the twelve Olympian gods and their Roman counterparts, there were many other deities, both Greek and Roman, some of whom appear only in a few of the myths. Some of the Roman gods that are described here, particularly the earliest among them, do not appear in any of the more well-known myths, but did have cults of worship among the people of ancient times. These gods of secondary importance are discussed here in alphabetical order.

Eos/Aurora

Eos, in Greek mythology, and known as Aurora in Roman myths, was the goddess of the dawn. According to Hesiod, she was the daughter of the Titan Hyperion, and sister of Helios and Selena. She mated with Astraios and gave birth to the stars and the wind.

As in many other cases in the mythology, whereby love affairs of the gods hurt those who were the objects of their passion, the love of Eos caused suffering to those she desired. Her love for Orion the hunter, for example, the giant son of Poseidon, brought no good at all to poor Orion. The gods did not look favorably upon Eos's desire for Orion, to say the least – in fact they were so annoyed by this relationship that Apollo caused Artemis, his sister, to kill the handsome hunter by shooting an arrow at him.

Eos, as one who was always waiting for the dawn to bring new possibilities along with the promise of each new day, found that lovers always slipped "between her fingers" and she never found much joy and satisfaction with any of them. Eos seemed always to choose the unattainable male, in that he could not or would not remain committed to her.

She continued to fall in love with "the wrong men" – Cephalus, son of Iolus, King of the winds, was another woman's mate – in fact he was freshly married and in love with Procris. He too, like Orion, was a great hunter. Eos fell in love with him, and right away, without consideration for his feelings, she grabbed him and tried to force him to return her affections.

This type of love, we learn from the myths, has no chance, and Cephalus ' heart belonged to another! He neither forgot nor forgave Eos's behavior, and he certainly did not return her love. Eos was forced to let him go and to allow him to return to Procris, but not before she planted in his heart the seed of jealousy and a suspicion that his wife had been unfaithful to him. Like most stories of love between a god and a mortal, here too, the mortal was the one to suffer. According to the Greek version of this story, Cephalus accidentally caused his wife's death.

Eos did not learn her lesson, and she continued to fall in love with mortals. The next man to suffer from her cursed attraction was the Tithonos, Prince of Troy. It seemed that this time Eos found a solution to her problems – she asked Zeus, father of the gods, to make the prince immortal! However, as a goddess whose fate was a beauty that would last forever, Eos forgot to ask Zeus to ensure that her lover would have the same. Zeus gave Tithonos everlasting life, but not everlasting youth!

In due time Tithonos turned elderly and infirm. At first Eos continued to care for him, but when he became too dependent on her ministrations, and was so old he was barely functional, Eos locked him into a room so that she would not have to be reminded of the unfairness of everlasting life in a broken down body. Some accounts claim that she turned him into a grasshopper.

Ops

Ops was a Roman goddess of riches and plenty, and a protector of Rome. Her husband was Katornus, the parallel Roman god to the Greek Kronos.

Ilithyia

Daughter of Zeus and Hera, Ilithyia was the goddess of childbirth. Her Latin name was Lukina. Hera would often use Ilithyia to punish the women that copulated with her husband by withholding midwifery care during their confinements. Leto suffered childbirth pains for nine days and nights as a result of this deed, and Alcmena, the mother of Heracles, also suffered from Hera's wrath in a similar manner.

Iris

Iris was the goddess of the rainbow. She was the daughter of the Titans, Thaumas and Electra. Homer described her as devoted to Zeus, but other writers say she was closer to Hera, and often stayed close to her and at her service. There are very few stories about Iris, and she had no cult of worship. In ancient works of art she is depicted with wings on her back and on her shoes.

Erinyes/Furies

The three Erinyes - Alecto, Megaera, and Tisiphone - were the goddesses of revenge and blood vengeance. According to Hesiod, Gaia, goddess of the earth, produced them from the blood of Uranus after his castration at the hands of his son Kronos. The Erinyes chased after liars and murderers who had escaped justice and forced them to look at their shocking faces and serpent topped heads, causing the criminals to go mad with fear. According to some of the myths, Athena was able to appease and calm the Erinyes, and they later even became known as the "benevolent" goddesses!

Eris

Twin sister of Ares, the god of war, and daughter of Hera, Eris was goddess of jealousy and quarrels. Some myths recount that the twins were born to Hera after she came into contact with a particular herb or plant, in which case theirs was a fatherless conception.

Eris assisted her brother, the most hated of the gods except for Hades, in his task of inciting wars among men and gods. In one of the most famous myths, dealing with perhaps the most notorious war in mythology, it was Eris who started the conflict. She was not well-liked among the gods, and they did not invite her to the wedding of Paleus and Thetis. Eris was not content to be left out, however, and she showed up without an invitation, ready to ply her talent for causing rows and disagreements. She brought with her to the celebration a golden apple on which was engraved "For the fairest goddess of them all", and tossed it into the wedding hall among the assembled guests. Sure enough, three of the goddesses argued over who should get the prize; Hera, Athena, and Aphrodite, each claimed to be the loveliest indeed. Paris, Prince of Troy was asked to judge the contest and award the golden apple. Aphrodite promised Paris that she would cause the beautiful Helena to fall in love with him, a bribe Paris could not resist. Afterwards, feeling deserving of his reward, Paris kidnapped Helena, and the Trojan War began!

Hesiod, in his essay *Works and Days,* claims there were two Eris' – Eris the Bad, who caused jealousy and quarrels between people, and Eris the Good, goddess of competition, who motivated mankind to ambitions of success and development.

Dione

In the earliest Greek myths, Dione is the wife of Zeus. Only in the later literature does Hera take her place in Greek religion. The famous shrines of Dodona, Epirus and Athens continued to consider Dione Zeus's wife.

In some of the myths Dione appears as Zeus's concubine. In later times she was considered the mother of Aphrodite and daughter of Uranus and Gaia.

Hebe

As the goddess of youth, Hebe provided the Olympians with their nectar, the special drink of the gods. When Heracles became mortal, he married Hebe.

Horae

The three Horae were the goddesses of hours and seasons. Daughters of Zeus and Themis, they enforced the law and protected the law. The Horae were Irene – goddess of peace, Dike – goddess of justice, and Eunomia – goddess of order.

Hygieia

The Greek goddess of health, Hygieia was the daughter of Asclepius, the famous physician. She was highly regarded in her own right, and there were numerous statues in her likeness in Greece, though often together with shrines to her father.

Hypnos

The son of Nyx (night), Hypnos was the god of sleep. His brother was Thanatos, the god of death. Hypnos was actually the personification of the concept of sleep. He was described as a winged youngster that brought on slumber by touching the forehead of a tired person, or by sprinkling sleep liquid from a horn he carried. Hypnos was married to Pasithea, and lived on the island of Manos, or according to Hesiod, in the underworld, and together with his brother, he accompanied the deceased on their journey to the land of the dead.

Hymenaeos

God of the Greek wedding.

Helios

The sun god, Helios was the son of the Titans Hyperion and Thea. Selena (moon) and Eos (dawn) were his siblings. Traveling each day carrying the sun in his chariot across the heavens, Helios lit up the world for humankind. He had the unique ability to see everything that took place on the face of the earth. Since Helios saw, heard, and knew all, he was often called upon to bear witness in trials and to resolve disagreements where conflicting versions of events were involved. Similarly, the gods sometimes asked Helios to confirm suspicions they held about one another. It was Helios who told Demeter that Hades had indeed kidnapped her daughter, and who let Hephaestus know that his wife had betrayed him. Aphrodite, in her anger at Helios for his "gossip", caused him to fall in love with a mortal, an event which caused suffering to all mankind, since in his compromised state and out of his desire to spend time with his beloved, Helios began to waver from his course in the sky, and even to abandon his chariot at inopportune times. Sometimes he was late bringing on the dawn, and other times the sunset was delayed.

One of the most well-known myths concerning Helios is the story of Phaethon, his son by Clymene. Phaethon grew up believing that Merops was his father, and when his mother later revealed to him that actually he was the offspring of the sun god, he quickly made his way to Helios' palace. Helios was overjoyed to see his son, and in celebration of their reunion, he offered to give Phaethon whatever his heart desired. To his surprise, the youngster requested the only thing that Helios truly did not wish to give him – a chance to drive the chariot of the sun for a whole day. Helios knew that this could be extremely dangerous for the inexperienced lad, and it was with a heavy heart that he turned over the reins of the chariot to his son.

The horses quickly sensed that an inexperienced hand was driving them, and they started to run amok. First they rose too high, trying to reach the outermost reaches of the heavens, and in so doing they scorched a streak in the sky which became the Milky Way. The earth became colder and colder as the chariot moved father away. Then the horses reversed their course and descended quickly - this time coming to close to the earth and scorching it, which created desserts, dried up lakes, and threatened an uncontrollable outbreak of fire. Then the chariot changed direction again and began to climb quickly back up into the sky. By this time Phaethon realized his foolishness and regretted his wish, but it was too late. Zeus, seeing what was happening and wishing to avert any further disaster, let loose a mighty thunderbolt and flash of lightening, stopping the chariot in its tracks and killing Phaethon instantly. The horses returned to their stable, and Phaethon's body plunged to Earth, where it sank to the bottom of the Eridanus River.

According to the myths, Helios returned every night from the west to the east in a golden basin, made by the artisan Hephaestus. The Greeks saw him as a Titan, and worshipped him only rarely. The exception to this was the Island of Rhodes, which according to legend

Helios asked that Zeus give him, and was named for his wife Rhoda. Rhodes became the center of the cult of Helios - he was worshipped there as a deity of some importance and a yearly festival took place in his honor.

Hecate

One of the earliest Greek goddesses, Hecate was the daughter of the Titan Perses, and Asteria, goddess of the dead and the underworld. Zeus gave Hecate an awesome responsibility – authority over the seas, the heavens, and the earth. It was unusual for Zeus to trust so much to one goddess during the times of the Titans.

Hecate was goddess of the crossroads, and of witchcraft. Three-headed statues of the goddess were often erected at crossroads. She was able to cause success of any kind – political, material, or military. She was generally thought of as a goddess of women, and was often turned to by those who wished to bring a child into the world. She had ties with the realm of magic, and would often be seen in the company of the wind, dogs and wolves, and lit torches.

Hecate was sometimes identified with Artemis or with Selena, and even with Persephone, due to her connection with death and dying. Her Roman name, Trivia, meant "triple crossroad". In Rome she was thought to bring tragedy on anyone those who failed to pray to or appease her.

Victoria

Roman goddess of victory. Parallel goddess to the Greek Nike.

Tyche

The goddess of luck, fate, and chance, Tyche's name meant "whatever happens to man". Her cult was mainly based in Athens and Thebes. Her symbol in many works of art is the wheel of fortune.

Telos

The Roman goddess of the earth, Telos was also called Terra Mater (Mother Earth). She was identified with Gaia (also earth), and sometimes with Hestia, goddess of the hearth fire.

Triton

Son of Poseidon and Amphitrita, and grandson of the Titan Oceanus, Triton was a god of the sea.

Triton's upper body was that of a human and from the waist down he was fishlike. His name became synonymous with "sea dwellers", and "Tritons" were the male counterparts of the female mermaids.

Triton dwelled with his parents in a golden palace under the sea where he ruled. By blowing a huge trumpet made of a spiral-shaped shell, Triton commanded the sea and its inhabitants. One mighty blast of the trumpet could cause a great storm to rise over the waters. Mapmakers in ancient times would often draw tritons and the mermaids on their maps in the belief that travelers who used them would indeed come in contact with these creatures on their journeys!

Charites/Graces

Daughters of Zeus and Eurynome (though some sources say their mother was Aphrodite), the Charites personified all the best qualities of humankind – beauty, grace, intelligence, fun and celebration, and more. According to Homer, there were two Charites, but Hesiod mentions three: Euphrosyne, goddess of mirth; Aglaea, goddess of splendor; Thalia, goddess of happiness. Each was thought both to be and to represent the quality of her name. The rose and the myrtle were their sacred plants.

Janus

The Roman god of gates, Janus had two faces, which looked in opposing directions. Thus he was the only god with the ability to see behind him. The northern gate of the Roman forum was consecrated to Janus' name. It would open when war broke out and lock down again when the war was over.

Lukina

The Roman goddess of childbirth, Lukina was sometimes identified with Diana and Juno. Lukina was the parallel goddess to the Greek Ilithyia.

Liber

The ancient Italian god of productivity, Liber is sometimes compared to Dionysus in that he is closely tied to the making of wine. The center for his cult was mount Aventino, where Keres, the god of punishment, and Liber's female counterpart, Libera, thought to be the daughter of Keres, were also worshipped. A festival in honor of Liber, who was called by many "Father" took place every seventeenth of March.

Muses

The nine Muses were the daughters of Zeus, father of the gods, and Mnemosyne, goddess of memory. They were the goddess of the fine arts and sciences. The Muses were born on Olympus and mount Likon in Boiaotia was consecrated to them. When they matured, this mountain became their place of entertainment, from which they always returned in the evening to Olympus.

Hesiod tells of the Muses: "Mnemosyne bore nine daughters, all of the same spirit, carefree and full of song and dance ...lovely verses come from their lips, singing the laws and the ways of immortals with their beautiful immortal voices."
(Theogony, 60-69)

Thalia – Muse of Comedy

Thalia was the muse of laughter, fun, and entertainment.

Melpomene – Muse of Song and Tragedy

Melpomene was the patroness of singing, especially at special occasions and celebrations, as well as at times of grief.

Clio – Muse of History and Fame

Clio assured that the greats received the notoriety they deserved.

Euterpe – Muse of Pleasure

Euterpe played the flute, and was the patroness of song lyrics.

Erato – Muse of Poetry and Mimicry

Erato was also the arouser of love and the muse of erotic music.

Terpsichore – Muse of Dancing

Terpsichore would whirl and dance to the music of her stringed instrument.

Polyhymnia - Muse of Hymns

Polyhymnia was the goddess of holy music and consecrated song.

Urania – Heavenly Muse

Urania gave the astronomers their abilities to research the heavens.

Calliope – Muse of Epic Poetry

Calliope was the eldest of the Muses. Hesiod said of Calliope that she was the most important Muse, and that she rose above the rest, and that she was the faithful attendant of kings and princes. The name Calliope meant “she of fair voice”.

Apollo, patron of song, was the leader of the Muses. The Muses danced in honor of the heroic gods, and judged important art competitions such as the contest between Apollo and Marsyas. The singer, Thamyris dared to announce that he was more talented than the Muses, and was punished by blindness and the loss of his ability to play music.

The word museum means "place of the Muses" and the first museums were built around the shrines of the Muses. Although officially the Museum was dedicated to the worship of the Muses, in actuality these were institutions of learning and research. Lectures and lessons were held within their auspices and a special hall was built for when kings were in attendance.

Moirai

The Moirai were the Greek goddesses of Fate, and indeed were often called the Fates. The Moirai were sisters of the Horae, and daughters of Zeus and Themis. Most sources speak of three fates, although in Delphi only two were worshipped (the Fate of life, and the Fate of death). According to Hesiod's Theogony, the names of the three Fates were: Klotho, Lachesis, and Atropos.

Klotho spun the thread of life. Lachesis determined the length of life, and Atropos, whose name meant "inevitable", would cut the thread when life came to an end. The name of Atropos is familiar to us until this day in connection with a well known drug called Atrophine.

The Moirai were seen as responsible for the individual destinies of humans.

Morpheus

Son of Hypnos, the god of sleep, Morpheus was the personification of dreams and imagination. He was an expert at changing himself into human characters and appearing as such in the dreams of mortals.

Matuta Mater

Roman goddess of the dawn, Matuta Mater was given a major festival every year on June eleventh.

Metis

Metis was the wisest among gods and humans. Her name meant "wise advice". She was the first wife of Zeus, father of the gods. The Titans Gaia and Uranus, Zeus's grandparents, prophesied that the second child of Metis would be so wise and clever as to be able to challenge the prevailing god for sovereignty over all men and immortals. Zeus, in order to circumvent this prophecy, swallowed Metis when she was pregnant with their first child, preventing a second from ever being conceived. By taking Metis into his body he took on her wisdom and her ability to discern good from bad. Their child, Athena, was born through Zeus's head an already mature woman, carrying a weapon and sounding the call of battle.

Nike

The personification of the concept of victory, Nike was the Greek goddess of winning. She was the daughter of Athena and sister of "competition", "strength", and "power". Nike symbolized victory in all areas of conflict, especially military battles and sporting events. She is depicted as a young woman with wings, accompanying the winners as they receive their awards.

Nike's symbols are her crown and scepter, her sword, and her helmet. Some believe that Nike was not a god at all, and looking at ancient artwork strengthens this belief by which she is actually the victory prize offered by Athena and Zeus. These gods were usually represented with small winged hands.

Nemesis

Goddess of just rewards, of punishment and revenge, Nemesis was the daughter of Nyx, the night goddess.

During the earliest part of the Iron Age Nemesis left humankind, along with Aidos, the god of shame. There is one version according to which Nemesis became the mother of the beautiful Helena of troy, after Zeus mated with her in the form of a swan. She laid an egg and Helena was hatched. Nemesis meted out punishments for pride and pretentiousness, and served as the personification of the anger of the gods over man's impudence and insolence.

Nereus

Nereus was an early Greek god of the sea, and was sometimes called "Old Man of the Sea". Nereus was the son of Gaia and Pontus. By coupling with Doris, daughter of the Titan Oceanus, he fathered the Neriads (sea nymphs), and lived with them in the depths of he ocean. His daughter Amphitrite was Poseidon's wife, who gave birth to Triton.

Nereus was thought to be kind hearted, just, and wise. He had knowledge of the future, but did not often expose it. When Heracles wanted to know the way to the Garden of Hesperides, he had to shackle Nereus in order to get the information he needed. Nereus used his talent for transformation to try to evade Heracles but to no avail.

Silvanus

This Roman god was the spirit of the forest and other wild places in nature, but he also protected the domesticated fields and crops of humans. Silvanus was a close friend to the Satyrs and the Sileni. He was very territorial, and it was important to him to monitor all entrances and exits from his domain. He was identified in later myths with the god Pan.

Selene

The Greek goddess of the moon, Selene was the sister of Helios and Eos, and daughter of the Titan Hyperion.

Like Helios and Eos, Selene drove a chariot across the sky. Selene fell in love with the handsome shepherd Endymion, and gave birth to five daughters. She was blessed (or cursed) with eternal sleep. According to one version of the myth, she asked that Zeus give her sleep and he provided what she requested, but other versions claim that the sleep was punishment from Hera who found out that Zeus had fallen in love with Selene.

Selene is sometimes depicted as the mother of the Nemean Lion, as well as the sprinkler of dew and as the goddess of the "hours". The Greeks identified Selene with Artemis and Hecate. The Romans equated her with Luna, the Italian moon goddess who was in turn associated with the goddess of childbirth as personified by Juno and Diana.

Pan/Faunus

The Greek god of nature, Pan was the son of Hermes and one of the Nymphs. Pan had a human torso, the legs of a goat, and a beard. Originally an ancient god of fertility and fruitfulness, his goat-legs symbolized the lustfulness of the goat! Like the goat, Pan was a chaser of females – nymphs and goddesses.

From Pan's name came the word "panic", since according to myth, Pan would disseminate fear and uncertainty among the shepherds and the flocks during the hottest hours of the afternoon. When we study the myths of Pan, and seeing his origins in nature, and the comparative unimportance of his place in relation to the Olympian gods, we see how the worship and respect for nature itself enjoyed a low level of reverence. In the end Pan was the one and only male god of nature, and the other remaining deities of that realm were female.

Pan's image, that of a bearded man with the legs and horns of a goat, was a widespread one in the Christian world, especially in the middle ages, as the image of Satan.

Faunus was the Roman god of shepherds and flocks, and later became associated with the Greek Pan. Faunus was called the "speaker" and was given credit for the voices and messages sometimes heard in the forests and mountainsides. Faunus was said to have prophetic abilities. Every February fifteenth a festival was held in honor of Faunus, during which his priests would whip the participants with leather belts. The women believed that these floggings would bring them many children!

The Pans (plural) were the Roman parallels to the Satyrs, and they were described as humans with goat – legs. Fauna, the feminine parallel to Faunus, is still today the term we use for the members of the animal world.

Fortuna

The Roman goddess of fate and destiny, Fortuna was an ancient goddess whose cult had many names, each associated with a different group. She was the "Men's Fortuna", the "Women's Fortuna", and the "people's Fortuna", as well as the goddess that provided a safe return home from war. At the shrine of Fortuna fortunes were told on pieces of wood engraved with short lines which would need interpretation. Later, Fortuna became associated with Tyche, the Greek goddess of luck, success, and chance.

Flora

Flora was the goddess of the flowers of spring, and of all vegetation in nature. Her April twenty-eight festival was happy and gay, celebrating the fullness of the earth's bounty. Flora had a sexual nature and would perform crude shows of mimicry and strip-tease dances. She hunted goats and rabbits. Today the word Flora depicts the plant world.

Persephone/Proserpina

The goddess of the underworld, wife of Hades, Persephone was the beautiful daughter of Demeter and Zeus, Demeter's brother, father of the gods. Originally, Persephone was a para-Hellenistic goddess whose identity was parallel to that of Kore. The lovely Persephone had no intentions of becoming queen of the land of the dead. She lived on the surface of the earth and was a happy, carefree and contented young woman. It was her bad luck, however, that Hades, king of the underworld, fell in love with her. He asked her father, his brother Zeus, for her hand in marriage, but Zeus knew that Demeter would be terribly angry should he agree to let Hades take the girl. On the other hand, he did not want to quarrel with his brother. So he refused to give an answer one way or the other. The frustrated Hades then simply rushed off and abducted Persephone from a field where she was innocently picking flowers.

For nine days and nights Demeter desperately searched for her daughter. When she finally learned that Persephone had been kidnapped by Hades, she ran angrily from Olympus, and placed a curse on the earth, forbidding all growth of vegetation until her daughter was returned to her. This of course caused untold human suffering, and Zeus knew that it was an intolerable situation which could not be allowed to continue. He decreed that Persephone must be returned to her mother, assuming she had not yet tasted any of the food of the deceased.

During the nine days and nights of her captivity Persephone had indeed refused to take any nourishment, so Hermes, as messenger to Zeus, was instructed to go down to the land of the dead to retrieve the girl and return her to earth. Demeter rode in the chariot with Hermes and was overjoyed to be reunited with her daughter, but just as the excited party was about to leave the underworld, one of Hades' gardeners let out a great shout, and claimed that he had been an eye witness to Persephone's having ingested seven kernels of pomegranate from the food of the dead. This meant that Persephone had to be returned to Hades where she would remain forever!

Demeter was inconsolable, and in her anger and grief she swore that she would never again return to Olympus. Furthermore, she would never allow growth of trees or other vegetation on the earth.

Zeus again stepped in to resolve a matter which had gone too far. He turned to Rhea, Demeter's mother, and asked her advice. Rhea proposed a compromise whereby Persephone would be returned to earth, but that for three months out of each year she would go back to live in the underworld and function as the wife of Hades. Hecate was called upon to make sure that all parties carried out their part in this agreement, which they did, and Demeter allowed the green to again flourish on earth.

In other variations of this myth, Hades fed Persephone the pomegranate himself in order to ensure that Persephone would forever belong in his realm, and some of the stories say that Persephone lived in the land of the dead for six months each year, rather than three. Either way, this story explains the desolation on earth for several months of dry season each year. The months of draught correspond with the time Persephone is in the underworld, and when Persephone is with Demeter the earth flourishes and turns green.

In the oldest of the myths, Persephone is the goddess of growth. Her earliest name was Kore, and in Roman Mythology she is called Proserpina. The connection between Kore (Persephone), Demeter, and Hecate arises from an even earlier image from the mythology – the Triple Goddess. Just as the moon can be full, half, or invisible, the triple goddess could be a virgin, a mother, or a crone.

Usually, the cult of Persephone worshipped her in tandem with that of Demeter.

In European religion, Persephone was thought to be the mother of Dionysus.

Thanatos

Son of the night, brother of sleep, Thanatos was the god of death and the personification of dying. His task in the mythology was marginal, and he appears in only a few of the stories. When the end of mortal or immortal life was discussed, it was usually in connection with Hades and the underworld – the realm of the dead. Alternatively, it was Tartarus, the hellish pit where the dead suffered. Thanatos would sometimes be called upon to carry, along with his brother Hypnos, soldiers fallen in battle or other deceased humans. Thanatos had angelic wings and a soft face, as opposed to his brother's gloomy and disheveled appearance.

Folk Gods, Spirits, Nymphs, and Members of the Gods' Entourage

Not only gods, but also various nymphs and numerous spirits of nature were part of the popular cults during the Para-Hellenistic period and earlier.

The cult of the natural spirits spread to many places in the world and lasted many years. In Europe, for example, until a relatively recent period, it was still customary to lay gift offerings at the openings to caves and near bushes which served as altars to the spirits of the forest. In the Greek tradition too, there were many spirits of nature, but with the spread of the cult of the Olympian gods, their importance waned and they were usually seen only as adjuncts to the more major deities associated with nature. Even these gods (of nature) gradually lost their perceived power.

The various folk gods - guardians of travel, home, and family - gradually became quite marginal, while belief in them quietly remained quite widespread, and privately they were still worshipped by many along with the great gods of Olympia.

Folk Gods

Oceanids

The three thousand daughters of the Titans Oceanus and Thetis were the Oceanids. Some of them were goddesses of the sea, and others were more like nymphs.

Oreads

The Oreads were nymphs of the trees of the forests and mountain slopes.

Aeolos

Lord of the winds.

Graeae

Their name meant "gray" and they were called such because they were born already showing signs of old age. Daughters of Phorkys and Keto, the grays were three in number, yet they shared one tooth and one eye with which they all ate and saw.

When Perseus wanted them to direct him to the nymphs of the north, he stole their eye as they were passing it one to the other, and they were forced to tell him what he wanted to know.

Hesperides

Daughters of the night, their name meant "maidens of the evening". The Hesperides' task was to guard the trees on which grew the splendid shining golden apples. Taking care of these apple trees was not simple and they were aided in their job by the mighty dragon, Ladon. When Heracles succeeded in felling Ladon, he took the golden apples.

According to another myth, it was Atlas who picked the apples for Heracles.

Charon

Charon was the old boatman who brought the spirits of the dead to Tartarus on the River Styx. His boat was a decaying canoe of bulrushes. He would charge for his services, so the Greeks would leave golden coins under the tongue of the deceased. When there was no coin to pay for passage, the body would be left on the banks of the underworld river and would not receive a proper burial.

Virgil describes Charon as a white-haired man with a burning gaze. On rare occasions the living had reason to be transported in his boat – Heracles of the great strength, Orpheus of amazing singing ability, and Inias who showed Charon his golden wing. Charon did not take payment from Heracles, and was punished for this by Hades who kept him in chains for an entire year.

In artwork depicting the transportation of the dead to Tartarus, Charon appears monstrous, holding a hammer with which he hits the heads of the dying in order to hurry them into the next world.

During the Roman gladiator battles, it was customary to send a slave in the image of Charon to kill the Gladiators as they neared death.

Lares

The Lares were Roman household gods, protectors of family, farms, and property. They were the gods who watched over pedestrians and travelers. Each family had its own Lare. The Lare shrine would be placed near the household fireplace and sometimes on the paths leading up to the house.

The simplest citizens were among the worshippers of the Lares – manual laborers, servants and freed slaves. In ancient art they appear as young handsome gods carrying horns of plenty.

Nymphs

The nymphs were the spirits of nature that lived near the rivers, springs, seas, and forests, as well as within the trees themselves. They resembled young beautiful women and protected the areas in which they resided.

As far as their place in the hierarchy of Greek deities, they were not considered goddesses, but were actually closer to mortal women.

Still, they usually had special powers. The nymphs would appear in the entourages of other gods, such as Apollo, Artemis, and Dionysus, and accompany them in song and dance, and sometimes in archery contests.

The nymphs usually appear in love stories. Sometimes they were the love objects of the most powerful of gods – even Zeus

himself, and sometimes they had love affairs with mortals. When they did love mortals, they tried to bring them into their world of trees, springs and forests. Often they were described as wild, and even dangerous, and were often seen in the company of Pan's Satyrs.

The nymphs of the springs, the rivers, and the seas, were called Nyads. The tree nymphs were Driads, and sometimes Hamadriads. They were born and died among their beloved trees. The source of the Driads' name is the word for "oak" and they were called thus because of their special affinity for oak trees. "Hama" means "together". The nymphs of the largest forest trees on the mountains were called Oriads.

The worship of the nymphs took place for the most part in the forests and in caves.

Satyrs

The Satyrs were male spirits of nature, parallel to the female nymphs. They had human heads and torsos, and lower bodies, beards, and horns of goats.

The Satyrs accompanied the various gods of nature: Silvanus, the Faunas, Pan, and Dionysus. They were wild, lustful, and quick to fight. Hesiod called them "useless".

The Satyrs symbolized untamed and undomesticated nature, desire, lust of the flesh, and mischievousness. The Satyrs were the cohorts and companions of Dionysus, and they sometimes wrapped their heads in crowns of ivy which resembled his crown, and even carried his wineskin.

The Satyrs mated with the female followers of Dionysus, the Maenads, and they are shown in numerous works of ancient art chasing after the Maenads and nymphs in an effort to have sex with them.

Silens

The Silens, like the Satyrs, were spirits of the forests and hills. They had flat noses, horse-like ears, and sometimes even the legs and tails of horses. The most notorious of the Silens, Silenus, was usually depicted in the myths as drunk. Despite his habitual inebriation, however, Silenus was the wisest of Dionysus' protégé's and a respected member of his entourage. When King Midas caught him in his garden, drunk as usual, he regaled the king with wonderful stories....

Socrates used to say that he was like Silenus in that he was wise... and ugly...

Silenus personified the archetype of the drunken bum who lives outside of regular society but somehow always "gets along". His drunkenness was only a disguise for his deep wisdom.

Centaurs

In the Greek myths the Centaurs were creatures with human heads and torsos and set on the lower bodies of horses. They were thought of as a strong tribe of impulsive, wild, and raging creatures. The Centaurs shared what they had between themselves, and never used anything without the permission of the other Centaurs. Violations of these rules brought about severe punishments, sometimes involving bloodshed.

In many classic works of art and in numerous myths the Centaurs are depicted in the company of Dionysus, god of wine, and yet in others their names are associated with acts of rape and violence. Heracles killed the Centaur Nessus when he tried to rape his wife Deianira, and the war between the Centaurs and the Lapiths began when the Centaurs were invited to the wedding of the King of the Lapiths; they got drunk and tried to rape the female guests. A cruel and difficult war ensued, but in the end the Lapiths succeeded in beating the Centaurs, who later surprised them by fleeing quite a distance from the kingdom.

Though most of them were wild and unrestrained, the most famous Centaur was Cheiron, who represented intelligence and good-heartedness and taught some of the most important heroes. Cheiron was the teacher of the legendary hero Achilles and the esteemed doctor Asclepius, among many others.

Certain traditions of Greek mythology hold that Cheiron asked to exchange his immortal life for death in order to save Prometheus. Another version tells that he gave up his immortality after Heracles shot him by mistake. Heracles dropped in to see one of his Centaur friends, Polos, and not using common sense, he impulsively incited his friend the Centaur to open a bottle of wine from the common collection of the Centaurs. The Centaurs hurried to punish Polos, and Heracles, in an effort to defend his friend, accidentally shot Cheiron, who had not even been taking part in the scuffle. Cheiron's wounds caused him great suffering, and Zeus, father of the gods, agreed to allow him to die to end his pain.

Spirits

Boreas

Boreas, son of Eos and Astraeus, was the north wind – bringer of darkness, snow, and frost. He was depicted as a winged man with wild hair and a long beard. It seems that many worshipped Boreas out of fear of inciting his wrath, and his cult enjoyed a fairly wide base of worship among the people of Greece. According to Homer, Boreas assumed the image of a "dark-maned horse" in order to copulate with the twelve mares of King Erichtonius. Boreas fell in love with the daughter of the king of Athens Oritia, and abducted her to Thrace where she bore him two sons.

This "marriage" formed a relation between the north wind and the Athenians. Acting on advice from the Oracle, the Athenians requested help from Boreas against the naval fleet of the King of Persia, and he indeed successfully assisted them in pushing back the approaching ships. In southern Italy as well, Boreas was appreciated greatly for being the hero who turned back a threatening enemy.

Attica was the main center for the worship of Boreas.

Zephyr

Another son of Astraeus and Eos, Zephyr was the East Wind. He was the father of the swift horses of Achilles. Zephyr was sometimes mentioned as the husband of Iris. The most notorious myth about Zephyr concerns Yakinton (Hyacinth), the handsome young man with whom Apollo fell in love. Zephyr too, fancied the youth, and was jealous that Yakinton seemed to prefer the company of Apollo to his own. He did not hesitate to use the wind at his command, and during a discus competition between Apollo and Yakinton, he blew the disc off its course and caused it to hit Yakinton. The young man died of his wound.

Notus

The South Wind – bringer of winter rains and stormy weather.

Euros

The East Wind.

Mythical Monsters

Echidna

Daughter of Phorkys and Keto according to one version and of Gaia and Tartarus according to another, Echidna was the mother of many monsters including the dog of Geryon, Cerberus, the Hydra, Chimera, Sphinx, and the Nemean Lion. Echidna had half the body of a woman and half that of a snake. She lived with Typhon who fathered many of the monsters.

Argos

Argos was the "all-seeing" – he had one hundred eyes, some of which were open even when he slept. When Zeus turned the hapless girl Io into a calf out of frustration at not being able to spend time with her alone, Hera found out that a love affair had taken place between Zeus and Io. She then added insult to injury by making sure that Io would remain a calf and ordering Argos to serve as her ever-watchful guard.

The Nemean Lion

A monstrous lion, the son of Typhon and Echidna wandered the valleys around Nemea, terrorizing the farmers in the area who could not live securely and safely under its constant threat. No weapon could hurt the lion and the people despaired of ever doing him in. Heracles to the rescue – he killed the lion by strangling him with his bare hands.

From the skin of the Nemean lion Heracles fashioned himself a garment, and he made a helmet from the skull.

Gorgons

The three Gorgons were female monsters with bodies of winged dragons and hair made of snakes. A glance from a Gorgon could turn one to stone. Daughters of Phorkys and Keto, their names were Sthenno, Euryale, and Medusa.

Two of the Gorgons were immortal and the third, Medusa, was mortal. Thus Perseus was able to chop off Medusa's head. He did so without looking at her, of course. Rather, he followed her movements in a mirror. Afterwards, he donned a cap which made him invisible but able to see, in order to protect himself from the revenge of Medusa's sisters. His winged sandals helped him escape quickly.

As Medusa died, from her blood sprang Pegasus and Chrysaor. From one of her veins the blood of life flowed, and from another, the blood of death. Asclepius, the legendary physician, gathered and preserved them both.

Harpies

Disgusting winged monsters, the Harpies had heads and torsos of women and the lower bodies of birds. They were dirty and repulsive, and often swooped in and stole food from humans or polluted the food they were about to eat.

The Harpies were thought to be daughters of Neptune, and were also sometimes called "Zeus's hounds".

In the Greek myths the three Harpies stank horribly. They were feared and hated, and sometimes even carried off small children and other weaker humans. They were thought to be carriers of sudden death, and personified all that was destructive in the female nature. Some see in their characters a symbolization of the male fear of the female temper.

Hydra

A monster in the shape of a water snake or a dragon, the Hydra was born of the mating between Typhon and Echidna and nourished by Hera. He was killed by Heracles with the help of Athena and Julius.

Later myths describe the hydra as a nine-headed monster, or seven-headed in some cases. One of the heads was immortal and could regenerate itself time and again after being decapitated. Heracles was able to gain control of all the heads by having Julius press a burning torch to the neck of each of the cut off heads, preventing the immortal head from growing back.

The hydra was blind, which some believe points to her being a symbol for the power of animals. Some believe that the number seven (seven heads) was significant and may have been tied to the planets and their influences.

Typhon

A monstrous dragon, nicknamed Tiptoes, Typhon was the son of Gaia and Tartarus. Typhon had one hundred fire breathing heads, one hundred different voices, and one hundred hand and legs. He was the creator of the most violent storms.

Typhon is sometimes called the father of Hydra, Chimera, and Cerberus, some of the monsters of Echidna. According to Homer, Typhon was the son of Hera, the product of a virgin pregnancy, which angered Zeus. Homer says he was raised by a female dragon near Delphi.

In his war against Zeus, Typhon was able to injure his rival seriously, but with the help of Hermes, Zeus overcame the monster, killed him, and buried him under a mountain which from then on tended to periodic volcanic eruptions.

Charybdis

Two monsters were greatly feared by sailors, of which Charybdis was one. She lay in wait on the seashore and three times daily she caused a huge storm to threaten the vessels on the water. Her name meant "she who sucks", because she would suck in whole ships, swallow them, and then regurgitate their wreckage back onto the water. This ability was given to her when Zeus, angry that she had stolen an ox from Heracles, struck her with a mighty bolt of thunder which turned her into a monstrous swirling vortex. Charybdis was the daughter of Poseidon and Gaia.

Chimera

The name Chimera meant female goat, and indeed by all accounts she was a monster with a goat's body, though there is some inconsistency in reports about her head(s) and tail. Some said she had a serpent's head. Homer described her as having a lion's head, a body of a goat, and a snake for a tail. Hesiod describes her as having three heads – a lion's head facing forward, a goat's head to one side, and a dragon head facing backward. All agree that the huge and agile monster would blow frightening flames from her mouth or mouths. Like many of the other monsters, Chimera was the daughter of Typhon and Echidna.

Chimera was a complicated symbol for evil, storms and anger, and danger on land and sea. Like other complicated creatures, such as the Sphinx and the Unicorn, Chimera represented a season of the year – the period consecrated to the queen of the skies.

Pegasus the flying horse killed Chimera.

Lamya

Lamya was a demonic character which according to Greek folklore was able to assume various forms. She would suck the blood of human beings and eat children whole. (The children could be retrieved alive and well from her belly.)

In one myth, Lamya was one of the hapless lovers of Zeus who received harsh punishment from the jealous Hera. Hera caused Lamya to become insane and murder her own children. In her sorrow over her deed Lamya went permanently insane and turned into an ugly monster.

Another version describes Lamya as a beautiful but evil queen who turned into a wild animal because of her cruelty.

Some myths refer the Lamyas in the plural, and describe their hideouts as similar to those of the dragons' caves and desserts.

Minotaur

The Minotaur's name was a combination of King Minos and the Greek word for bull. Thus "Bull of Minos".

When King Minos wished to sacrifice a fine white bull to Poseidon, he prayed that such a bull would be delivered from the sea. When the lovely bull indeed swam ashore, however, Minos was so taken with it that he decided to keep it, and sacrificed a different bull instead. This did not sit well with Poseidon, who punished Minos by causing the king's wife to fall in love with the beautiful bull! So great was the queens passion for the bull that with the help of a mock cow, she succeeded in mating with him.

This coupling resulted in the birth of Minotaur – a monster with the body of a man and the head of a bull which enjoyed consuming human flesh.

Minos was humiliated by the entire affair and turned to the Oracle at Delphi for advice on how to rid his family of this shame. The Oracle advised Minos to have Dedalus, the famous carpenter, fashion a complicated labyrinth in which to hide Minotaur. This was done, and Minotaur was fed on young male and female virgins who were sacrificed by the Athenians every seven years in payment for having killed one of Minos' sons. The young men and women were placed in the labyrinth to wander until they met their death as a meal for Minotaur.

Minotaur represents the power of the baser animal instincts over those of the human mind. The Centaurs, with their human heads and bestial bodies, represent the opposite.

Seirenes

The Seirenes appear most often in Greek mythology as birds with heads of human women. They also appear at times as mermaids, and in some works of ancient art they even have male heads with beards.

The Seirenes would sing sweetly in the ears of sailors, arousing them so intensely with their beautiful sounds that if they did not lash themselves to the decks of their ships they jumped right into the sea after the bird-women.

But the sweetness of their song hid a monstrous and evil intention. When a sailor jumped into the water and swam after the sound, or when the captain dropped anchor at the island of the Seirenes, they would meet certain death at the hands of the bird-women.

Odysseus and his crew succeeded in escaping the loud and

insistent song of the Seirenes only because he ordered everyone to plug up their ears with wax. Odysseus himself so desperately wished to hear the wonderful music just once that he had his men tie him strongly to the flagpole of his vessel to prevent him from jumping into the water and trying to swim to the island.

In post-Homeric literature, the Seirenes are described also as human woman who accompanied the dead to the underworld, comforted them, and watched over them. Some writers even equated them with the Muses.

The Seirenes can be seen as symbols of the fear that men have of the power of women to seduce them and lead them to danger and foolishness, and even to death. The sexual act itself is equated with death in that it means the loss of the man's individualism. Some see in the Seirenes a symbol of the illusory quality of the power of desire and the fact that the senses can lead a man astray. The Seirenes appeared to the sailors after hard days and exhausting nights on the sea, when their imaginations were ripe to run away with them. The Seirenes taught them that following their illusions can be fatal.

This myth is so widespread that the belief in it continues even today among certain cultures of sailing men.

The Seirenes are symbolized by the harp and the flute.

Sphinx

Daughter of Echidna and Typhon, the Sphinx was generally considered to be a benevolent monster, despite her habit of consuming humans! She was a creature with either a man's bearded head or that of a woman, with the body of an ox, feet of a lion, and wings of an eagle.

The Sphinx is an important image in the history of the city of Thebes and King Oedipus. She was sent by Hera (or according to a later myth by Apollo), to punish the people of Thebes. The Sphinx would sit on a rock near the gate to the city and stop anyone who passed by with a riddle: *What animal in the morning goes on four, at noon on two, and in the evening on three?* Passers by who could not answer were gobbled up by the Sphinx. This effectively paralyzed the population since all feared passing the Sphinx and stayed in their homes. The city was suffering and in hunger when finally, Oedipus solved her riddle. Oedipus' answer was: A man. In the morning of his life he crawls on all four, he then rises onto two for most of his life, and as his life wanes he adopts a can as a third "foot". The riddle itself symbolized the mortality of man – the fact that he would grow and then decay and ultimately cease to be.

The Sphinx was so distraught at the fact that a human was able to solve her riddle that she committed suicide on the spot.

The symbol of unsolvable mystery – the idea that there is an ultimate knowledge which man cannot share with the immortals was symbolized by the Sphinx. Such knowledge was meant to be kept forever out of the reach of humans. According to Jung, the Sphinx symbolized the "threatening mother" who has the power to take back what she gives.

Skylla

Skylla was a beautiful sea nymph with whom a fisherman named Glaucus fell deeply in love. Glaucus would fish from his perch

on a grassy slope that touched the sea. One day, when he'd finished, he arranged his catch on the grass in order to count them, when suddenly he noticed that the fish were moving about and trying to jump back into the sea. Surprised by this unusual display of energy by the fish and their obvious desire to get back to the water, he decided it must be the grass on which they lay that imparted some kind of magical powers to the fish. He plucked some blades of the grass and began to chew on them, hoping that he too would be imbued with unusual strength and ambition. Indeed, like the fish, Glaucus felt a sudden irresistible longing to be in the sea. The desire was so strong that he ran straight to the water and was swallowed up by the waves. The gods of the sea welcomed him warmly, and asked Oceanus and Thetis to allow him to become immortal. One hundred maidens poured their waters over him, and he fainted. When he came to, Glaucus discovered that he had become a sea god, complete with the tail of a fish and green hair that looked like seaweed.

One day as Skylla was bathing in the waters where Glaucus lived, he suddenly rose to the surface, unwittingly frightening her. Skylla ran quickly to the safety of an overhanging cliff and looked back toward the sea at Glaucus, not sure if he was a god or a monster. He beseeched her to come down, claiming to have fallen in love with her at first sight, and trying to convince her there was nothing to fear, but Skylla ran off and disappeared from sight. Determined to win the nymph's affection, Glaucus turned to a sea sorcerer, Circe, for help. Circe, however, fell in love with Glaucus and wanted for herself. She tried to convince him to forget about Skylla, but Glaucus was not interested and insisted that Circe compose a love spell meant to bring Skylla into his arms.

As often happened in the Greek myths, the jealous female punished not the object of her love, but the object of his. Circe would not hurt Glaucus, for whom she cared so deeply, but she turned her envious wrath on poor Skylla. Instead of preparing a potion which would cause Skylla to fall in love, she mixed a potent poison and hatched a plan. Circe spilled the poison into the waters where Skylla habitually bathed, and as soon as the nymph entered the surf her body began to sprout the heads of snakes and dogs. Skylla was livid with anger and grief at her monstrous appearance, and became a dire and violent threat to all who passed her way, especially sailors.

Odysseus, Jason, and Vainius were forced to deal with the now horrid monster as they plied those same waters.

According to a different version, it was Amphitrite, Poseidon's wife, who turned Skylla into a monster. The motivation in this version was the same – Amphitrite's jealous rage when Poseidon fell in love with the beautiful nymph.

Skylla the monster inhabited the gulf of Mecina along with Charybdis, the monster who caused huge storms and dangerous vortexes. Charybdis would suck up all the water in the bay, and spit them out three times each day, together with the wrecks of all the ships and fishing vessels that happened to be in her way. Skylla, who now had six heads and six vicious dogs permanently tied to her body, would gobble the boats back up.

Another version holds that Skylla was actually a huge boulder. Whichever was the case, from this story comes the Greek saying "caught between Skylla and Charybdis", which means "between a rock and a hard place."

Pegasus

The wondrous winged horse Pegasus sprang from the blood of Medusa the Gorgon when Perseus beheaded her. It was said that he never grew weary of flying and that he moved through the air at the speed of light. Springs were formed in the earth where the hoofs of Pegasus stamped the ground. Pegasus is described as having a mind with human characteristics, despite the fact that he did not speak as did many of the other god-creatures in the mythology.

Pegasus was admired by the young Bellerophon, a handsome and heroic figure whose ambition was to catch the winged horse and become his rider. This finally came true after he spent a night in fervent prayer to the goddess Athena, who provided him with a magical golden bridle with which to subdue Pegasus. Bellerophon placed the bridle on Pegasus with no trouble, and together they rode off to fight against Chimera, whom Bellerophon succeeded in killing. According to the legend, both the horse and his rider enjoyed their relationship, until Bellerophon became too arrogant and tried to ride Pegasus to Olympus for a visit to the gods. By one account, Zeus was annoyed by Bellerophon's presumptuousness and as the pair neared the Mount he sent a gad-fly to sting Pegasus, causing him to throw his rider. Another version holds that Pegasus himself decided to teach his companion a lesson and tossed him off his back, causing him a crippling injury from his fall.

Pegasus himself went up to Olympus where he was given a place of honor in the stables of the gods.

Pegasus symbolizes the desire of mortal man to be like the gods. As long as man keeps this ambition in check, he remains in the gods' good graces, but when he commits the sin of pride, and begins to see himself as like unto the gods, as did Bellerophon, he loses his spiritual power, and brings about his own downfall.

Phoenix

The size of a great eagle, the phoenix was a legendary bird that rose out of flames. She is the universal symbol for eternal life, and for rebirth through fire.

The legend has it that when the Phoenix saw death approaching, she would build a nest in a sweet smelling tree (usually a palm tree), and line it with resin, spices, and herbs. The heat of the sun's rays caused the nest to catch fire and the Phoenix went up in flames. The Phoenix would then remain dead for three days (the period that the moon is dark) before rising from the ashes and coming back to life. The Phoenix also symbolizes the cycles of the moon – its disappearance and reappearance, but more often she represents the sun as the "bird of fire".

The Phoenix had a nonviolent character – she did not prey on any living creature and never harmed anything on which she alighted.

Obedeus, the Roman poet, tells a slightly different version of the story of the Phoenix according to which the Phoenix lived to the age of five hundred years. She then built herself a nest of spicy grasses and ended her life in it. At the moment that she found her death in flames, a new Phoenix arose from the ashes and carried the nest, with the dead bird in it, to the shrine of the sun god in Heliopolis. This is apparently the older of the two legends of the Phoenix.

The Hebrew tradition has a bird of this type as well, called the "sand bird", which is born again from dust. In Roman culture, the Phoenix represented the rebirth of the Roman Empire.

Psychological analysts have seen the Phoenix in each one of us as the possibility to rise above any adversity and to cheat death. Falling asleep and rising again in the morning are sometimes equated with the death and rebirth of the Phoenix.

Kerberos

Kerberos was a giant triple-headed dog (in some accounts he had five heads). Around his neck were coiled snakes, and sometimes his tail was depicted as a snake as well. Kerberos, in his three-headed version, represented the three worlds, and it was his job to guard the gates of the underworld of Hades. He made sure that the souls that entered the land of the dead could not escape back up to the "middle world", where redemption was possible.

Kerberos was born of the mating of two famous monsters – Typhon and Echidna. He ate live flesh, and according to Hesiod, his voice was brassy. The crafty Kerberos would welcome everyone who entered the underworld with a friendly wag of his tail, but if someone should try to leave, his angry teeth would leave their mark. The heroes who succeeded in subduing Kerberos included Heracles - using his brute strength, and Orpheus – who used his hypnotic playing of his instrument.

Gods of Ancient Egypt

Foreword

Herodotos, the noted Greek historian and scientist, tells of the singularity of Egypt in his description of one of his visits there: "Just as the Egyptian river [The Nile] is different in nature from all other rivers, so are the laws and customs of the people different from those of others. The woman does the buying and selling while the husband sits at home and spins. The men carry burdens on their heads, and the women carry them on their shoulders. Women void standing up and men void sitting down – they do this in their homes and bring the output to the street, since they believe that such things should be hidden from view, while the pleasanter things should be shared in public. While no woman is given to the service of any god or goddess, men must serve the gods, male and female. Sons are under no obligation to support their parents, but daughters must always do so..."

For hundreds of years Egypt was protected from enemies by the fact that she was surrounded by hostile dessert – a natural barrier to invasion. The Egyptians were proud of their uniqueness, and called themselves the Black Nation, after the black mud of the Nile River banks. Others called the Egyptians the Red Nation, after the red clay of the mountains.

The black Nile was the source of life for the Egyptians, and they developed thriving agriculture along its shores. The yearly flooding of the river kept the fields irrigated and lessoned the need for working and tilling of the land.

The Nile was extremely important and central to the lives of the inhabitants of Ancient Egypt. Every aspect of their existence was tied to the Nile and its surroundings. The early Egyptians believed that the world was a sort of mound of earth, through the center of which flowed the Nile, and which was surrounded on all sides by the great ocean. Nun, the first ancient goddess, was the personification of that ocean, and the river and the rains were believed to come from her. Above the earth were spread the heavens, which were held aloft by four sturdy pillars at the four corners of the world.

Ancient Egypt was divided into two sections: Upper Egypt and Lower Egypt (South and North, respectively). Echoes of this division can be found in the myth of the war waged by Osiris and Horus against Set. Horus was the god who symbolized the unification of the two Egypts, and every Pharaoh was an incarnation of Horus.

The cult of burial of the dead was associated with the myth of Osiris. The sun-god, Ra, was also central, as Ra was considered the creator of the world. Atum, according to one of the creation myths, created himself from nothing, and according to another, he was the sun of Nun, who emerged from the primordial waters in the shape of a hill.

During the rule of the Pharaoh Akhenatun (1366-1387 BC), an effort was made to change the basic beliefs of the Egyptians and to unite their worship under one god – Atun, while letting go of belief in all other gods, but this was unsuccessful. The myth of Osiris, his death and rebirth, was planted too strongly in the minds of the Egyptian people. This myth reflected the yearly rebirth of the Nile, and ran too deeply and was too closely tied to their very survival to be routed out. Under the scepter of Osiris, in the underworld, lived the souls that had achieved immortality after they were judged and found worthy by Osiris himself.

Departing from the Mesopotamian religions, in which the king was given his sovereignty by the gods, in Egypt the king himself was considered a god.

Ogdoad

The Ogdoad was a group of four couples (god-goddess) of gods, each couple representing a different aspect of Chaos.

Nun and Naunet represented the deep primordial waters. Hu and Hauhet stood for the empty spaces, infinity. Amun and Amaunet were the powers of creation - the powerful secret unseen forces, and Kuk and Kauket were the infinite darkness and mist over the waters from which all that is was created.

The gods of the Ogdoad were sometimes depicted as frogs and snakes that lived in the prehistoric swamp, or as baboons that existed before the dawn. The worship of the Ogdoad gods took place in Hermopolis. According to legend, the sun first shone in this place, on an "island of fire" which sprang from the cosmic swamp which the Ogdoad produced.

Ennead

A council of nine ancient Egyptian gods who took part in the creation of the world made up the Ennead. The nine were said to be the greatest gods of Heliopolis. The source of the name is the Greek word Ennea, meaning "nine". The first of these was Atum, or Ra-Atum, who lived on a hill created for him by Nun, the dark primordial waters. Ra-Atum planned out all of creation, and began his work by taking his own semen into his mouth, and spitting out the next generation – the twin gods Shu (the God of Air) and Tefenet (the Goddess of moisture).

Shu and Tefenet set out to explore Nun, the primordial waters that were their environment. Atum feared his offspring had gotten lost, and taking out his eye, he sent it to search for them. The eye itself was a powerful heavenly force and was thought of as a "daughter" of Atum. When the eye found the wayward gods, Atum wept with joy and relief, and each of his tears turned into a human being. Shu and Tefenet mated and their children were Geb (god of the Earth) and Nut (Goddess of the Sky). Geb and

Nut also paired incestuously and clung so tightly to one another that their father, Shu, had to pry them apart in order to allow Nut to give birth.

Their offspring were four of the most important Egyptian deities: Osiris, Iris, Set, and Nephthys. Osiris, the oldest of Nut's sons, would be the first ruler of Egypt.

Geb divided the earth into the upper (southern) and lower (northern) sections, giving the lower to Horus, and the upper to Set.

Osiris

One of the most central gods to the Egyptians and the first ruler of Egypt, Osiris was the son of Geb, god of earth, and Nut, goddess of the sky. His siblings were Set, and Isis, who later became his wife as well. As the eldest son of Geb and Nut, Osiris was named the first Pharaoh and ruler of the land.

Osiris was considered a benevolent king and god by the humans to whom he taught the secrets of culture and agriculture. As god of vegetation and growth, he gave them the bounties of the fruits of the earth. Osiris instructed mankind to respect the gods, and taught them the various ceremonies that were to be conducted in their honor. As king, he was responsible for passing and enforcing the laws of the land.

Osiris was also called "Un-nefer", or Lord of Lords. According to myth, he walked the entire length of the earth, and the human inhabitants of the places he visited were given the gifts of culture and knowledge.

Osiris' death and his subsequent rebirth symbolized the afterlife and the nighttime cycle of the sun (Ra stood for the daytime sun).

Evil enemies plotted against Osiris' rule of Egypt, the most insidious of these being his brother Set, who in the end managed to cause his death. The myth of the murder of Osiris by Set is a central theme in ancient Egyptian culture, and has various and numerous versions. The most common of them tells that Set became jealous of his brother's sovereignty. He coveted not only the kingship but also the love, honor and respect afforded Osiris by the mortal population.

Set and seventy of his friends plotted the downfall of the benevolent Lord of Lords. They built a painted wooden trunk which they decorated sumptuously with precious stones. This trunk had the exact measurements that would be needed for a coffin for Osiris. Set then invited his brother to take part in a large celebration attended by many gods and men. During the party, the wondrous trunk was revealed, and all of the revelers (who had been instructed to do so beforehand) shouted it's praises loud and long. Set suggested a game – the beautiful trunk would be given as a gift to anyone who could fit inside it and prove it to be exactly his size.

One after the other the guests tried on the trunk for size, but none fit exactly to its measurements. Set's friends then approached Osiris and urged him to take part in the game. Osiris agreed, and no sooner did he lie down inside than Set's friends snapped the lid shut tightly and nailed it into place. They then proceeded to seal the openings of the trunk with lead, making escape impossible. The trunk, with the king inside, was thrown into the depths of the Nile, and Set took over as Pharaoh of Egypt.

One of the most important and oft-retold stories from the Egyptian mythology is that of Isis finding Osiris body and bringing him back to life.

One version tells that Isis searched for the trunk tirelessly until she finally located it in the depths of the river. Using her magic, Isis was able to recover the body. Anubis, the god with the head of a jackal, pulled the body from the water and embalmed it, creating from it the first mummy. Using her magic again, Isis turned herself into a hawk and hovered over her husband/brother's mummy. As she flapped her wings, the breath of life was breathed into Osiris' lungs, and he returned to life for a short time – time enough to mate with Isis and conceive their child.

Some versions of this myth say that Set cut his brother's body into fourteen pieces, and buried each piece in a separate hidden grave. Isis succeeded in recovering all but one of the pieces – his sexual organ, and that she somehow became pregnant regardless. In any case, she bore a son, Horus, and raised him in hiding for fear that Set would do him harm. When Horus came of age, he did battle against his evil uncle, avenged the wrongs that had been perpetrated against his father, and won the kingdom for himself. This myth had widespread importance in that it symbolized the taking over of the kingship by the Pharaoh's son. In all subsequent generations, the Pharaoh was called Osiris after his death, and his son was called Horus.

Osiris remained powerful after his death, as king of the underworld, or land of the dead. At first, Osiris was characterized as the leader of the demons, but later he was seen as the judge of all souls of the deceased who could give the righteous the right to live forever in paradise.

Since Osiris was also considered the god in charge of the growth of the yearly crops, the harvest of grain was likened to the murder of the god and the dissection of his body.

In time, the worship of Osiris overshadowed that of the other gods, such as the gods of the sun and heavens, and their characteristics and powers were added to his. In the city of Avidos, huge festivals were held in his honor, during which the highlights of his life and death were reenacted – his death, resurrection, and the revenge of his son on his enemies. Along with the large public ceremonies, additional special services attended by small numbers of worshippers took place inside his shrines.

The most prominent worship of Osiris took place every spring when the waters of the Nile receded, revealing the wet, fertile strip along its banks. The Egyptians fashioned statues of Osiris from the Nile clay, and planted seeds of grain within the images. When the grain sprouted the images grew, keeping their shape intact. Ceremonies were conducted thanking Osiris for the renewal of life and the hope of a good harvest.

Every Egyptian, upon his death, was met in the underworld by Osiris who judged whether he was worthy of eternal life in the land of the deceased. Those who passed would gain immortality and continue to exist much as they had on earth, in the land of the dead.

The worship of Osiris and Isis spread to all corners of the Middle East and even to such far-off locales as the river Rein in Europe and certain places in England. In Rome and Greece large public rites were held around the rebirth of Osiris.

Usually, Osiris was depicted with his head wrapped and topped with a crown plumed with two large feathers. He was also described as a green mummy, green being the color of fertility and growth. Osiris' hands were often crossed over his chest and held the symbols of his position – the kingly scepter, the judge's whip, and the staff of long life (a stick with the head of a serpent). On each side of his body were drawn Nephthys and Isis, each with wings, as symbols of the breath of life that brought him back to life in order to give Isis a son.

Atum (See: Ra)

Isis

Isis was the most important goddess in the Egyptian Pantheon. The daughter of Nut and Geb, sister to Set and Nephthys, and sister and wife to Osiris, Isis was the most powerful and influential of goddesses. She was thought of as the mother – goddess of Egypt. Isis' son, Horus, avenged the death of her husband, Osiris, by killing his murderer, Osiris' brother Set.

Isis was usually described as a loving and giving mother to her son. In drawings and paintings she is depicted with cow's horns, and between them a sun-disk. She was sometimes identified with Hathor, the nurturing cow goddess.

According to myth, Isis came into her amazing powers by use of cunning. In order to become a goddess, Isis had to guess the secret name of the god Ra – a name that gave eternal life to all who uttered it. In order to uncover the name, Isis took advantage of Ra's advanced age and less than alert state to trick him into providing her with some of his saliva. She mixed a bit of clay earth with the saliva and using magic she fashioned a snake from the mixture. She placed the snake on the path which Ra usually traversed and waited for the god to arrive. As expected, the snake attacked and bit Ra as he passed. Ra writhed in pain and begged for relief, which Isis promised to provide if only he would reveal the secret name. Feeling he had no choice, Ra told Isis the name, and the moment she uttered it she gained a portion of the great god's powers. Thus she became the goddess of protection against snakes and other biting creatures, as well as the goddess of relief from pain and disease.

Isis is portrayed most often in the Egyptian mythology as the loving and faithful wife of Osiris, the first earthly king. Osiris' arch-rival was his brother Set, who coveted his sovereignty and plotted his overthrow and death. When Set succeeded in murdering his brother he hid the body exceedingly well, but Isis would not rest until she had found the special coffin Set had tricked her husband into putting himself into. No sooner had she found it than Set stole the body back, however, and cut it into fourteen parts, only thirteen of which Isis was able to retrieve. Using various magic skills, Isis was able to bring the dissected body of her husband back to life.

Horus, the hawk-headed god who represented the struggle of the light against the darkness, was born to Isis after she succeeded in mating with the revived Osiris. Isis turned herself into a giant bird that hovered over Osiris' body and by flapping its wings breathed life into the murdered god. When Isis discovered her pregnancy, she went into hiding to protect her child from the wrath of Set, who she knew would come after the offspring of his brother, the new heir to the kingship. Isis gave birth to and raised Horus in hiding in the Nile delta. When he reached adulthood, Horus emerged and avenged the wrongs done to his father. Isis was behind the return of the throne to Horus, the rightful heir. The battle between Set and Horus was fierce, and Isis stood at her son's side throughout. When the fight seemed endless and neither side was able to achieve a clear victory, Isis tried to sway the judges in the council of the gods in Horus' favor, but they too had difficulty reaching a decision. Isis appealed to her husband, now king of the underworld, in a letter beseeching him for council. Osiris sent back the message that if his son was not made Pharaoh forthwith, he would send dark and horrible spirits from the land of the dead to haunt the gods. The council then quickly decided in favor of Horus, who quickly became King.

Isis was worshiped in all corners of Egypt, in Greece, and even in Rome. The Greeks equated her with Aphrodite, Demeter and Io. Her cult spread to all areas of the Middle East, where she was thought of as goddess of the heavens, the earth, and even of the underworld, where she was said to rule together with Osiris.

In Greece, Isis was identified with the goddess Io. According to Greek myth Zeus fell in love with Io, and Hera did everything in her power to make life difficult for the object of her husband's desire. Hera turned Io into a calf, and sent a fly to bother her unceasingly, driving Io half mad. According to the legend, Io tried to run from the fly, and covered the length and breadth of Europe, Asia, and Africa in a futile attempt to escape it. When she finally arrived in Egypt, Zeus changed her into the goddess Isis.

Imhotep

Imhotep was one of the mortals who changed into a god. He was the architect responsible for the building of the famous Step Pyramid in 2650 B.C. When Imhotep became immortal it was as the god of medicine, wisdom, and magic. He was depicted in ancient art as a priest with shaved head, carrying rolled papyri on which healing spells were written. Imhotep was thought to support learning of all kinds, and was appealed to for success in studies. According to tradition, Imhotep was the son of Ptah, and the daughter of a mortal woman.

The Greeks identified Imhotep with Asclepius, the much admired physician, who was the son of Hermes.

Ammon/Amun

Ammon was the ram headed god who stood at the head of the Egyptian Pantheon. He as portrayed as the all-powerful god of creation, as well as the god of fertility. The cult of Ammon was especially strong in the sixteenth century B.C., when the Egyptians widened their influence eastward to Canaan. Ammon then became the national god of Egypt. Ammon and the sun god Ra were linked and eventually became one god, known as Ammon-Ra.

The only rival for the top of the Egyptian Pantheon that

Ammon experienced was Atun and that only for a short time, when the Pharaoh Akhenatun tried to unify all the gods into a single entity and declared that Atun was that one deity.

Ammon was thought of as the god who created all the others. According to one version of this creation myth, Ammon, in the shape of a serpent, was the first creature ever to exist on the waters of Chaos. Ammon was sometimes depicted as a man in a hat or crown with two feathers, and other times as a man with the head of a ram. Ammon's partner was Mut, goddess of the sky, whose form was that of an eagle.

The name Ammon meant "hidden", that godlike aspect which contained all the mystery of the unknown and unknowable.

Ammon was king of the heavens, creator of all that existed, and guardian of the pharaoh's dynasty. Prayers directed to Ammon emphasized his generosity and kindness. The Greeks equated Ammon to the fatherly figure of Zeus.

In the year 331 B.C., Ammon's priests welcomed Alexander the Great at the dessert and from then on Alexander saw himself as the son of Ammon, and therefore immortal as well.

Originally, Ammon was the god of Thebes, where he was worshipped as the god of air and fertility. When Thebes became the official capital of Egypt, Ammon became the protector and leader of the nation. Thus began his identification with Ra, who was then seen as god of the sun, but also as god of creation.

When the Pharaoh Akhenatun (who had changed his name from the original Amnopis), tried to put and end to the cult of Ammon and to replace it with that of a single god, Atun, his efforts were for naught. One of the main reasons for this failure was the power base held by the priests of Ammon. Their strength was so influential when Akhenatun insisted on adherence to the new single deity; he was forced to build himself a new city, quite a distance away.

Ammon-Ra was the only Egyptian god to have "divine consorts" – mortal virgins, usually princesses, who slept in the temple of the god, but refrained from sexual activity of any kind. They saw to the continuation of the dynasty through adoption. The princess who acted as the wife of Ammon eventually became his priestess.

During the Festival of Ammon which took place in Egypt in the tenth month, the god crossed the Nile together with the Pharaoh in a magnificent boat made of wood and covered in gold and precious gems.

The daily ceremonies of the cult of Ammon included the careful cleaning and anointing of the revered statues. The priests burned incense and left food offerings for the god at the feet of the anointed statues.

Ammon-Ra's standing was lessoned somewhat when Egypt changed its capital and the local gods rose in importance, including Osiris who became ever more popular.

Ammut

A monstrous goddess with the body of a hippopotamus, lion, and alligator, Ammut would swallow up souls that were judged unworthy after death.

Amenhotep

Amenhotep, like Imhotep, was an admired mortal architect who was raised to immortal status. He too was connected with wisdom, and the healing of the sick.

Anubis

Egyptian god of the dead, Anubis was sometimes called Anpu. He had the body of a human and the head of a jackal. Before the rise of the cult of Osiris, the later god of the dead, funeral prayers were addressed to Anubis. Anubis was thought of as guardian of the tomb and the god of embalming, and it was he that accompanied the soul on its way to the land of the deceased. Anubis was god of the dessert and of the city of the dead (Necropolis). Later, he was cast as assistant to the great god and judge of the underworld– Osiris.

Anibus was the son of Osiris and Neptune (she too was connected with death). After Osiris was torn to pieces by Set, Anubis helped Isis to reassemble him. He bandaged Osiris' body tightly into wrappings and Isis used her magic to bring her husband back to life. Worship of Anubis spread to all parts of Egypt and even parts of the Greek-Roman world.

Astarte

The origins of Astarte can be found in the ancient East, in Mesopotamia, where she was called Ishtar in Canaanite mythology. She was the goddess of battle, and was thought to be the wife of the god Set and the daughter either of the sun-god Ram or the creation god Ptah.

Apiss

The ox, Apiss had the most devoted following of any animal god. Apiss was believed to be the embodiment of Ptah.

The crowning of the ox Apiss took place during an impressive ceremony in Memphis during the celebration of the new moon. The ox was chosen from among all others because of special markings on his body. After the coronation, the Apiss was brought out through the eastern gate of the temple and displayed to the people. After this viewing, the ox was taken to a temple yard where he was kept and never brought out again, save for during holy processions.

When the ox died, he would be embalmed and preserved just as human princes. The ox was laid to rest during with an elaborate funeral and burial in a special cemetery for Apiss oxen. Only after the burial was the Apiss' successor chosen. During the Hellenistic period, the Apiss was connected to Osiris, and Osir-Apis, was worshipped as well. In ancient art the ox is depicted with a cobra, symbol of kingship, between his legs.

Apep

Known also by the name Apopis, Apep was a gigantic serpent or dragon who threatened the sun god as he sailed the heavens in his boat through the underworld. Again and again the armies of the souls of the dead with Set at their command overcame Apep.

Atun

Like the god Ra, Atun too had a round form, the shape of the sun.

This god was singular among the Egyptian deities in that only one Pharaoh supported his cult, and he was part of the Egyptian culture for only a short time.

Amnopis the fourth (1387-1366 B.C.) lived during the period when most of Egypt's economic and practical culture was under the leadership of the priests of Ammon. Amnopis took an interest in religion much deeper than that of former Pharaohs. He decreed that all the gods must be united into the one entity which would be called Atun. Atun was to be worshipped exclusively. Amnopis then changed his own name to Akhenatun, or "Devotee of Atun".

Akhenatun, the unusual Pharaoh, tried to cause all the people of Egypt to accept his decree of one god. He even did something which until that time had never been tried – he attempted to do away with the priests of Ammon, who at that time controlled

Egypt in all matters religious and economic, and whose influence and regard was widespread and strong. It is not surprising that his efforts met with staunch resistance.

The Egyptian people were entrenched in the ways of Ammon, and their many institutions, including medical and educational, were based on the worship of Ammon. When Akhenatun realized the difficulty he would face in bringing the exclusive worship of Atun to the populace, he decided to distance himself from the centers of population and to build himself a new city where the new practice would be initiated.

Akhenatun established his city between Thebes and Memphis, and called it Akhtaton. Atun, according to Akhenatun, was the father of humanity, the creator of humankind in all its colors and forms who gave human beings their different languages, cultures, and countries. He gave Egypt the Nile, and to all people he gave the rains.

Of course, the followers of Ammon did everything they could to prevent Atun from becoming the one and only deity of the Egyptian people. Akhenatun and his city were isolated, and became thought of as strange and outside the mainstream.

Despite his best efforts and his fierce belief, Akhenatun did not succeed in implementing the worship of Atun as the one god, and Atun soon disappeared from the myths. There was no place in the mythology for a god whose very existence would negate that of the entire Egyptian Pantheon!

Thus, after the death of Akhenatun, Tutankhamen returned the seat of the kingship to Thebes, and soon all traces of the worship of Atun disappeared.

Bes

Bes did not cut an imposing physical figure. He was characterized as a long-haired, heavy eye-browed dwarf with bowed legs, a flat nose, and huge ears. Depictions of Bes in ancient art are quite different from those of the other gods, who are usually seen in profile. Bes was drawn from frontal perspective. The only other deity depicted in this manner was Ketesh, whose origins were Asian.

Bes was the god who protected children, family, and households. He especially looked after women in childbirth. He was also known as the god of enjoyment and entertainment.

Bastet

A goddess with the head of a cat and the body of a human woman, Bastet was at first identified with wild lions and not with domestic cats.

The house cat was thought of as a holy animal for a long period in Egyptian history. The danger of rats and other rodents was considerable since the economy was based in large part on the growing of grain crops. The domesticated cats brought relief from this threat, and they quickly became well-loved and blessed. When a cat died from unnatural causes, its owners' grief was prolonged and acute, and when the death was natural, the owners would shave their eyebrows. Bastet was worshipped mainly in the city of Bobastis, which was the dedicated city of dead cats, where it was customary to embalm them.

During the yearly festival of Bastet, all hunting of lions (a sport much loved by the Pharaoh's) was suspended.

Geb

Son of Shu, the god of air, and Tefenet, the goddess of moisture, Geb was the god of Earth. His twin sister was Nut, goddess of the sky. Nut and Geb were so close that their father had to separate their bodies in order to allow the birth of their children. Geb, along with eight additional heavenly entities, supported the sky as it covered the earth. The separation of earth from sky allowed the existence of all the earthy creatures.

The mating of Geb and Nut brought forth two sets of twin gods – Osiris and Isis, and Set and Nephthys.

Wepwawet

Like Anibus, Wepwawet had a canine look, and took part in funeral rites and ceremonies. Wepwawet was a guide who helped the dead find their way to the underworld. Egyptian leaders carried the symbol of Wepwawet when they marched into battle, and later in celebrations of victory.

Hapi

The Nile River played such a central and vital role in the lives of the Egyptians that it is not surprising that the river had its own god – Hapi. Hapi was depicted as a substantial figure carrying a sheaf of grain, symbolizing the plenty which the Nile Delta brought forth.

The god Hapi enjoyed the exchange of gifts. After the yearly flooding of the banks of the Nile, which fertilized the land for planting, Hapi would be brought offerings of food and objects of beauty such as precious stones and gems.

Horus

Horus was the hawk-headed Egyptian god of the heavens. He was the light that battled against the dark. His wife was the cow-goddess Hathor.

The origins of the cult of Horus were in Upper Egypt, where he was the sun god, and as such may have been one with the god Ra. In fact, he was thought of at first as the son of Ra and sister of Set, but later myths, where the god Horus appears with the head of a hawk, tell of his birth to Isis and her brother/husband Osiris, after the rebirth of Osiris.

According to the myths, Isis gave birth to Horus in a secret hideout at the far end of the Delta and raised him there, in order to keep him safe from Set, who she feared would kill him. When he matured, Horus avenged his father's death at the hand of Set. (Horus - light, battled Set – darkness). During the skirmish with Set, Horus lost one of his eyes, but still came out victorious, killing (or according to another version, castrating) his rival uncle. When the eye was restored to him by Thoth, Horus gave it to Osiris, and put in its place a snake god which later became the symbol of the royal family. Horus then took his place in the continuation of the dynasty of Osiris.

Every Pharaoh, upon his death, was said to turn into an Osiris, and every subsequent Pharaoh was called a Horus.

According to another myth, Horus won the kingship back from Set due to the intervention of Isis. In this version, the fight for the throne was long and there was no end in sight. Set declared that he alone could rule since only he could watch over the sun each night while it passed through the underworld. Some of the gods of the council set up to judge the conflict tended to agree with Set, but Isis tried to convince them that her son Horus was indeed the proper ruler. Her powers of persuasion were so strong that the council had to remove itself to a deserted island and forbid access to Isis while they deliberated. Isis used her cunning to gain entrance nevertheless, with the help of Nemti, who was punished severely for aiding her – his big toes were amputated. Still the gods could not reach a decision as to the kingship of Egypt – Horus or Set?

Finally, Isis appealed to Osiris in a letter sent to him in the underworld. Osiris responded by threatening to send evil spirits to haunt the gods if they did not award the throne to his son Horus. This proved the deciding factor, and Horus became the sovereign.

Horus appears in the mythology in two aspects – that of the innocent child, sucking his finger and that of the mighty adult. The eyes of Horus symbolized the moon and the sun, and he was the guardian of all creation and its laws. He was called the "shepherd of the people", and the watchful "eye of Horus" appears often in ancient Egyptian art.

Horus had four sons whose task was to watch over the jars containing the vital organs of the deceased. The ancient Egyptians always removed these organs before mummifying the dead, and they were mummified and buried along with the body in separate containers. Hapy (not the Nile River god Hapi), who was depicted as a mummy with the head of a monkey, guarded the jar containing the lungs, while Imsety, with his human head, looked after the liver. The jackal-headed Duamutef was in charge of the stomach and Kebehsenuef watched over the intestines.

Khepry

Khepry was the beetle headed god who heralded the dawn and the coming of the sun-god, Ra. The beetle was one of the most revered of creatures in Ancient Egypt and considered the symbol for life itself. The dung beetle, which rolled its eggs into a ball of excrement symbolized, renewal, birth, and the daily reappearance of the sun.

Hathor

Sometimes called "the Golden one" and "Madame of Dendera" (after the city which served as the center of her cult), Hathor was the goddess of love, beauty, and fertility. She had the form of a cow which wore a sun-disk between its horns, or a woman with horns of a cow between which shone the sun.

Hathor was the protector of women and lovers. She was the goddess of marriage and was present at the birth of babies as a helper to the midwife. Sometimes she was identified with Isis. The god Horus, who later became her husband, gave Hathor her cow likeness after she provided milk for him in infancy.

As the goddess of beauty and love, the Greeks equated Hathor with Aphrodite. Hathor was the wife of Horus, and she visited him once a year during the festival of the Het-Hert. During this festival the statue of Hathor was taken from Dendera and stood at the shrine of Horus. After the festival it was ceremoniously returned to its place.

The complicated image of Hathor had still another facet. She was associated not only with love, marriage and birth, but also to death and rebirth. In the underworld, it was Hathor that received the newly deceased souls and who provided them with food and sustenance after they passed judgment of Osiris.

According to legend, during the rule of Ra, Hathor was a blood seeking lion. Ra wanted her by his side, and asked Thoth to bring her to him. They convinced her to come to Egypt, land of wine and happiness. Hathor agreed, and upon arriving in Egypt she gave up her wild ways and changed into the symbol of love and benevolence.

Taweret

Guardian of women and children, Taweret gave assistance at the rebirth of the dead in the primordial waters of Nun. The image of Taweret was a combination of an alligator, a lion, and a hippo, with utters hanging from it. She was sometimes considered the wife of Set, who also appeared at times in the form of a hippo.

Maat

Goddess of truth and justice, Maat was the daughter of Ra and the wife of Thoth. She was usually depicted with a single large feather plume. In the underworld, Maat would weigh her feather against the heart of the deceased. If the heart weighed more than the feather of Maat, the soul of the dead was considered unworthy and his body would be gobbled up by a monster. If the heart weight less than the feather, the soul was free to continue its path to everlasting life in the land of the dead. Maat represented and guarded the cosmic social order. She took care that justice would always be done, in the land of the living as well as in the underworld. While other deities would sometimes take part in conflicts of this or that nature, Maat was never involved in trouble of any kind, and was considered the friendliest of the gods. Indeed they all depended on her to keep the order and balance that ruled all of their existences.

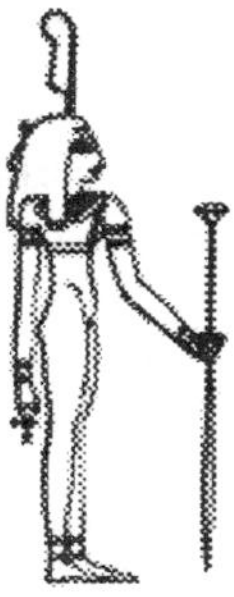

The four seasons and the rains obeyed Maat's orders to appear at the appropriate times, and day and night came in appointed cycles due to her watchful observance.

An image of Maat was a gift coveted by the gods themselves. The head of the high court of Ancient Egypt was thought of as the priest of Maat and the judges would carry small likenesses of the goddess on their persons.

Min

Min was the God of nomads and hunters, whose cult was mainly in the cities Panopolis and Kontos, in Lower Egypt.

Min was identical to the Greek god Preapos, who appeared with two long feathers and a scepter which looked like a boat oar. His sexual organ was depicted at its full erect length and girth. Min was one of the gods of the dark, and he ruled the eastern dessert, thought to be the domain of nomads and hunters. He was the god of sexual prowess, masculinity, and renewal. The most important festival held in his honor took place each year at the beginning of the harvest season. Apparently the lower castes of Egyptian society would take part in these wild and raucous, and very popular festivals.

Meresger

The goddess whose task it was to watch over the tombs of the kings, Meresger, in the form of a serpent, sat at the top of a mountain overlooking the graves of Luxor. Meresger was thought of as a good and benevolent goddess, with powers to cure human diseases of all kinds, but she was also able to bring about just those ailments as punishment for sinners

Nanuet

Along with her partner, Nun, Nanuet was the personification of the primordial waters. Nun and Nanuet were two of the eight gods of creation, called the Ogdoad.

Nehebkau

An evil spirit that haunted the souls of the newly deceased, Nehebkau had the body of a snake and the hands and feet of a human. Legend tells that after Ra, the sun god, broke him in and trained him, he became his loyal servant.

Neith

Neith was the ancient mother-goddess. According to one myth, she sprang from the primordial waters and created all the rest of the gods and humankind. When she spit into the waters, she created Apep, the serpent that fought with the sun god's boat as it made its way through the underworld each night.

During the struggle between Set and Horus over the kingship of Egypt, the gods on the council that was trying to make a decision wrote to Neith asking for her advice. Neith decided that Horus was the appropriate leader, but as compensation for Set, she suggested he be awarded two non-Egyptian goddesses. Some believe that Neith did not consider Set worthy of marriage to an Egyptian goddess.

Neith was associated with war and the hunt. Her symbol was a shield with two crossed arrows. The center of her cult was at Says, in the Nile Delta.

Nut

The Egyptian god of the heavens, Nut sprang, along with Geb, from the coupling of Shu (God of air) and Tefenet (goddess of moisture). The mating of Nut and Geb produced some very important gods: Osiris, Set, Isis, and Nephthys. Nut was depicted as a giant naked woman whose eyebrow was supported by Shu and contained the sky.

According to legend, the sun would enter Nut's mouth each evening, and pass through her body during the night, reappearing again in the morning.

Nun

According to ancient Egyptian tradition, Nun was the name of the primordial waters. The god Nun was described as a man standing in the water up to his thighs, and holding the boat of the sun god over his head with his outstretched arms.

The waters were thought to encircle all of creation and held a central and important place in the mythology. There is not, however, as opposed to other mythologies of the world, any traditional flood story in Egyptian myth.

From Nun, the primordial waters, Atum was born, and he created Shu and Tefenet – air and moisture. The energy of Chaos contained the potential for all forms of life within it. The mating of Shu and Tefenet brought about Geb, god of the earth, and Nut, goddess of the sky, whose offspring were Osiris, Set, Isis, and Nephthys.

The chaos of the primordial waters had four aspects each of which is represented by a pair of gods:

The Deep. Nun and Nanuet
Infinity. Hu and Hauhet
Darkness. Kuk and Kauket
The unseen. Amun and Amaunet

Together these eight gods made up the Ogdoad of Hermes, the City of Eight.

Nekhbet

The eagle-formed goddess that flew the heavens of Upper Egypt, Nekhbet, along protected the Pharaoh by spreading her wings over his palace.

The Greeks equated Nekhbet with their goddess of childbirth, Ilithyia, daughter of Hera.

Nephthys

Daughter of Geb (earth) and Nut (sky), and sister to Isis, Osiris, and Set, Nephthys' name meant "Castle Dweller".

Nephthys appears less often in the mythology than her illustrious siblings, and is associated mostly with funeral rites and burial ceremonies. Nephthys married Set, but the pair never produced offspring. After Set killed Osiris, Nephthys abandoned Set, and grieved along with Isis, for their brother.

During Egyptian funerals it was customary for two women to stand next to the mummy of the deceased and lament his passing just as Isis and Nephthys had mourned for Osiris.

Sekhmet

Like Bastet, Sekhmet had the head of a lion and was thought of as a cat-goddess. However, Sekhmet had a far more frightening and less domesticated countenance. She was called "the powerful", and had a forbidding and foreboding character. When the god Ra wished to punish humanity, he sent Sekhmet to do the job, but he had to be careful to prevent her from destroying the human race altogether. Sekhmet was the goddess who brought the wrath of the gods down on humankind, and epidemics and natural disasters were thought to be her doing. This bloodthirsty goddess was thought to cause wars, famines, and all manner of bad events that affected mankind, and she was greatly feared. Criminals were sacrificed to Sekhmet in an effort to appease and honor her. Memphis was the center of her cult of worship.

Numerous archeological findings point to the immense popularity of the goddess, including many lion-headed statues. Ironically, along with her threatening features, Sekhmet was thought to have strong healing powers, and special ceremonies were devoted to asking her to lift epidemics and soothe the sick. Also in contradiction to her frightening aspects, Sekhmet was thought to be protector of the king and thus of the entire people.

Selket

Selket was depicted as a human being with a scorpion on her head, or as a scorpion with the head of a woman. She looked after the mummified bodies of the deceased during their burial, and attended women in childbirth. Selket was one of the goddesses that assisted Isis when she gave birth to Horus and helped her to keep the infant hidden from Set.

Seker

Seker was another funeral god and Necropolis was the center of his cult of worship. His form was that of a mummy, with the head of a hawk. Seker was said to control one of the areas of the underworld – where the spirit Nehebkau, with his serpent head and human hands and feet, waited for the dead.

Seker was sometimes associated with Osiris, god of the dead, who also was depicted as a mummy.

Serapis

Serapis was the god of the city of Alexandria and the Ptolemy dynasty (305-30 B.C.) and his cult of worship spread throughout the Greek-Roman world.

Serapis was depicted as a bearded man with curly hair, whose head was topped by a basket of wheat sheaves, symbols of plenty and the goodness of the earth. The cult of Serapis grew out of that of the ox Apis, and he was actually a combination of Osiris and Apis, such that Isis was considered his wife as well.

In Greece, Serapis was associated with Hades, the underworld god, with Helios, the sun, and even with Zeus, father of the gods. Like Hades, Serapis was accompanied by the dog Kerberos. In the basket on his head he carried the blessings and gifts of all the deities of the underworld.

Serapis was the lord of the darkness, a title given him by Osiris, and as such oversaw fate and was able to give eternal life. Serapis had the power to heal using dreams and to provide waking visions.

Serapis had forty two alters of worship in Egypt, of whish the most prominent were in the cities of Memphis and Alexandria. The Greeks called his temple "Serapion". His temple in Alexandria was a destination for pilgrims from all over the world who sought his healing powers, as well as a center for learning and study.

Sobek

The son of Neith, Sobek appeared in the form of a crocodile. He ruled the rivers, streams and lakes and was one of the deities that protected the Pharaoh's of Egypt. Along with this, however, in certain areas he was associated with Set, enemy of Osiris, the first Pharaoh. His temple had a pool of live crocodiles that were considered holy by his followers.

Set

Set was the son of Geb (earth) and Nut (Sky), and the younger brother of Osiris and Isis. Nephthys was both his sister and his wife.

Findings from the third millennium B.C. present the image of Set as a god who resembles a donkey – his ears are large and wide, his legs and long and his tail straight. But in time, his image evolved, and later in later depictions Set looks more like a large dog, a characterization appropriate to the myths about him. The best-known of these is the story of the murder of Osiris and the subsequent war between Set and Horus, his nephew, Osiris' son. According to this myth, Set coveted his brother Osiris' kingship as well as the fact that Osiris, as provider of culture and economic plenty was well-loved and respected by the people of Egypt and by the other gods. Set therefore plotted to overthrow his brother and take over himself as Pharaoh. He made a special box to the exact proportions of Osiris and tricked his brother into getting into the box, under cover of a party game. Once Osiris was nailed into the coffin, set threw it into the Nile, and from there it floated into the sea. Osiris' wife, Isis, after a protracted search, located the box and was able to use her magic to become impregnated with Osiris' child. The infant, Horus, was raised in hiding out of fear that Set would take out his jealous wrath on Osiris' rightful heir. Set then mutilated the body of Osiris by cutting it into fourteen parts and buried them in separate places all over Egypt. According to one version of the myth, Isis found the pieces and managed to put her husband back together, save for one piece.

Set was the opposite in character to Maat, the goddess of justice and peace. Just as she personified love, Set personified hate. As she was beautiful, he was ugly. He stood for rebellion, upset, and violence. The belief was the Set held the power to cause humans to become irresponsible criminals. Any social unrest was blamed on the influence and activities of Set. The ancient Egyptians feared his awesome power and some even adopted his name in an effort to honor him and appease him into providing them with protection from destruction.

Set's brutal character was vital, however, for his important role as guardian of the sun that passed through the underworld each night on its way to the dawn. As Ra sailed through the land of the dead he was attacked each night by the serpent Apep, and Set, with his armies of dead souls, was his protection, allowing him to safely complete his trip through the underworld and to bring the light of a new day to Egypt. This nightly battle symbolized the eternal conflict between the forces of light and the forces of darkness.

In some places Set was symbolized by a fish with a long narrow beak, and these fish were considered holy. Wars were sometimes fought between communities when one was perceived to have desecrated this holy fish.

The Greeks considered Set the same as their god Typhon, the monstrous god who did battle with Zeus.

Ptah

In the beginning, Ptah, the god of the city of Memphis, was considered the original creation god. He created himself out of himself, when the earth and heavens did not yet exist. He then created the entire world by his utterances, including humankind. Ptah was the father of the arts, metallurgy, and sculpture. In Memphis, the center of his cult of worship, Sekhmet was his wife and Nephertem his son. According to ancient myth, Ptah existed first as Nun, the primordial waters, and he created the world by speaking words. It was even said that it was Ptah who created Atum, one and the same as Ra in the creation myths.

Legend had it that Ptah was the god of creative abilities and artistic endeavors, and that just by imagining the form of a god and speaking that form with a word, the god came into being. Precious metals too, were formed by Ptah into images. The Greeks saw in him a counterpart to Phaistos, the patron of the arts. Some considered him an additional god of fertility.

In the beginning, Ptah was described as the image of a man, wrapped like a mummy, with a beard and a hat. He held the ankh, the symbol of life, in his hand. Later depictions of Ptah show him as a dwarf with a flat head.

Ketesh

Ketesh was originally an Asian goddess, who later became the Egyptian goddess of love. Like Aphrodite in the Greek/Roman world, Ketesh was the Egyptian personification of love and beauty. In ancient art, Ketesh appeared as a naked woman standing on a horse, shown from the frontal view, and not in silhouette as were almost all of the other gods. In one hand she carried a bouquet of flowers and in the other a snake. She was considered the concubine of the gods, although sometimes she was identified with Isis and Hathor.

Ra

Ra was one of the most prominent and important gods in the Ancient Egyptian Pantheon. Appearing as the sun god as well as a creation god, he had several aspects: The morning sun was Ra the child, or the holy beetle, the scarab. Ra as the afternoon sun was depicted as a man with a hawk's head, surrounded by a sphere. As the evening setting sun, Ra was called Atum, or Ra-Atum, and looked like a human wearing the crown of an Egyptian Pharaoh. As the "nighttime sun", Ra appeared as a man with a ram's head.

According to one tradition, the sun (Ra) was born every dawn to Nut, goddess of the sky. In the afternoon he matured and in the evening he became elderly. At night, he sailed his ship through the underworld, the land of the dead, where Set and the souls protected him from attacks by the monster Apep, serpent of the void. At dawn, he emerged born again from Nut's womb, and sailed across the sky toward evening, only to repeat the cycle again.

At the altar to Ra in Thebes, daily ceremonies and prayers were held in Ra's honor to assist him in his battles against Apep. The Egyptians believed that even after the sun rose, the serpent could raise his head out of the clouds of the underworld and do battle with the light. In the daily service the priests would hold a statue of Apep and write on it in green ink. They then broke the statue into pieces and threw it on the ground. The priests whispered over and over the chants meant to increase the power and strength of Ra.

According to one of the myths, Ra first lived on the surface of the earth, where he ruled mankind and the gods. He tired of the earthly existence, however, and Nut, goddess of the sky, carried him up to the heavens where he created the stars and a heavenly paradise. Every morning, Ra, as the sun, would traverse the skies, but at night he would go down to the underworld and keep light from shining on the earth. He created Thoth, the moon, to shine at night in his stead.

Also according to this version, Ra appointed Osiris to rule mankind on earth, but expected that one day Osiris too would tire of this burden and return the world to chaos again, from which it would have to be created anew.

Another tradition holds that Atum-Ra was the son of Nun, the primordial waters – the first creation to spring from the hill she created in the waters. It was then Ra who planned the rest of creation, and formed it all from his saliva and sperm. He made the air – the god Shu, the moisture – the goddess Tefenet. They in turn created earth (Geb) and sky (Nut). From his tears, Atum-Ra created the human race.

The Benben stone at Heliopolis was sanctified to the belief that in that spot Ra began the creation of all that is.

The creature that represented Ra was the Phoenix, the immortal bird that rebirthed itself from ashes.

Ra never lost his place in the pantheon of gods, although he was often identified with other gods, or combined with them, such as Amun-Ra.

Beginning in the third millennium B.C., the Pharaoh's often called themselves "son of Ra", and this considerably strengthened the worship of Ra. Amnopis the fourth, who called himself "Akhenatun" wanted to convert all of Egypt to the worship of just one god, Atun, who most agree was a form of Ra.

It was Ra's task to raise the soul of the departed Pharaohs to heaven. Ra and Horus would set up a ladder in the tomb of the deceased Pharaoh which would enable him to climb up to the palace of the gods.

The belief in rebirth, which was very strong in the cult of Osiris, was overshadowed by the worship of Ra, which did not emphasize this.

Shu

God of air, Shu was the offspring of Shu and Tefenet, the goddess of Moisture. The mating of Shu and Tefenet brought about the gods of the earth and the sky, and from them the rest of creation sprang.

Thoth

The god of scribes, wisdom, and the moon, Thoth was the main god of Hermopolis. He was described as an ibis-headed man or as an ibis. At first, Thoth was thought of as one of the creation gods, along with Amun and Atum-Ra, but in time he became identified more closely with writing and learning, and was known as patron of the scribes. He crew up the laws, invented hieroglyphic symbols and was privy to the secret magic spells written on the holy scrolls. According to myth, Thoth penned the first book of magic, which included numerous spells for getting rid of suffering and disease. The Egyptians would pray to Thoth to deliver them from ailments using his magic. According to one of the myths, Ra, the sun, created Thoth to be his assistant, by shining at night as the moon, when he, Ra, was traversing the underworld and the earth was dark. Thoth's knowledge of math and numbers, along with his ability to tell the time, was said to help him plan the moon's cycles. Thoth was accredited with the invention of the calendar and he was also known as the first historian, faithfully recording the events of the time.

One of Thoth's duties was to check the balance of the scales used at the entrance to the land of the dead to decide the worthiness of the deceased. It was his responsibility as well to examine new temple buildings and to assure that they were built according to law and tradition.

Thoth's symbols were the writing tablet and desk.

Hermopolis, Thoth's city, had the most famous library in Ancient Egypt. Thoth was called the "tongue off Ptah", because of his speaking abilities, and it was thought that with his help Ptah uttered the words necessary to bring about all of creation.

Another name for Thoth was "the heart of Ra" - the creative mind. Thoth was able to create whatever he wished simply by bringing it to mind and imagining it.

The Greeks identified Thoth with Hermes Tirsmegistus.

Tefenet

Goddess of moisture, Tefenet, along with Shu (air) sprang from Atum, who came from the primordial waters – Nun. Geb (earth) and Nut (sky) sprang from Shu and Tefenet.

Persian Mythology

Foreword

The ancient Persian religion before the spread of Islam was unique and different from the rest of the Eastern faiths. The faith of Zarathustra, which Western researchers have called Zoroastrianism, erased all trace of any gods or beliefs which preceded it.

Today most researchers see the faith of Zarathustra as dualistic. Dualism asked the question: "What exists?" Is everything of god, or is there a real separation between the body and the soul, between spirit and matter? (Dualism is not the opposite of Monotheism). The religion was based on the belief in two opposing forces – good and bad, which engage in constant battle one with the other within humans. According to the religion of Zarathustra, all of the good and the bad that exists in the world are expressions of these two warring energies.

At the same time, it is possible that the source of the ancient Persian religion was actually Monotheism and its development in a world mostly ruled by polytheism caused a strengthening of the belief in evil, and thus a larger role was later played by the battle between good and evil.

The two main active forces in the religion of Zarathustra were the Ahura Mazda (or Ormazd) – the god of creation, and Ahriman – the god of evil, keeper of the dark forces of Angra-Mainyu. Actually this was not true dualism since it was not the god Ahura Mazda directly pitted against Ahriman, but rather the holy spirit Spenta-Mainyu that battled the forces of evil.

Ahura Mazda was the holiest deity, the lord of all creation. He brought forth light and darkness, sleep and wakefulness, morning, afternoon, and evening. Since he created everything, he was the originator of both good and bad, life and death, truth and lies, and of the constant wars between these opposites.

Zarathustra passed on to the human race the commandments of Ahura Mazda, which were to choose the right side, to choose the good, the truth, and the light – to choose Ahura Mazda. He warned the people against the temptations and sins along the path of Ahriman. In the end, according to Zarathustra, the powers of the light would win out over darkness and evil.

In time, the constant philosophical battle between good and bad was personified into a competition between opposing gods, and this solidified Zoroastrianism into a true dualistic faith.

The will of man played an important role in Zoroastrianism. Each person freely chose between thoughts of good or evil, good or bad words, and good or evil deeds. After death, each person's thoughts, words, and actions were weighed and judged. It was believed that a soul that had faithfully followed the ways of Ahura Mazda and had chosen on balance only good could cross the bridge of into a life of eternal reward. The deeds of these righteous ones would turn into lovely maidens who met them at the foot of a bridge and accompanied them across it to their everlasting paradise. A person judged unworthy – one that had followed the ways of Ahriman and lied or committed evil deeds would be met at the foot of the bridge by the personification of the sum total of his wrong-doings – an ugly maiden. The ugly one would lead him across a very narrow and treacherous path, through dangerous mist, their bodies wracked with pain as they groaned their way to the gates of the "house of lies" – the hell which was their punishment.

Zoroastrianism divided the history of the world into three periods, describing the process of the conflict between good and evil. The first period was before the creation of the earth, when the two forces did not yet exist. With the creation came the dawn of the second period, when good and evil met, clashed, and fought. The third period was to take place after the ultimate victory of good over evil. Any remnant of evil would be definitively separated from the good. The world would be renewed, and amid fire and brimstone the evil ones would be exorcised and removed from the earth. Rivers of molten metal would flow through across the land, and the righteous would walk along these burning streams as if through warm milk, while demons would be consumed by the molten current.

The end of the world would be heralded by the weakening of the known natural order, the positive order around which life is organized.

Zarathustra described another dichotomy in his philosophical teachings. He saw the world as made up of two aspects – the physical and the spiritual. When Ahura Mazda first created the world, it consisted as a spiritual thought-form only. Later these thoughts turned into physical phenomena. Thus, in our world, there exist both physical and non-physical aspects and they are intertwined with one another. Every physical manifestation has a spiritual cause and counterpart.

Each person has within him a basic element that is non-physical and this part returns, after physical death, to the world at large, to the spiritual realm. When the good wins out over evil, there will still exist a physical aspect to creation, but it will have been purified of all that is negative or bad.

Ahura-Mazda, the god of all that is good, presided over the kingdom of the light. The kingdom of darkness was ruled by the god of evil. Between these two kingdoms existed an infinite void. The spirit of evil saw the light, gathered it to itself, and tried to consume it. Ahura Mazda created the physical world in order to bury within it the spirit of evil. Thus the potential for evil exists within every human, bringing with it the desire for destruction, and the possibility for guilt, dishonesty, and vulnerability. This potential will remain in man until such time that good finally triumphs over even once and for all.

Man's task was seen as bringing true love and truth to the battle between good and evil. He was commanded to follow truth, to choose the righteous path, and to banish his own evil spirit. The overcoming of personal internal demons would facilitate the ultimate triumph of good.

Zarathustra did away with the sacrificing of cows which used to take place in Ancient Persia, and he also ended the national cult of the mind-altering "Hauma" – an intoxicating substance which caused degeneration and profligacy in those who consumed it. He did not forbid its use altogether, however. At the central shrine of Mazda a ceremony was held which was connected with the preparation of the holy Hauma drink.

Fire held an important and highly regarded place in the religion of Zarathustra. Flames were considered the ultimate cleanser and purifier.

It was commanded to destroy certain animals – those thought to personify the evil demons of the world.

Burial of the dead was forbidden – corpses were left exposed in order to be consumed by birds that feasted on rotting flesh.

Zarathustra encouraged marriage between first degree relatives, such as father and daughter, and sister and brother.

Ahura Mazda/Ormazd

The central and most exalted god in Persian mythology, Ahura Mazda, or Ormazd, took many forms. The most common of these were the sun and the eagle, both of which symbolized the all-seeing vantage point from on high from which the god looked down on earth. Ahura Mazda meant "the wise god". (Ahura – god, and Mazda – wise), and he ruled the kingdom of the light. Ahura Mazda had nine wives who lived with him in the heavens. He was the personification of all that was good and pure, and all that was true, kind, and generous. His entourage included Vohu Mana ("the good soul" or "the good thought"), Asha ("truth" or "higher order"), and Hashthrah ("dominion"), all of whom sat to his right. On his left were Armaiti ("holy devotion"), Haurvatat ("wholeness" or "health"), and Amaratat ("immortality"). In front of Ahura Mazda sat "Obedience".

Ahura Mazda's enemy was the Angra Mainyu, the spirit of destruction, the force of evil, which Ahura Mazda created as part of himself.

According to Zarathustra, the prophet who lived in during the sixth or seventh century B.C. and established the religion Zoroastrianism, Ahura Mazda was the god of all gods.

Zarathustra considered Ahura Mazda the only god worthy of admiration and worship. He saw Ahura Mazda as the sole creator of the world, having formed everything that existed from his thoughts – including all mankind and the other gods. Everything came from him – the ability of fire to heat, and of water to flow, the growing of vegetation – it all came from the great of greats – Ahura Mazda.

Ahura Mazda created and established the "perfect order", called Arta, or Asha. Arta was precision and truth, the fundamental basis for all life. Man lived according to the principles of Arta, and after death, rose to a brilliant paradise.

In order to receive the reward of the afterlife,

man was required to live righteously and to choose the path of good. Their choices aided Ahura Mazda in the battle against Angra Mainyu, and the spirit armies of Ahriman.

The evil Ahriman was, according to one of the myths, the twin brother of Ahura Mazda. He chose evil, and brought death to the world. Ahura Mazda was not responsible for Ahriman's choice... and Ahriman's continuation along the path of evil strengthened the existence of bad on earth. According to another tradition, the force of evil was created by Ahura Mazda himself, in order to have something to measure and compare himself against.

Ahura Mazda was at first identified with the god Mitra, ruler of the day. This was before the religion of Zarathustra raised him to the status of most powerful deity.

Ahura Mazda was symbolized by flame and fire. The heavenly fires and the godly spark which exists in every man were thought to be given by Ahura Mazda. Eternal fires were tended at his shrines.

Ahriman

According to the ancient Persian mythology, Ahriman personified evil, and was the god of the forces of darkness. He may have been a later form of Angra Mainyu, the destructive spirit, the opposing spirit to Spenta Mainyu – the holy and blessed spirit.

Ahura Mazda, the wise god, gave all of mankind the ability to discern and choose between good and bad, right and wrong, and between himself and Ahriman – whom he himself created.

He who chose truth and right chose Ahura Mazda, and he who chose evil chose Ahriman.

It was Ahriman that brought death to the world, just as he brought disease, the freezing of winter, and the heavy heat of summer. He tried to break the spirit of the good which was Ahura Mazda, and to rule the world by evil and destruction. It was a war waged between the Angra Mainyu (Ahriman's spirit) and Spenta Mainyu (the spirit of Ahura Mazda).

For purposes of this conflict, Ahriman brought the dragon, Azi Dahaka, to help him fight for the powers of evil. When Ahura Mazda created the starts in the sky, the cruel dragon jumped into the fray and created the planets and the astrological sings in order to use their powers to bring evil to the world.

According to another myth, Ahura Mazda and his evil twin Ahriman were the offspring of an earlier deity called Zurvan Akarna – infinite time. When Zurvan Akarna swore that his firstborn shall rule the world, Ahriman tore open the womb which held the twin fetuses and emerged first in order to seize the ultimate power. Zurvan Akarna declared that Ahriman would rule for a limited period of nine thousand years, after which Ahura Mazda would take over according to his will.

Ahriman's main weapon was sexual desire, which he received from Zurvan Akarna. With the help of this weapon, Zurvan told him, he would be able to consume everything, even his own creation. Ahriman willingly received this gift, since it suited his nature to perfection.

Az

A female being, Az was the personification of the sexual passion which was given to the evil god Ahriman by Zurvan Akarna. Az was unbidden sexual desire, an evil passion the overshadowed and overcame wisdom and common sense. She weakened the powers of the mind using doubt, and the subsequent loss of faith. Az caused the destruction of all who came into contact with her. When Zurvan Akarna gave Az to Ahriman, he explained that she was a powerful weapon that would destroy all he used it against. She could even harm Ahriman himself – like a black hole that sucks every victim that passes into its abyss.

In the hands of the evil Ahriman, this weapon was perfect for his purposes, and he accepted it from Zurvan gladly.

Atar

The flames of heaven, Atar was the son of Ahura Mazda. He personified the fires of good which fought against the evil dragon Azi Dahaka, who was created by Ahriman, god of evil. The heavenly flames were the source of the spark of holiness present in every human being.

Azi Dahaka

The three-headed dragon which for a certain period ruled the world, Azi Dahaka was created by Ahriman, the evil god. He in turn created the planetary system, astrology and horoscopes, and turned them against mankind. The rule of Azi Dahaka brought pain and suffering on the world in the form of famines and droughts, excessive heat and cold, jealousy and misery, old age, and death. Atar, the son of Ahura Mazda who personified the fires of the heavens, fought Azi Dahaka and succeeded in sinking him to the depths of the ocean (or according to an alternate myth, tying him to a mountain peak). Azi Dahaka escaped after a short period however, and brought destruction to a third of the world's population, before he was finally killed.

Anahita

The ancient Persian fertility goddess, Anahita was the source of the cosmic sea, and all of the waters upon the earth. She was also the source of human culture. Anahita was identified with Aphrodite and with Venus, and became popular throughout the Near East, and in some parts of the West.

Angra Mainyu

Evil incarnate, Angra Mainyu was the spirit of Ahriman. According to the religion of Zarathustra, Angra Mainyu was the enemy of Spenta Mainyu, the holy spirit of good identified with

Ahura Mazda. According to this concept, Ahura Mazda was the supreme gods, creator of all, who created the Angra Mainyu as well as Ahriman. The true conflict was no between Ahura Mazda and Ahriman, but between the holy spirit (Spenta Mainyu) and Ahriman.

The existence of Angra Mainyu gave man a choice – between the good and the bad. Man's ability to choose gave him some power over the course the world in its entirety would take, and he influenced his own destiny.

Apaosha

The demon of drought, Apaosha was beaten by Tishtria, the god of rain.

Gayomart

Personification of prehistoric man, according to Persian myth, his name meant – Expiring Life. Gayomart existed for thousands of years as a spirit, before being given the form of a young and handsome man. When he reached the human age of thirty years, Ahriman, god of the forces of evil used Jeh, the whore, to poison him. From the seed of Gayomart were born the father and mother of humankind, Mashai and Mashain. They abandoned Ahura Mazda, the god of the light and the forces of good, and worshipped Ahriman. For this their punishment was everlasting life in the land of the dead.

Haoma

The Persian counterpart to the Indian Soma, Haoma was the drink of life. Its consumption was said to afford the unification of upper and lower, of earth and heaven.

The origins of the Haoma ceremony are found in Ancient Persia, where it had orgiastic aspects. Zarathustra was against the cult of Haoma and called it the habit of "filthy drunkards". The Haoma did not disappear, and even grew in prevalence lessoned as the religion of Zarathustra took hold. The practices surrounding the drinking of the Haoma gradually became more moderate and were eventually assimilated into Zoroastrianism itself.

Zurvan Akarna

The god of time, Zurvan Akarna was called "infinity" in the Persian creation myth. He was the father of Ahura Mazda, the god of good, and of Ahriman, the god of evil. According to this myth, the two were twins, born of Zurvan, the first being to exist. Zurvan swore that his firstborn child would rule the world, and when Ahriman heard this, while still in his father's womb, he tore it open and emerged first. Zurvan had to make good on his promise, so he promised Ahriman sovereignty over the universe for nine thousand years, after which rule would pass to his brother, Ahura Mazda.

Yima

According to Persian myth, Yima was the first human being and father of mankind. Zarathustra maintained that Yima was a sinner, because he allowed people to eat the meat of the ox. This transgression cost them dearly – the punishment for eating ox meat was mortality – the loss of eternal life. Sacrificing the ox to gods other than Ahura Mazda may have carried an even stiffer penalty.

The myth of Yima's kingdom was prevalent in Persia for a long time – it even persisted after the Arab invasion. According to the myth, Yima ruled for seven hundred years, during which time he succeeded in ousting all of the demons and taking over their lands, widening the territory of his kingdom in order to make room for subsequent generations of humans and the many animals which multiplied and thrived during his time.

No golden age can last forever, however, and Ahura Mazda ordered Yima to have a huge underwater shelter built to protect the humans from the onslaught her foresaw of rain, snow, and hail. Yima was to bring only the good men and women to the shelter, and the best of the plants and animals. He was ordered to bring them in pairs and to leave behind any specimen that showed illness or weakness. No creation of Ahriman's was to be allowed in the shelter.

It was believed that in time Yima and all those he had preserved in his shelter would be returned to their land.

Mashye and Mashyane

Mashye and Mashyane were the father and mother of humanity. They were conceived from the seed of Gayomart which saturated the ground as he died. The pair then sprang from the earth (their mother) and grew much as plants until Ahura Mazda made them the first humans. Like Adam and Eve in the Garden of Eden myth, Mashye and Mashyane were given a choice between good and evil – between Ahura Mazda and Ahriman. They abandoned righteousness and good and worshipped Ahriman, the god of evil. Their punishment for this choice was a life of living hell.

Mithra/Mithras

The Iranian-Indian god Mithra, whose worship was common even in other parts of the world, is not mentioned at all in the writings of Zarathustra. Therefore researchers conclude that he was one of the original Iranian gods that Zarathustra rejected. Nevertheless, many other documents afford him a prominent place among the deities. Apparently, during the early time of Para-Zoroastrianism, Ahura Mazda and Mithra were twin gods of the heavens, and were considered the two "guardians of creation". Later, as Zoroastrianism took firmer hold, Ahura Mazda emerged as the major deity, but Mithra retained importance as well. It was believed that Ahura Mazda himself held Mithra as worthy of reverence and admiration.

Mithra was very popular among the Persians, who considered him the son of Ahura Mazda. Mithra was the rising son, and like Helios, the Greek sun god, he was the observer of all that took place on earth. Nothing escaped his sight. Mithra witnessed every event however small and prosaic. One of Mithra's tasks was to assist mankind in maintaining peaceful relationships, friendships, and truthfulness. In addition to his identification with the sun, he was associated with other heavenly bodies, such as the stars. Mithra was also thought of as the god of abundance and of the growth of vegetation. He was a generous and friendly god. In the ancient Iranian writings – the Avesta, Mithra is depicted as rising each day like the sun, standing in his chariot which is pulled by two white horses. From this vantage point he used his thousand eyes to observe all of creation.

Mithra also had a cruel streak, however. He was the god of soldiers and of war, armed with a long javelin and horrible arrows of death. All who tried to oppose him were punished without mercy. Mithra would inflict them with fatal diseases or set wild boars upon them.

There are also mentions in the writings of Mithra in the role of judge in the land of the dead. As such, he was peace and war at once, as well as good and evil. The name Mithra meant "friend", and he indeed befriended all who chose the path of Ahura Mazda, but woe to he who chose the path of evil, and the worship of Ahriman.

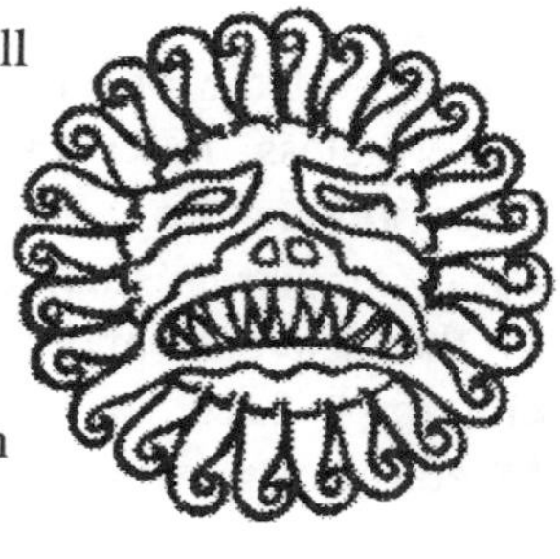

When the religion of Zoroastrianism all but erased the importance of Mithra in favor of Ahura Mazda, Ahura Mazda took note of Mithra's complaint that he was no longer worshipped as before. Ahura Mazda, out of his kindness and understanding, invited Mithra to share in the cult of Hauma, which at that time was central to Zoroastrianism. Mithra's participation in the cult of Hauma paved the way for him to morph into the mysterious god – Mithras.

The cult of Mithras was shrouded in mystery as it spread throughout the Roman Empire. Its source was the late entry of Mithra to Zoroastrianism as the god of mystery. The first evidence of the worship of Mithras outside of Persia came from Asia Minor in the first century B.C. and by the second half of that century the cult of Mithras had spread to the rest of the known world - From the Black Sea to Scotland, Africa, Spain, the Balkans, Germany, and Italy. Mithraism was at its height during the third century but when Christianity took over the Roman Empire, in the fourth century, the influence of Mithras slowly died out.

Plutarch wrote that the Persians considered Mithra to be the mediator between Ahura Mazda and Ahriman. As such, his character had aspects of both these major gods – the pure good and the pure evil. The Roman worship of Mithras was based on Mithras' promise to deliver abundance and fruitfulness to the world, as well as eternal life in the spirit world after physical death.

A central myth to the worship of Mithras was the story of the killing of the cow. The symbolism of the cow was expressed in the growth of new life from its blood, bones and semen. From these were said to have sprung many new forms of animal life. In Ancient Persian temples it was the custom to adorn the walls with pictures of Mithras in the act of killing the cow.

According to Mithraism, the killing of the cow by Mithra returned the rule of Yima to a world in which no hunger or death had yet been suffered. Believers practiced a special ceremony which exalted the killing of the cow, and which was to bring those who took part eternal life. For this reason, Mithras was very popular among warriors and soldiers who would perform this ceremony before setting out to battle.

Those wishing to take part in the mysterious cult of Mithras had to undergo a training period, after which they were sworn to secrecy and put through initiation rites. They then underwent a complicated series of tests. The believers were ranked and could move up the ranks in time as they proved their devotion. The ranks were as follows: Raven, Bride, Soldier, Lion, Persian, Sun-Courier, and Father. The holy feast was one of the most important customs of Mithraism.

As the god of war, Mithras gained the respect of the Roman Empire, and his cult spread from the Danube all the way to Britain. He was depicted mostly in human form with the head of a lion, with a snake coiled about his torso. Other animals as well were perched on his form. Sometimes he was shown with horns and with keys or a torch in his hand.

Mithra joined Verona as a Euro-Indian god.

Saoshyant

It was believed the Saoshyant – the Savior, would appear at the end of the world and renew life again.

Saoshyant would push aside evil wrought by Ahriman and deliver the world to the "second creation" or "second coming" when all souls that had passed on would return to their bodies. Even souls that had worshipped the evil god Ahriman would be revived along with those that had followed Ahura Mazda, the god of all that was righteous and good. There would be a mighty fire and rivers of molten boiling metal would flow, through which the righteous could walk without pain, as if through warm milk. Thus all of humanity would be returned to Ahura Mazda, purified of all sin, delivered into joy and light.

Spenta Mainyu

The holy spirit, Spenta Mainyu was the opposite of Angra Mainyu, the spirit of evil. Spenta Mainyu was the spirit identified with Ahura Mazda, the god of good, but was not the god himself.

Sraosha

The name Sraosha means "to listen". Sraosha embodied the quality of "listening" in Persian myth. During the period of Zoroastrianism, Sraosha was the "ear of Ahura Mazda". He heard every cry for help that emanated from humankind when the spirit of Ahriman was causing them suffering. Since most of the evil activity took place under cover of darkness, Sraosha would come down to earth at sundown and chase down the guilty parties, the sources of violence and anger that were his enemies.

Like Mithra, Sraosha was a mediator between the humans on earth, and the deities in heaven, and he was the special glue that united them. In the heavenly kingdom Sraosha was the only deity allowed to stand before Ahura Mazda. Sraosha survived the Arab period as Sorosh, messenger of Allah, who was identified at times also with the angel Gabriel.

Rapthiwhin

The god of heat and summer, Rapthiwhin started out as ruler of the entire year, until the demon of winter appeared. When winter reigned, Rapthiwhin took refuge underground in order to watch over the heat of the waters of chaos. He returned to the surface of the earth in springtime when the winter demon retreated.

Rashnu

Judge and keeper of justice in Persian myth, Rashnu, along with Mithra and Sraosha, evaluated the soul of a person according to his deeds.

For thirty days, Rashnu would weigh the deeds of person and at the end of that period he declared his judgment. The ancient Persians believed that the soul sat alongside the body of the deceased during these thirty days, waiting for Rashnu to decide its fate. If the soul was found worthy, it would be assisted in crossing the "bridge of decision", by a lovely maiden who was the personification of all the person's good deeds. The righteous soul would then be allowed to take its place among the heavenly bodies, and shine in the full light of happiness and joy. A soul found unworthy, however, would find the bridge narrow and treacherous, and would slip from it into the depths of the underworld, where a monstrous entity which embodied the person's evil deeds awaited its arrival. The soul was then delivered to the demons that would torture it mercilessly as punishment for worldly sins.

Tishtrya

The ancient Persian god of rain, Tishtrya succeeded in overcoming the terrible demon of drought, Apaosha.

Gods of Ancient Sumaria and Mesopotamia

Foreword

The ancient Mesopotamian religion is the oldest about which written evidence has been preserved and discovered. Based on the faiths of the Sumarians, it included spiritual and practical guidance, explanations of the secrets of life and death, and a very colorful and detailed mythology. The Babylonians and the Assyrians who in the footsteps of the Sumarians accepted most of the gods and the customs of the Sumarian religion, but not without leaving their mark and making some changes suited to the character of their own civilization. The influence of the Sumarian heritage comes through clearly in the mythology of these times.

The Sumarians were a very practical people, and they loved order and organization. They enjoyed material abundance, successful agriculture, prestige and reputation. Sumaria, which in classical times was called Babylonia, covered the lower half of Mesopotamia, from the area of Baghdad of today to the Persian Gulf. The climate in this part of the world is desolate and parched.

Notwithstanding the considerable industriousness of its inhabitants, the land remained dry and bare, and lacking in resources. The Sumarians were a strong people, however, and their agricultural skills and their inventiveness were extraordinary. Thus, they were able to eke from Sumaria a fertile and abundant life. They became the center of world culture by the third century B.C. Their intelligence and decisiveness developed the most advanced culture known in the ancient world. They invented irrigation, and by draining the floodwaters of the Tigris and Euphrates rivers, which were rich in silt, were able to nourish their fields.

Since stone was not plentiful in Sumaria, clay from the rivers, which could be formed into a strong and substantive mass, was the most prominently used building material. Sumarian architects were the first to use vaulted ceilings, domes and arches in their construction. They developed methods for the formation of bricks from river silt for the use in the building of homes.

The Sumarians are credited with the invention of several types of vehicles, as well as pottery, the sailboat, the plow, and the casting of bronze and copper. They originated writing upon clay tablets, and revolutionized the system of writing that had been in use for two thousand years. Many of their writings have survived until today, and our knowledge of Mesopotamian culture is based on the study of these.

The Sumarians turned out a wide range of literature. The Sumarian academic community revolved around an academy called the House of Manuscripts, which served as the education and instruction. This academy was deemed so important that the day to day activities which took place within its walls were recorded on tablets, many of which survive to this day. The scribes of the academy continued to write essays in the Sumarian language even after the infiltration of the Semites into their land and the subsequent end to Sumarian as the spoken language.

According to the Sumarians, the earth was flat and round, surrounded by a gigantic void, and covered by sky which was spread out above the earth.

The universe was called “An Ki”, or “Heaven Earth”. Surrounding the void above the heavens and below the earth was an infinite sea, which anchored the universe in place.

The water, as in many other ancient mythological traditions, was everlasting and basic, the source of all that is.

According to one of the myths, in the midst of the primordial waters there rose a cosmic mountain (similar to the mount in the myth of Nun) which consisted of a combination heaven and earth. From this union of heaven (personified by the god An) and earth (personified by the goddess Ki), the god Enlil, god of air, was born. Enlil separated his parents, the heaven and the earth, and by union with his mother, he formed the human race. In the empty space that was formed between "mother earth" and "father sky", the stars, sun, and moon were born. The Sumarians believed that a huge dome encompassed the entire world, keeping the stars, moon and sun in their places, and ensuring the lighting of the earth. Below the earth, they believed, was a cold and frozen underworld, kingdom of the dead and home of demons.

The Babylonian creation myth was borrowed from that of the Sumarians, with the addition of the popular Babylonian god Marduk. According to Babylonian myth, before creation there was only a great body of fresh water, called Absu, and a sea called Tihamat. Absu and Tihamat mated to create the gods. Later Absu hatched an evil plot against the gods, and the wise Enki destroyed him. This greatly angered Tihamat who then fought the gods, but neither side won and neither would back down. Marduk, the son of Enki and offered his assistance at bridging the conflict. He demanded that if he should succeed, he would be awarded the task of head of the gods. The gods met and discussed this suggestion, and agreed to accept Marduk's terms. Marduk had to fight with all his strength, but in the end he succeeded in bringing Tihamat down. He then used half of Tihamat's body to create the sky, moon, sun, and other heavenly bodies. He then created humankind out of the blood of a god that stood at Tihamat's side. The council of the gods, full of admiration for Marduk, built a magnificent temple in his honor, and held a feast during which they pronounced Marduk a god of fifty names. After the feast, the gods presented the earth to mankind that he may rest upon it.

The great and mighty beings that were responsible for the creation of the world, according the Sumarians, were the "Dingir" (gods). They had human form as well as many other human characteristics such as passion and emotion. Unlike humans, however, the Dingir were immortal and possessed super-human strength. The Sumarian Pantheon, according to documents that survive, was wide indeed, and included hundreds of deities which ruled over various areas of activity. The gods were ranked by importance, and the most powerful were those that ruled over the four main domains of life: An – the sky god, Enlil – the god of air, Enki – the god of water, and Ninhursag – the great goddess of mother earth. These four gods created the basic elements of the universe, and the secondary gods. According to Sumarian myth, the creation was quite simple – the gods had simply to decide that they wished to create something, and their thoughts would materialize into reality. This belief was common to all of the ancient religions – the word or thought of a god had ultimate creative power.

However, even with this awesome ability, the lives of the gods resembled those of human beings. They ate, drank, celebrated, married, had children, and displayed varying personality traits such as jealousy, friendliness, cruelty, anger, happiness, and sadness. The gods sometimes suffered from disease, and they needed sleep and shelter, just as mortals did. They fought their enemies, and sometimes even died, after which they simply carried on in the underworld. They usually preferred honesty and integrity in their behavior, but there were gods who lied and cheated as well.

During the fourth millennium B.C. when the city of Ur presided over Sumaria, An, the sky, was the main god of the Sumarian pantheon. We might be surprised at this, since the water was such a strong element in the mythology, and in fact came before the creation of the sky. However, the hierarchy of the gods was identical to that of political rule, where the top position was held by a male. Therefore the god of highest rank had also to be male.

When Ur lapsed in its power, so did An, and Enlil, the god of air, took over.

It was believed by the Sumarians that mankind was created from the blood of a god who was beaten and killed, and that the creation was for the good of the gods, as humans would serve them, and worship them, and provide them with food and shelter so that they may rest from their tasks of organizing and ruling the world. Man was considered a creature of no power to affect change, and of little consequence compared to the enormous powers of the gods. Since man could not fathom the motivations and causes of the gods, they were insecure and full of doubt. When a person died, he was believed to be sent below to the cold and forbidding world of the dead.

Given their perceived place in the order of things, the Sumarians never tried to affect the decisions of the gods, even when they seemed unjust and unfair. The Meh was perceived as the final cause of everything that took place in the world. The Meh was fate – or the preordained plan according to which everything that happened was set into motion, for better or for worse. Lies and truth, health and disease, judgment, worry, and sorrow – it all rose from Meh.

The highest and most powerful gods, namely Enki and Enlil, were seen as far removed indeed from man, and not in the least accessible or approachable. There was never any hope in the hearts of the Sumarian people that these gods might come to their aid or intervene in their lives. Only the lower ranked deities were seen as available for petition – those with lesser powers, but with the ability to mediate between humans and the higher gods.

Thus, the belief in "personal gods", gods who took care of the individual and his family, was established. Every male head of a family had his personal god, to whom he would turn as one might to a father.

Worship of the gods was of central importance in Sumarian life. The priests held a variety of ceremonies on a regular basis. Over the years, houses of worship became huge building complexes made up of sanctuaries and temples, and which houses a large staff of priests, including the High Priest or Priestess, and many secondary clergy and clerks. The main priests would preside over the most important ceremonies, and the "everyday" worship was run by the lesser among them. There were also special priests whose task was to make sacrifices to the gods. The complex was populated in addition by musicians whose job it was to entertain the gods, and by those who supposedly told fortunes and interpreted signs and dreams. Servants and workers of all kinds including those who did the buying and cooking for the temple were also in residence.

Every major city in Mesopotamia altars were erected where daily sacrifices were offered to the gods. Meat, vegetables, wine, perfumes and more were burned in sacrifice by the presiding priests along with the city's citizens.

The calendar sported a variety of holidays and festivals, and for each the gods were worshipped in elaborate ceremony. The most important of these was the celebration of the New Year, which took place in the spring. Observance of this holiday lasted twelve days, with the central worship service being the "Sacred Marriage" which took place on New Year's day itself. The marriage was between the king and the High Priestess. The King took the part of Tamuz, and the Priestess enacted the role of goddess Ishtar. The purpose of the sacred marriage between the king and the goddess was to ensure continued prosperity in the coming year, as well as good health and long life for the king, as husband to the goddess. The origins of the sacred marriage are found in several songs, poems and practices whose motivation was to ignite the king's desire for the goddess. In the end, as in the myth of Tamuz and Ishtar, there was frustration and catastrophe.

Adad/Hadad

In Sumarian myths, Hadad was the thunder, lightening and winds of a storm. He was called the "rider on the clouds". Sholat and Hanish ran before him as his heralds.

Adad was the central god of Aramaic people – the forerunners of today's Syrians. He was like Hadad in that he would cause the earth to tremble with shock by shaking the mountains and uprooting trees. The ancient governors of Damascus called themselves "sons of Adad", and several kings called themselves the same.

Adad was thought to be the son of the god Anu. He was associated with destruction, on the one hand, due to his causing of earthquakes and storms, but he was also the god who assisted the growth of plant life. As god of storms, he symbol was thunder and he was sometimes compared to the ram, which symbolized strength and productivity. The cult of Adad spread throughout the early East. It was customary to shout his name in curses upon enemies and in prayers to bring the rain.

Utu/Shamash

Utu was the mythological Sumarian sun, and one of the most important deities. He was depicted as a human man with rays of sun emanating from his head and lighting the world. He had a long beard, wore long robes, and on his head there was either a hat or a crown.

The Acadians, as well as the Assyrians and the Babylonians called him Shamash. His father was Nana – god of the moon, and his mother was Ningal and his sister was Inana, the goddess of love and war (the Acadian counterpart to Ishtar). Sin, Ishtar, and Ningal made up the Babylonian triad. Sin's wife was Aya, the morning star.

Utu, in addition to being the sun-god, was also the god of justice, and as served as the highest judge. Humans would turn to him when they had grievances and he would see to their complaints. Like Helios, the Greek god of the sun, Utu was the all-seeing surveyor from the heavens. He also had the ability to interpret dreams.

Utu had a chariot (like the other sun-gods, Helios, and Ra), but he sometimes made his way across the heavens on foot. According to Babylonian myth, Shamash brought the laws down from the sky, and presented them to Hamurabi, the king of Babylonia.

In the Sumarian underworld, the same high judge would evaluate the souls of the departed. Utu's symbol was the disk of the sun as it rose up between two mountain peaks.

Since the sun was all-seeing and all-knowing as it made its way across the daytime sky, he was prayed to often and fervently. When a crime was committed, it was clear to all that the sun had seen the wrongdoing and that the perpetrator would be brought to justice.

The sun's helpers were Giro, the god of fire, and Nosku, god of light. The temples of Utu were placed on mountainsides and called "apabar" – houses of light.

Inana/Ishtar

Inana, Lady of the heavens, and also called Irnina, was the goddess of love, fertility, and war in Sumarian mythology. She was guardian and patroness of the city of Ur, but her worship spread to all corners of Mesopotamia. She was the most important goddess in the Sumarian Pantheon.

Inana was the daughter of An, and sister of Ershkigal. Inana was depicted as a woman wearing a dress and holding a staff in her hand. At her side appeared her symbols – gateposts on which were hung cloth flags. The flags perhaps stood for home and war, the two areas of her influence. By the power of Inana, life resulted from love, or death from war. Inana was also called the goddess of eternal laughter who was always pleased.

Inana became famous in Sumarian mythology for successfully making Ur the most important city in the land. Ur became the major center for culture of the entire ancient world. Inana did this after she succeeded in ousting the Meh – the laws governing all that took place – from the grasp of Enki, god of water. She arrived at the palace of Enki in the depths of the sea, and did not need to try very hard in order to get the Meh away from Enki. Enki organized a celebration in her honor at which he became so drunk that he gave her Meh after Meh as gifts! When she had amassed a large amount of Meh, Inana escaped in her boat, accompanied by her wise and loyal servant, Ninshubur. When Enki came to his senses and realized what he had done, he sent his servant Isimud along with a group of sea monsters to chase after Inana. He ordered Isimud and the monsters to leave Inana unharmed, but to return with the Meh.

Inana's servant, Ninshubur was able to outsmart the pursuers and Inana succeeded in bringing the Meh back to Ur and to raise the city to its glory as the religious and cultural center of Ancient Mesopotamia.

Another myth puts Inana in a very human light. This is the legend of Inana and her Huluppu tree. Inana discovered the Huluppu tree on the banks of the river Euphrates, and was impressed by it as she had never been by any tree before. She uprooted it and brought it to her garden in Ur, where she cared for it and planned to make a new staff and a royal throne from its branches when it grew large enough. She waited expectantly and impatiently for the tree to grow and to be able to fashion the

items she wanted from it. An evil serpent coiled itself around the tree and put a strange curse upon it. In addition, an Anzu, a bird of ill-intent roosted in its bows, and a lilith made its home in the trunk. The branches of the cursed tree continued to grow, but bore no leaves.

In her great sorrow, Inana knelt near the tree and cried out for help. Gilgamesh heard her lament, and came to her assistance. The hero killed the snake, expelled the lilith and the Anzu bird, and uprooted the tree. He presented it to a happy Inana who used the wood to build the throne and staff she desired.

Inana had a strong and aggressive nature, and she was extremely ambitious. She was not satisfied with her rule upon the earth, and wished to be sovereign over the world of the dead as well. After she wed Tamuz (Dumuzi), Inana went down to the underworld to pay a visit to Ershkigal. She dressed in royal robes and adorned herself with jewels. In order to get to the palace of Ershkigal, Inana had to pass through seven gates. At each gate, she was requested to remove one of her pieces of royal jewelry or robes, so that when she finally reached the entrance to the palace she had taken off all of her finery, and appeared before the throne of Ershkigal completely naked. Seven cruel judges and Ershkigal herself looked at Inana with the evil eye of death, which in fact caused Inana to die. Inana's corpse was hung from a meat hook on the wall of the palace.

Inana had foreseen this possible disaster, however, and had warned her trusty servant Ninshubur, telling him to get help from the gods if she should not return from the underworld within three days. The gods consulted the Meh (the laws) of the underworld, and realized that one could return from there alive only if another creature took one's place in death. The loyal Ninshubur begged Enki, the powerful water god, to help Inana. Enki created two creatures that had no volume – creatures that could slip through gates undetected and therefore not be stopped from entering the underworld. These went down and found

Inana's corpse, bathed it in the "water of life" and fed it the "food of life". Inana indeed revived, but she was unable to return to earth unless a replacement for her could be found.

Inana returned to the land of the living along with guards from the underworld who warned her that her return was only temporary – until she could find someone to replace her in the land of the dead. If she failed, she would be returned there herself. She had several opportunities to kidnap some lesser gods for her purpose, but she passed these up. She made her way to her city, Ur, where her husband, Dumuzi, high-handedly and happily ruled. He was glad to be rid of his aggressive wife, in whose presence he had always felt overshadowed. His happiness was short-lived however, since Inana had returned, and had her husband kidnapped and taken to the underworld in her place.

Inana's Babylonian name was Ishtar. Ishtar, as the morning star, was the personification of war. As the evening star, she was love and desire. Like the Greek goddess Hera, Ishtar always remained a virgin. She did not lack for intimate relations, but like Hera, she bathed in a particular lake, which each time she entered its water, caused her to regain her virginity.

Ishtar's faithful and ever-present servants were Ninata and Kolita.

The Babylonians and the Assyrians also called her Milita. Herodotus, the ancient Greek adventurer who whose memoirs are still studies, tells a fascinating story of the cult of Milita – Ishtar: "Babylonian tradition forces every woman in the land to come once in her lifetime to the temple of Aphrodite (Ishtar) and to lie with a man who is a stranger to her. From the moment that she arrives at the temple, the woman cannot leave, until a man throws silver to her and has relations with her outside the temple. When the man chooses her and throws the coins toward her, he must say "I command you in the name of Milita". After the sexual union, the woman is consecrated to Milita. She returns to her home, and there is then no bribe large enough to buy her benevolence again. Attractive women, of course, were able to carry out this deed quite easily and were quickly returned home, but some women waited in vain for a man to throw her some coins and allow her to complete the obligation. Sometimes these women lingered at the temple for years. A similar custom took place on Cyprus"

Men that suffered from impotence would pray to Ishtar for a cure.

In the Babylonian myths, Ishtar was the sister and wife of Tamuz. Ishtar went down to the land of the dead, as a cruel and threatening countenance, such that even Ershkigal, Queen of the underworld, was frightened by her. Nevertheless, Ishtar succumbed there to death, which caused all of the vegetation on earth to wither and perish. The god Ea revived and freed her,

by sending a brilliant eunuch to trick Ershkigal into giving Ishtar the water of life.

Ishtar was hailed in Assyria especially as a goddess of war. She was depicted carrying a bow and arrows, and the look in her eye was warlike. She even sported a long beard!

According to Babylonian myth, when Ishtar fell in love with Gilgamesh, she beckoned to him, only to be firmly rejected. Gilgamesh found many ways to express his feelings about Ishtar's character, telling her that she was a cold hearth on a frigid day, a door that would not shut in a storm, like a castle that served as the tomb of its inhabitants, and like tar that dirties the hand that touches it. He accused her of being unfaithful to all her previous lovers.

When Ishtar heard Gilgamesh speak these words, she was so filled with wrath that she called on her father, Anu to bring forth the powers of the heavens. After at first denying her, Anu struck Gilgamesh's companion, Enkidu, dead.

Ishtar was as powerful a female force as can be found in the mythology. She was never willing to take no for an answer – even from the king of the gods.

An/Anu

An (Anu was his Acadian and Canaanite name) was the god of the heavens and the personification of the sky. He was the son of Namu - the primordial sea, the brother of Ki - goddess of the earth, and the father of Enlil. The star was the symbol of An. In the Sumarian creation myth, An is attached to Ki, the earth, by way of a cosmic mountain that rises out of the primordial waters.

The connection between Ki and An produced Enlil, god of the air, who was later to divide his parents, and mate with his mother to bring about the rest of creation.

During the fourth millennium B.C. when the city of Uruk was the most important center in Sumaria, An was considered the king of the gods. Later, his place was overtaken by Enlil. An was always considered a distant god, however just and righteous. He would not intervene in the day to day goings on of humanity, but instead left human kind to its own devices, and let his son Enlil rule them as he might. He himself stayed far away, high in the heavens.

The Temple of An in Uruk was called Ayana, and was used also for the worship of the goddess Inana.

The Assyrian-Babylonian mythology also mentions An, as Anu, god of the heavens, but he was not as active as other gods such as Marduk and Ashur.

According to Canaanite myth, in the beginning the world was covered with water, when Apsu and Tihamat, the first heavenly couple, appeared. After them came additional couples, and only later was Anu, god of the sky, born.

Anu, Ea, and Enlil formed the mighty triumvirate of gods, of which Anu was thought to be the first in time and space.

The three great gods divided the world between them (just as the three greatest Greek gods did – Zeus, Poseidon, and Hades). They tossed a die in order to decide the details of the division. The sky was won by Anu, and a crown was placed on his head, and a scepter in his hand. The kings of the land were to be his offspring.

During the flood, Anu provided shelter for the gods, and they turned to him with many and varied complaints, all of which he listened to with attention. On the other hand, in all that concerned human beings, Anu was distant and unreachable.

In the Hittite creation myth, Anu expelled Alulu, the first great king of the sky. The god Kumarbi (who bears similarities to the Sumarian Enlil) declared war against Anu, and bit off his penis in battle.

Acadian myth tells of Adapa, a priest of the god Ea, in the city of Eredu, who met Anu. One day, while Adapa sat in his fishing boat, a sudden south wind came up and capsized it. In anger, Adapa stopped the South wind, which caused the land to become parched from not receiving the moisture usually carried on the wind.

Anu called Adapa to his palace in the sky, in order to pass judgment on his deeds. Ea, whose priest Adapa was, warned Adapa not to touch any item of food or drink that Anu offered, as consuming it would surely kill him. In actuality, the food and beverage that Anu offered had the ability to give him immortality. When Adapa refused them, Anu understood that Ea had given him the wrong advice, preventing him from receiving eternal life. Anu laughed, and sent Adapa back to the earth's surface. The ancient text ends here, however we assume that in the end Anu gave special rights to the city of Eridu and its priests.

Anunki

The Anunki were huge gods that dwelled in the underworld, the offspring of Anu - father of the gods, and god of the sky. The Acadian-Sumarian legend tells that the Anunki were hungry and lacking for garments. They did not know how to eat bread, or how to dress themselves. All of their food was vegetables and grain, which they took directly into their mouths, like animals, and their water they drank straight from the stream. Enlil and Enki provided them with cattle, crops, a plow and an ox to pull it, but the Anunki did not know how to use these things to better their lives. They cried before an that they were hungry, tired and cold.

The gods found a solution to the Anunki's problems. They created human beings, and from then on the work of seeing to the needs of the Anunki fell to them. The humans provided for the Anunki by making sacrifices to them.

Enlil

The Acadian-Sumarian Enlil was the god of air, and later also the god of the earth. He was born from the mating of An and Ki (sky and earth). He later divided the pair, and An took over the sky and Enlil the earth. At first, Enlil was considered a lower god than An, but as Uruk lost its standing, and the city of Nippur rose in importance over Uruk as the political and cultural center, Enlil, the patron god of Nippur, became the main god in the Sumarian mythology. Enlil shared most of An's attributes. The name Enlil meant "lord of air". According to myth, after his parents parted, Enlil mated with his mother, and produced children with her. (The continuation of creation)

Enlil was called the "father of the gods" and the "king of the world". Enlil created all that was needed in the universe. He invented the hoe, and presented it to the humans so that they might succeed in agricultural pursuits. And the Sumarians did succeed. They were a very productive people and their economy, including agriculture, flourished.

As the head of the Pantheon, Enlil was sought by the other gods who wished to have his blessing bestowed on them. Enki from Erido, after building his magnificent sea house, hurried to travel to the temple of Enlil in order to receive his blessing. Nana, the moon and patron of the large city of Ur, sailed with his boat loaded with gifts for Enlil to ensure the continuing success and thriving of his city.

According to tradition, Enlil founded the Meh, the system of universal laws which governed all of existence, and all of creation was bound by these laws.

While it was Enlil who drew up the Meh, he also brought about his own downfall when he desecrated those same laws. Enlil's strong sexual drive was at fault for what happened. According to one of the myths, the event occurred while Enlil was walking in the streets of Nippur. Human beings had not yet been created, and Nippur was populated only by gods. As he walked about the city, Enlil noticed a beautiful goddess, the young Ninlil, as she bathed in a stream. The moment he saw her Enlil was strongly sexually drawn to Ninlil and wanted to possess her immediately. Ninlil tried to stop his advances, exclaiming that she was still too young, but Enlil would not listen to her refusals. He grabbed the young goddess and tossed her into a nearby boat, where he raped her. This unseemly act was a transgression of the laws of the Meh, and the gods banished Enlil to the underworld.

As a result of being raped by Enlil, Ninlil gave birth to Nana, god of the moon, and then she followed Enlil to the underworld.

The Meh, and the Enlil's place in the ranks of the Pantheon, were passed to Enki, god of water.

The rape of Ninlil was not Enlil's only crime. According to the myth of the flood, Enlil wanted to wipe out the human race. It may be, however, that this motivation was attributed to him since he was the god of air, and as such controlled the winds and weather.

Enki/Ea

Enki, from the city of Eridu, was the fresh-water god, as well as the lord of wisdom in Sumarian mythology. Ea was the parallel god in Acadian myths. Enki was a human-figured god who wore long robes, a beard, and a pointed hat. From his shoulders, wide rivers streamed toward earth. Enki was the god who provided the leaders of men their understanding and insight, and who gave the artisans their skill.

At first, Enki was of lower rank than Enlil, the god of air, so after his temple was built, he mad the journey to Nippur to visit Enlil and ask for his blessing. However when Enlil desecrated one of the holy laws of the Meh, Enki received the Meh into his keeping and he watched over them in Abzu, his underwater shrine. Once the Meh was in Enki's possession it raised him to the highest rank among the gods.

In his new capacity, Enki set out to continue the creation of the world in all of its detail. He decided on the levels of abundance that each land would achieve, and created the means for the inhabitants to reach his goals. He poured water into the rivers and streams, formed lakes and filled them with fish, and caused the rain to fall in its season. He planted the fields with crops and showed humans how to build barns and care for cattle.

In order to keep order in the world, Enki appointed special gods whose task it was to make sure that his creations worked properly.

The city of Eridu rose in importance in Sumaria as Nippur's influence lessoned in accordance.

Like Enlil, Enki too brought about his own downfall. As opposed to Enlil's case, however, it was not sexual drive that caused the problem, but gluttonous behavior. What the two did have in common however, was the involvement of a female, whereas in the case of Enki, it was the woman's ambition and not her attractiveness that caused the folly.

Inana, "lady of the heavens" and the goddess of love and

fertility, was the one that wrenched the Meh from Enki's grasp. Inana was the patroness of the city of Uruk, and was determined to make Uruk the most important religious and cultural center in Sumaria. To make this happen she needed to get the Meh away from Enki. Inana sailed in her "heavenly boat", along with her trusty companion Ninshubur, toward Abzu, the watery shrine of Enki. The great god welcomed her warmly and respectfully upon her arrival. His welcome was so magnanimous in fact, that he ordered a huge feast to be laid out in celebration of Inana's visit. Inana and her entourage partook of scrumptious cakes and fruits, and the date wine flowed like water. In his excitement, Enki, the host, imbibed far more than his guests. He washed down his cakes with glass after glass of wine, until his functioning and thinking were compromised and blurry. In such a state of intoxication, Enki became extremely generous, and began to gift his guest, Inana, with Meh. Inana amassed quite a lot of Meh by the time the party wound down.

Of course, Inana accepted the gift with great pleasure, and hurried to load them onto her boat. She and her helpers set sail immediately with the Meh onboard, before Enki could recover from his drunken state and realize his folly. When Enki did awaken from his drink-induced stupor he noticed at once that the Meh was missing, and was shocked when his advisors and servants explained that he himself had given it away go Inana! He swore that he would get the Meh back, and appointed Isimud, along with some sea monsters, to hurry after Inana, assuming she would have to stop at certain ports on her way back to Uruk. He ordered Isimud and the monsters to seize Inana's vessel along with the Meh, but to leave the goddess herself unharmed.

It was Inana's good fortune that she had included her wise and loyal servant Ninshubur among her companions. It was Ninshubur who succeeded in outsmarting the monsters and keeping them from overtaking the boat. Inana and her group arrived safely on the shore of Uruk with the Meh still in their possession. The people and gods of Uruk celebrated – and now that the Meh was within its walls, Uruk's standing in Sumaria rose appropriately to that of most revered and important city.

Enki's problems did not end here. Yet again, his gluttonous appetites caused him grief. This time the great goddess Ninhursag, goddess of the earth, was involved. This legend took place in Dilmun (near the Persian Gulf). Dilmun was in those days a glorious city. Its populace enjoyed excellent health, and never suffered from ailments of old age. The only problem that had ever concerned the inhabitants of Dilmun was the lack of water in the region. However the good-hearted Enki solved this dilemma when he ordered Utu (god of the sun), to bring forth water from the depths of the earth, and to supply it to Dilmun in abundance. Thus Dilmun enjoyed plenty of flourishing and luxurious plant life. In fact, the gardens of Dilmun were particularly lush and beautiful. Ninhursag grew eight special plants which were connected to the birth of several generations of goddesses, all of whom were descended from Enki. Enki was so impressed when he laid eyes on these beautiful plants that he ordered his servant Isimud to cut them down so that he might consume them. When Ninhursag heard that Enki had eaten the plants she was incensed and angered. In her rage, she cursed Enki to death, and she abandoned the house of the gods.

The terrible curse caused Enki to become ill in eight of his body's organs. The disease was indeed terrible, and Enki soon felt his life ebbing away. The gods even began to prepare for his funeral. They wanted him to recover, but they were helpless in the face of Ninhursag's curse. Unless she returned to the council of the gods, there could be hope for Enki.

A wise fox came to the aid of Enki, and mysteriously succeeded in convincing Ninhursag to return to the house of the gods. When she arrived, she created eight special heavenly beings, one to cure each of Enki's ailing organs. Thus he was saved the brink of death, and returned to health.

During the ceremonies of purification, Enki's priests would dress up as fish, to symbolize the purifying power of Enki.

The great shrine of Enki was in Abzu, and this became the word for "sweet water from within the earth".

Ninurta

The Sumarian god of War, Ninurta was the son of Mah, or Mahmi, the goddess who changed form at will, and of Enlil, the ruler of all the gods. He was depicted as large, strong, young, and brave. In addition to being the god or war, Ninurta was also responsible for the spring rainfall and for the lightning. Thus he is associated with the Zu, the thunderbird with the head of lion.

Ninurta was the hero of the conflicts between the cosmic order and chaos, of organization against anarchy and brutality, and of culture against savagery. He was an artist and craftsman who created metal and the tools which enabled human economy and culture to expand.

Ninurta's claim to fame as a warrior began after the winged demon Anzu's theft from Enlil. Anzu robbed the god of air of the wind, and of his most powerful tool in the rule of the world – the Meh. The gods met in council to discuss the crime, and to decide who should be sent into war against the powerful and terrible force of Anzu. As they deliberated, Mah approached and suggested that her young and handsome son Ninurta be the one to undertake the mission. It was decided that Ninurta would hide his young and strong figure under a disguise and would set out under cover of mist. That way, he could surprise his adversary and shoot him with his bow and arrow without exposing himself to possible injury.

Seven evil winds accompanied Ninurta up the mountain where Anzu resided. Shrouded in mist like the surface of the sea, he appeared before Anzu, while the demon was celebrating his acquisition of the holy tablets of the law. Anzu demanded that the Ninurta identify himself, by name and by kind, but Ninurta only gave the names of those who had sent him – the gods. Anzu ground his teeth in frustration. A deep darkness descended on the mountain and Ninurta shot his arrows at Anzu. The arrows did not find their mark, however, because Anzu quickly shot off magic words which caused the arrows to turn veer from their course fly back to the bow that shot them. Ninurta was upset by his unsuccessful attempt, and sent a messenger to Enlil with the report of what had transpired. Enlil advised Ninurta to send the seven evil winds to trap Anzu in a mighty storm. In such a situation Anzu would be unable to speak, and thus unable to deflect the arrows of Ninurta. Frightened and trembling, Ninurta gathered his courage and made his way back to the mountain. He did as Enlil had directed, and succeeded in clipping the demons wings and cutting his throat. The tablets of the Meh were returned to Enlil, and world order restored.

Meh

The Meh were the tablets of fate, and they held a vital place of importance in the Sumarian mythology as the system of universal laws according to which everything functioned. Everything and everyone was bound by the laws of the Meh, including all of the elements of nature, man, the gods, even the underworld of the dead. Enlil, lord of the air, was the supreme god in the Samarian pantheon, during the time that Nippur was the center of religion and culture of southern Mesopotamia. He is believed to have established the Meh. According to Sumerian myth, the Meh included more than one hundred laws. The laws governed every aspect of life from war and peace to the occupations and arts, and from the worship of gods to love, truth, and lies. The Meh guided the gods in their activities and informed them of their rights and responsibilities, and their privileges and limitations. Even Enlil, lord of the gods, was bound by the rule of the Meh and forced to function within its parameters. Desecration or disregard of the law of the Meh brought him ruin and fall from worship.

The immense importance of the Meh teaches us about the character of the Sumarian people. The rights and obligations of every human were spelled out clearly in the Meh, and living according to this law and order was vital. The Sumarians were first civilization to invent a system of law, and they preserved the laws on clay tablets in order that any misunderstanding of their letter be avoided.

Nammu

The ancient Sumarian water goddess, Nammu possessed a great strength and force. She encircled the entire universe, anchoring it in place. She was called the mother of both heaven and earth. Nammu was the first goddess, and from her came all that existed. She gave birth to Ki, goddess of the earth, and An, god of the sky. From their mating the rest of the gods emerged.

Nanna/Sin/Suen

The Sumarians greatly admired the god of the moon, as did the Babylonians, the Acadians, and the Assyrians. His Acadian name was Sin.

As the god of the moon, Nanna was the patron of the famous city of Ur. He was the eldest son of Enlil, god of air. Nanna's means of transport was a wondrous boat. He was the greatest of the heavenly bodies which made up the triumvirate which included his two offspring – Utu and Inana, as well as himself. He was depicted as a bearded figure sitting on a throne of royalty. In his hands he held an axe, a scepter, and a staff.

Nanna was born after Enlil raped Ninlil. This act was a desecration of one of the laws of the Meh, and caused the gods to banish Enlil to the underworld. His behavior toward her notwithstanding, Ninlil followed Enlil to the iand of the dead, and gave birth to his child there, in his presence. According to one of the myths Enlil escaped with Nanna's help, and turned into the light of the night sky. After this, Nanna was known as the god of the moon.

Other gods valued Nanna's cleverness and wisdom, and often visited him to receive guidance and counsel.

Nanna, or Sin, was also called "lord of the calendar". He was believed to have knowledge of events that were to occur, even those in the distant future, but he never revealed his plans to another god or man. Lunar eclipse was perceived as the gravest of signs. That Nanna should choose to hide his face was thought to herald a tragedy. Sin was sometimes called god of the morning flocks, and was associated with fertility, as were the moon gods in other mythological traditions. The moon was connected to the cycles of nature, and its fullness or waning tied to lack or plenty, to the birth of animals, and the natural feminine cycle.

According to legend, Sin fell in love with Ningal, the immortal mother of Inana, but Ningal rejected him. She would agree to live with him only after the banks of the rivers overflowed, wheat grew in the fields, the ponds were filed with fish, the forests teamed with wildlife, the dessert bloomed, and honey and wine flowed from the gardens. Only after all of this abundance was in evidence did Ningal agree to follow Sin to his home on the step pyramid of Ur.

Ninhursag/Ninhursaga/Aruru

Ninhursag was the "Mother Earth" of Sumarian mythology, and the source of all life both animal and vegetable. The name Ninhursag meant "the mother". Her Acadian name was Aruru, and she was also called Nintu. Together with An, Enlil, and Enki, Ninhursag was one of the first Sumarian deities. Enlil was thought to be her mate, but Enki was also her lover. She was responsible for the wildlife, especially the creatures of the mountains, and for the natural cycles of nature. She also had a hand in the establishment of the kingdom. Ninhursag was depicted in Sumarian artwork with a shining countenance, and she was presented in a front view, as opposed to most of the other gods, who were shown in profile. Her hair was long and looked somewhat like oats. Her head was adorned with a crown of leaves, and she carried a branch laden with leaves as a symbol of growth, fertility and vitality.

When Enki, the water god, ate Ninhursag's eight daughter goddesses (whom she planted and tended to in a garden), Ninhursag behaved as Demeter. (Demeter too, was usually a very kind and good-hearted goddess, until her child was threatened.) Ninhursag reacted violently to the destruction of her daughters. She punished Enki by afflicting him with a horrible disease that affected eight of his bodily organs. (Demeter too, had used disease as punishment) Ninhursag then left the house of the gods in anger. (Demeter too, had abandoned the home of the gods.) Unlike Demeter, however, Ninhursag was eventually convinced by a small but wise fox to give up her vendetta and return to the council of the gods.

She was merciful by nature, and agreed to forgive Enki. She created eight new godlike creatures that infiltrated the eight sick organs of his body, and healed them.

Ershkigal

Goddess of darkness, gloom, and death, Ershkigal was the sister of Inana (Ishtar). Her kingdom was the underworld. Ershkigal was a jealous goddess and guarded her territory with tenacity. When Inana came down to the land of the dead with the intention of taking it over from her sister, Ershkigal parted her from the royal robes and jewels she had come wearing, and forced her to appear before the throne stark naked before striking her dead. Ershkigal was the daughter of Anu, and she built herself her own kingdom in the underworld. The gods could enter her kingdom only with nothing hiding their nakedness. It was dangerous, and they could end up her prisoner. Ershkigal was thus usually excluded from the feasts that the council of god held, and she would be forced to send messengers to fetch her portion of the food and drink served at the events. At one of these feasts, when Nergal refused to sit next to the messenger of Ershkigal, she demanded that Nergal come to the underworld to tender an apology. In the end, Nergal not only apologized, but remained at Ershkigal's side and became her husband and co-ruler of the land of the dead.

Kur-Nu-Gi-A

Kur-Nu-Gi-A, the Sumarian and Acadian land of the dead, was the gaping void under the earth, the counterpart to the sky which was spread out above the earth. Kur-Nu-Gi-A was the place to which souls descended after physical death of their bodies. Major cities may have been thought to have had direct entrances to the underworld. As was true of the Greek land of the dead, a river had to be traversed in order to reach it.

The cold and misty underworld was ruled by Nergal and Ershkigal from a locked castle with seven gates. Their kingdom was also inhabited by other gods who served under them. Ninmul, Endokuga, and Nindukuka were offspring of Nergal who resided in the underworld. Mametum, a goddess responsible for fate, lived alongside Namtar, the god of ill-fate who carried out Ershkigal's demon tasks. The books of the dead were inscribed by Belit-Sheri, the official scribe of the underworld. Neti, keeper of the flame, kept guard over the gates. Seven gods who had "died" (the seven Anunki), served as judges. The underworld also employed groups of demons called Gala, whose job was similar to that of police officers. All of the gods of the underworld, except the Gala, needed the same types of living conditions as humans - food, water, clothing, shelter, and the like.

The underworld functioned according to a clear hierarchy. The souls of the gods and their highest ranked servants held the "best" positions. When a deceased soul arrived in the land of the dead, he or she was required to make sacrifices to those that had come before. It was the hero - god Gilgamesh who decided upon the rules of behavior to be followed in the underworld.

During the daylight hours the Sumarian underworld was shrouded in darkness. But as the sun set, it arrived, as in Egyptian mythology, in the land of the dead, under the earth's surface, passing through it on its way to another sunrise on earth. The moon too, during the time of the month that it was not seen by people on earth, was thought to have gone down to the underworld.

Utu, god of the sun, (the Acadian Shamash) was the main judge of the souls who arrived in the underworld. When a soul was found worthy, it could expect a pleasant existence in the land of the dead, forever.

Gilgamesh and Enkidu

"Two-thirds god and one-third man – thus the gods fashioned Gilgamesh. They gave him perfection: a lithe body, a brave heart, and the look of a wild bull that stood above his fellows and stalked threateningly about. He was unrivaled in battle, and was as the drum that called warriors to fight."

Such was Gilgamesh described in the Epic of Gilgamesh, King of Uruk. He was also called the "savage who rose from the depths of the wilderness".

Gilgamesh's mother was Ninsun, a low ranking goddess in the hierarchy of the Sumarian pantheon known for her outstanding wisdom. His father was Lugalbanda, the third king of the first dynasty of Uruk after the flood. Lugalbanda was half-god, half-human, a heroic warrior and a shepherd. Lugalbanda was apparently also Utnapishtim, the half-deity that Gilgamesh went in search of on his quest for immortality.

At the beginning of the epic which tells of his adventures, Gilgamesh is described as having a fiery, passionate character. His notable lustfulness was directed at Marusa, a warrior's daughter. Gilgamesh's rambunctious and conflict-arousing activities caused the nobles of Uruk to cry out to Anu, god of the heavens, for assistance in dealing with him. Anu heard their pleas, and called in turn for the help of the goddess of the earth, Aruru (the Sumarian goddess Ninhursag). He told her: "you made this man, now create his double!" Give the new one a stormy nature, just as the other has, and they shall fight between themselves and leave Uruk in peace!"

Aruru took a lump of clay, kneaded it in her hands and formed it into the giant Enkidu. Enkidu's entire body was covered with long hair, and he lived the innocent life of an animal. He grazed in the grass with the deer and drank from streams with the wild beasts, until one day he was spotted by a hunter who was taken aback by his strength and size. Terrified, the hunter hid inside his house with his dogs. Out of fear of Enkidu, and also because Enkidu would sometimes free animals from the traps he had set, the hunter sought council with his father as to what to do about the problem. The father suggested that he approach the powerful Gilgamesh, and ask him to send a concubine to arouse Enkidu's desire, thus distracting him from the plight of the animals. And so it was done.

Gilgamesh agreed that the hunter's father had a good plan. He provided the woman, and all believed that after Enkidu had sexual relations with her the wild animals would abandon him.

When Enkidu saw the woman, he did desire her, and indeed they had sexual intercourse. As planned, the animals did begin keep their distance from him. Enkidu immediately understood the significance of this, and asked the woman for her thoughts. She complimented him on his wisdom and strength, and told him about the hero Gilgamesh who lived in the shrine of Ishtar in Uruk. Enkidu decided to find Gilgamesh and engage him in battle.

A short time before these events, Gilgamesh had a dream. The dream was about "something" strong and mighty. All the inhabitants of the city had assembled to see this thing and gape at it. All of his friends kissed its feet, and he, Gilgamesh, was drawn to it as to a woman. Gilgamesh told his mother about the dream, adding that in the dream his mother had caused him to compete and fight against this "thing".

Gilgamesh's wise mother interpreted the dream. She told him that this "thing" was actually a man, a faithful friend who would never betray him – a strong and honorable man – and that she indeed would cause him to fight with Gilgamesh.

On their journey to Uruk to find Gilgamesh, the concubine taught Enkidu the ways of humans. She explained that he must dress in clothing, eat as a man, and wash, among other things. They came to a gathering of shepherds who wondered over the beast-man. A particular man with a gloomy countenance approached Enkidu and the harlot who accompanied him. The harlot asked why he had such a dark expression, and the man told of a recent event that had taken place in Uruk. Gilgamesh had burst into a wedding party, and announced a new law according to which Gilgamesh would have intercourse with every bride before her groom could touch her. All engaged women were fair game to him. When Enkidu heard this, he was filled with rage, and announced that he would soon show this Gilgamesh the range and strength of his might. As he strode purposely toward the shrine in Uruk, he saw that crowds had gathered in the market square, staring at him in shocked surprise - at this newcomer who so resembled Gilgamesh.

After nightfall, as Gilgamesh made his way to the home of a bride, Enkidu waited at the door. When Gilgamesh arrived, Enkidu jumped out at him, only to be felled immediately by Gilgamesh's quick leg-movement. They began to fight one another like lions. Gilgamesh managed to lay Enkidu out, and as Enkidu was prone on the ground, Gilgamesh recited a blessing him. He then helped him up, and the two formed an alliance. Enkidu explained to Gilgamesh that the power of a partial god was not something to be taken lightly, and that Gilgamesh needed to use his strength and gifts with responsibility and righteousness.

Gilgamesh took his brother's admonitions to heart, and decided to go out to the cedar forest to seek out the monster Huvava (Humbaba was his Acadian name). He saw getting rid of Huvava as a contribution to the routing out of evil from the world. In addition, he hoped to revive his reputation among the gods. Enkidu tried to dissuade Gilgamesh from undertaking such a dangerous mission, but was unsuccessful. Enkidu then insisted that at least Gilgamesh must visit the god Shamash, under whose jurisdiction the treacherous cedar forest fell. Gilgamesh agreed, and went to Shamash to request assistance and guidance.

Shamash gave Gilgamesh his blessing and reinforced him with an army of giants. He also ordered the four winds to follow Gilgamesh into battle with gale force storms. Gilgamesh was overjoyed with the help afforded him by Shamash, and when he returned to Enkidu, they ordered the artisans to begin fashioning weapons for their battle. They made him huge axes and gigantic swords. Gilgamesh's sword was especially sharp and powerful. It was named "bow of Anshan" after the city of Anshan, known for its mighty trees.

Like Enkidu, the elders of Uruk tried to stop Gilgamesh from what seemed a foolhardy action, but Gilgamesh appeared before them and before his mother, Ninsun, and asked for their support and help. Ninsun prayed for him to the god Shamash, and told Enkidu that although he was not her son, she adopted him in her heart, as she would an abandoned child found at the temple. She asked that he watch over his brother Gilgamesh, and return with him whole and unharmed.

Enkidu knew the area well and in fact had already come into contact with the monster face to face. The brothers walked a long way, and during the nights they both had prophetic dreams which hinted at what was to come. When they came to the bottom of the mountain, Gilgamesh drew his axe, and cut down a cedar tree. Hearing the sound of the falling cedar from far off in the distance, Huvava was furious, and he shouted, "Who dares desecrate my forest and cut down my tree?" This was immediately followed by the voice of Shamash which rang down from the sky, urging the brothers to continue their quest.

Suddenly Gilgamesh was overtaken by a heavy sleep and a feeling of weakness. Enkidu had a hard time rousing him, but he finally awakened. Gilgamesh put on his protective vest, and swore to go up against the monster. However, now Enkidu's motivation flagged, and Gilgamesh had to encourage him to keep up the will to fight. Gilgamesh instructed Enkidu to block the monster's path while he, Gilgamesh, would engage him in a sword battle.

Huvava came out of his cedar-wood house, swaggering and threatening. Gilgamesh began to entreat Shamash to come to his aid, and Shamash did not disappoint him. He sent storms from out of the four winds, and eight gales which flew into the eyes of Huvava and rendered him blind and immobile.

The battle begin with the cutting down of cedars, so Gilgamesh asked the giant Kardumi to assist him. Seven times he uprooted cedars and piled them at the foot of the mountain. Still Huvava restrained himself from reacting. When the fourth cedar was axed, Gilgamesh and his army marched to the monster's lair.

Huvava stood before them confused and teary-eyed and approached them like a prisoner. He promised Gilgamesh that he would be his servant, that he would build him a palace of cedar in his forest. Gilgamesh hesitated, unsure whether to release Huvava on this declaration. He consulted Enkidu as to how to proceed.

Enkidu assured Gilgamesh that if he did not cut off the monster's head he would never again return to his mother's arms. Huvava tried to pit brother against brother by insulting Enkidu. Huvava accused Enkidu of harboring jealousy toward Gilgamesh who gave all of the orders. In the end, however, Gilgamesh heeded Enkidu's warnings and let the monster have it with a blow to the back of his neck. Enkidu then moved in and delivered an additional hit. The third blow beheaded Huvava, and he fell. The brothers then uprooted all of the trees in the forest, all the way to the banks of the Euphrates.

Gilgamesh and Enkidu delivered the corpse of Huvava to the gods. They approached Enlil, bowed down before him, and presented the monster. Enlil did not react positively. He threatened the two with his never-ending wrath and punishment. Gilgamesh and Enkidu were cheered by the other gods, however, and they were hailed as heroes in Uruk.

The theme of this myth is the subduing of a creature of the forest, a wild being. In modern times, with our emphasis on the "return to nature", this seems a bit backward. Enkidu was blessed with the ability to come near the creatures of the wood with no fear, and to free them from the traps of those who would hunt and kill them. He lived with the creatures of the wild in perfect innocent harmony and when the time came he had to be taught the ways of human society. The cutting down of the great cedar forest in which Huvava resided was seen as an act of heroism. It seems that this tendency to want to subdue and overcome the powers of nature began during ancient times.

Another famous myth tells the story of Ishtar's love for

Gilgamesh. There was no deep affection here, but rather a desire to mate with a great hero in order to receive his sperm. Gilgamesh understood the motivations of Ishtar, and had heard about the bad luck of her previous lovers (notably Tamuz). He did not just refuse her advances, but even blasted her with verbal insults right to her face. This caused Ishtar to react with fury and to seek revenge, and by demanding and threatening she succeeded in convincing the father of the gods, Anu, that he should allow her to use the Bull of Heaven to destroy Gilgamesh.

The Bull of Heaven caused horrible disasters to befall the city of Uruk. His snoring brought about earthquakes, one of which almost swallowed up the hero Enkidu! He rallied however, and charged at the bull, grabbing his horns as he called out for Gilgamesh to come quickly and draw his sword. Gilgamesh stabbed and killed the bull, dissected him, tore out his heart, and placed it on the ground at the feet of Shamash. Ishtar climbed up to a platform between the highest towers of the city and from there called down a curse on Gilgamesh. "Beware, Gilgamesh! You have humiliated me by killing the Bull of Heaven!" Enkidu then slashed the bull's genitals from its body and threw them up into Ishtar's face, threatening that if he could catch her he would tie her up with the bull's intestines.

A huge and lavish celebration was held in honor of the heroes. Gilgamesh hung the bull's horns on the wall of his room. That night, Enkidu had a dream: The gods had come together for a meeting, during which they decided that Gilgamesh and Enkidu must be put to death as punishment for the desecration of the cedar forest and for the killing of Huvava and the Bull of Heaven. Enlil intervened however, and decreed that Enkidu would die, but Gilgamesh would be spared. Shamash cried out that the two had done their deeds with his blessing, which angered Enlil greatly.

Immediately after this dream Enkidu became ill, and as he lay alone in his bed his brother Gilgamesh received praise and was honored wherever he went. Enkidu knew that very soon he would descend to the underworld - alone. So intense was Enkidu's suffering that in his heart he cursed Gilgamesh. When the dawn broke and the first rays of light were seen, he feebly approached Shamash and asked him to curse all involved in his being tempted by a woman, and his subsequent meeting of Gilgamesh.

Shamash, sitting on high, heard Enkidu's request, and asked him why he would curse the woman that fed, clothed, and cared for him. And why would he curse his friend who had so much affection for him? Enkidu heard Shamash's words and was comforted by them slightly. After a ten day illness, he died.

Gilgamesh mourned the loss of his friend. He cried at the side of Enkidu's body for a week, until worms invaded the corpse and it was necessary to bury it. After the funeral, Gilgamesh ordered craftsmen, metal workers, and stone-cutters to fashion a statue. The statue was set up across from a table on which rested a small shrine to Shamash, Enkidu's god, and some honey and butter.

Gilgamesh wandered in the mountains and continued to weep for his deceased friend. The death of Enkidu had given Gilgamesh a new respect for the power of death. He began a new mythological quest – the search for the secret to immortality.

Still in shock over his loss, Gilgamesh decided to seek out his father, who was immortal, and to ask him about the matter of immortality versus mortality. On his way to the garden of the gods, he passed through an area completely devoid of light. When he reached the gods, he saw beautiful trees with precious stones sparkling among their branches. As he walked along a beach, wrapped in the skin of a lion he had hunted soon after Enkidu's death, he suddenly met Shamash. The god irately told Gilgamesh to stop strutting around like an animal and to stop his foolish and impossible quest for immortality.

Gilgamesh would not accept that he must someday come to the same mortal end as had his friend. He met Siduri, the barmaid to the gods and confided in her his great fear of death. Siduri led Gilgamesh to Utnapishtim, the only man to whom the gods had given eternal life. On the way to Utnapishtim Gilgamesh had to cross a terrible sea of death, but he managed to do so unscathed. He told Utnapishtim about his desire for everlasting life and his horror at the idea of mortal death, and he asked him the secret to immortality. In answer, Utnapishtim related to Gilgamesh the story of the great flood, which only Utnapishtim had survived. When he finished his retelling, he told Gilgamesh that he would attempt to convene the gods' council and would request that they give Gilgamesh immortality according to his wishes, on condition that Gilgamesh would remain with him for six days and nights. Before long, Gilgamesh dropped off to sleep, and remained sleeping for seven days. Each day that he slumbered, Utnapishtim's wife carved a mark on the wall and baked a loaf of bread.

When he awoke, Gilgamesh told Utnapishtim – "I slept for only a moment before you shook me awake!" Utnapishtim told him to count the loaves of bread and then he would know how long his nap had been. Gilgamesh apologized, and Utnapishtim instructed him to return by the same path he had taken when he arrived. When Utnapishtim's wife heard this, she reminded her husband of the many difficulties Gilgamesh had faced on his journey and suggested he supply the younger man with assistance.

Utnapishtim then told Gilgamesh about a wondrous prickly plant which had the ability to supply man with eternal youth. He suggested that Gilgamesh harvest some of this plant, which grew in the depths of the sea. Gilgamesh found a way to get some of the secret plant, and armed with this treasure, he made his way back to Uruk.

On his journey, Gilgamesh stopped at a well to bathe, and a snake that resided in the well recognized the scent of the plant. He grabbed the precious plant from Gilgamesh and escaped with it. After this, Gilgamesh despaired of ever changing his fate and achieving the immortality he so desperately sought. Sure enough, like every man, he eventually met his death. Only his memory was immortal, and the people of Uruk did remember his with honor and affection.

Gilgamesh, the great Sumarian-Acadian hero, in spite of being two-thirds god, was in the end just a man, and even had characteristics not usually found in mythical heroes. In the end he seemed more man than god. He was sensitive, and far from innocent of transgression. Gilgamesh was a braggart, but also moved easily to tears. He was not ashamed to admit having a very human fear of death. He did not fight his battles alone, but with the brave Enkidu by his side. The assistance of the god Shamash also played a significant part in his victories. All of this taken together, especially his intense but unsatisfied desire for everlasting life, makes him rather a unique and special hero. He was far from perfect, but even so, he was a hero to be remembered forever.

Huvava

Huvava (Humbaba was his Acadian name) was the monster that Gilgamesh went in search of in order to destroy. Huvava lived in the great cedar forest in the mountains of Amna (today's northern Syria). Huvava controlled all of the animal life and was able to hear every sound in the forest, even from great distances. He had a mighty roar, and he spit flames from his mouth. Enkidu, in the Epic of Gilgamesh King of Uruk, describes Huvava has having teeth like frightful fangs and the gaze of a lion. He could crush a tree just by looking at it.

Even with all his supposed fearsome power, Huvava was beaten by Enkidu and Gilgamesh without much of a real fight. The god Shamash helped the two by sending gale force winds, and they uprooted tree after tree until Huvava was desperately upset. When they tore out the seventh tree, he surrendered. He declared to Gilgamesh, "I will never know my mother, and I did not have a father, I was created from and nurtured by the mountain. Enlil made me guardian of the forest. If you let me go free I will serve you faithfully and you will be my lord. All of these trees which I have cared for will be yours. I will build you a castle of cedar and stone.

Huvava's pleas were to no avail, however, and Gilgamesh beheaded him. It is interesting to note that the name Huvava resembles the Aramaic word for "snake".

Tamuz/Dumuzi

Tamuz was the Mesopotamian god of growth and fertility. The name Tamuz appears in the Bible in the book of Ezekiel, where the ceremony is described that was commonly held in honor of the god. "The women sit weeping for Tamuz". Tamuz, also called Dumuzi, was a shepherd, and the lover of Ishtar/Inana, whom she preferred over her other lover, the wild Enkimdo. The myth of the coupling of Dumuzi and Inana was a typical fertility myth. Dumuzi's marriage to Inana was to afford him immortal life, and as such was doubly appealing. However, Inana was an ambitious goddess. She was not satisfied with being "merely" the goddess of the heavens. She wanted to rule the underworld as well.

When Ershkigal, the goddess of the land of the dead, heard about Inana's ambition, she hurried to cause her death. Inana would surely have remained dead forever, if Enki had not rushed to her aid. He sprinkled her corpse with the "water of life" and fed her the "food of life", and she revived. There was still a problem, however, in that according to the Meh (holy laws) of the underworld, any man or god who had passed through the gates of the underworld was doomed to remain there, unless an alternate soul was provided in place of the one that returned to the land of the living. Inana knew that she would have to return to the underworld if she could not find someone to take her place. Inana and her accompanying demons wandered from city to city, searching for such a replacement, whom of course, they would kidnap.

In the first two cities they passed through the gods of the cities greeted them wearing sacks, and frightened, they bowed down before Inana. She did not kidnap them, however. She kept going toward Uruk, her own city, and the seat of Dumuzi's kingdom. Dumuzi was now both king and god (due to the marriage) and sat on the throne feeling happy and good-hearted. He had been more than pleased when the news had come of the untimely death of his aggressive and controlling wife.

Inana was incensed at his disloyalty. She ordered Gala to kidnap him immediately. Dumuzi begged him not to, and appealed to Utu, the sun god who was Inana's brother (and therefore Dumuzi's brother in law), to come to his aid. Utu answered his request by turning him into a snake. This was not help enough, however, since Gala succeeded in capturing the snake, and torturing it to death. The dead snake was then taken down to the underworld.

Dumuzi would have had to remain in the land of the dead forever, as the replacement soul for Inana, but his loving sister, the goddess Geshtin-Ana, agreed to take his place each year for six months. This myth bears similarities to others, such as that of Atus and Adonis, in which the fertility god lives part of the year in the underworld – the part of the year which corresponds with the season of lack of green and growth upon the earth.

The main characteristic of the cult of Tamuz was that women mourned his death each year. Certain chapters from the Acadian epic, describe Ishtar herself wailing the loss of her husband. The wedding of Tamuz was celebrated yearly by his worshippers, and he was hailed as the god of lush growth of wildlife and vegetation. His yearly descent to the underworld heralded the yearly dry season, and his return marked the season of plenty. His cult ran in parallel to the agricultural calendar, and was very popular in Mesopotamia – even getting as far as to the land of Israel, carrying so much momentum that Ezekiel mentioned the Tamuz elegy reaching the gates of the Temple.

Marduk

One of the greatest of the Babylonian gods, Marduk was the son of Ea, the Acadian god of wisdom, and his mother was Damkina. Marduk's wife was Zerbanitu, and his son was Nabu. He was the god of the scribes and authors, and responsible for setting important ideas into stone. Ea was the offspring of two deities from the earliest stage of creation; Apsu – the fresh water, and Tihamat – the salt water. Along with him, other great and important gods were created, but Ea was the most powerful of them all, and it was he who became the father of Marduk. Ea wanted to rule all of creation, and to win this position he had to fight against Apsu. After his victory, the young gods (offspring of Apsu and Tihamat) had to endure the revenge of Tihamat. She used an army of demons driven by her son Kingu. The young gods sought advice – who should stand at the head of the forces which would fight the demons of Tihamat?

The chosen god was Marduk. He agreed to go to war against Tihamat and her monsters if in return for victory he would receive the title of god of gods. As the brave Marduk went out to battle against Tihamat, he sent an "evil wind" in her direction. Tihamat opened her mouth to swallow the wind, and it poisoned her body, causing her abdomen to swell frightfully. Marduk then shot a fatal arrow into Tihamat's heart. Marduk stood on her lifeless body and all who saw him ran out of fear for their own lives. He trampled his enemies under his feet, and slashed Tihamat's body into two pieces. With one half of the corpse he built a temple to Ashera, which reached into what became the sky. There lived Anu, Enlil, and Ea. From the second half he created the earth, the mountains, and the hills.

After this great victory, the Tablets of Fate (counterparts to the

Sumerian Meh) were rested from the hands of Kingu. Whoever held possession of these tablets was the undisputed leader and ruler of the universe. Marduk seized the tablets and killed Kingu. He mixed the blood of Kingu with earth, and created the human race in order that the gods would have worshippers and servants. All of the gods recognized the superiority of Marduk, both because of his victory over Tihamat, and because he now had the tablets of law. A great temple was built in his honor in the Acadian capital city.

Marduk stood at the head of the "new generation" of gods which stood for development and civilization, in contrast to the former gods, Tihamat and Apsu, who symbolized the great void and the vast and terrible powers of nature. Marduk took over the organization and arrangement of all creation.

When Era, the god of death, succeeded in tricking Marduk into getting off his throne, the world was turned "upside down". The sun's light turned to dark, and the paths and byways were

filled with danger. Human beings even began to behave cannibalistically. Order was returned to the world only when Marduk sat once again on the throne.

When the Acadians conquered Sumaria in 1900 B.C., Marduk became the most important god of Mesopotamia. A huge step pyramid was built in his honor, and it is possible that this structure was the one in the myth of the Tower of Babel which appears in Hebrew sources.

Nergal

The Babylonians greatly respected Nergal, the son of Enlil, the god of the skies. Enlil gave Nergal responsibility for the fate of human beings. He was a strong, impatient, blustering god, and was sometimes compared to a wild bull, or to a raging storm or flood. Wars and epidemics were among his favorite things. His was the kingdom of death, and as such he looked for death, and tried to make it come about. Nergal wore a crown on his head and fourteen terrifying creatures were his faithful servants.

According to one of the myths, Nergal became the husband of Ershkigal, the goddess of death, making him the lord of death, in the following manner: He refused to take part in a feast held by the gods, in order to demonstrate his dissatisfaction with the fact that Ershkigal had been invited. Ershkigal, of course, was angered and insulted by this, and insisted that Nergal come down to the underworld to apologize to her. According to one version, the gods decided that Nergal had to be replaced, and in order to get rid of him, Ea sent fourteen demons to accompany him to the underworld. Nergal passed through the seven gates of the land of the dead, and reached Ershkigal. He was charming and friendly to her, and Ershkigal fell in love with him. Then, however, leaving no warning, Nergal simply turned around and left the underworld, returning to his home.

Ershkigal's anger now knew no bounds. She wanted revenge! She demanded that the gods send Nergal back down to the underworld, and this time, she would never let him return. She threatened the gods, that if they did not return Nergal to her, she would bring about a horrible holocaust on earth. The gods saw no choice, and they sent Nergal back down to Ershkigal's domain. This time, though, the god appeared in his hard and angry form, thinking that if he had to stay underworld, he would at least be its ruler. He threatened Ershkigal with death, but she begged for mercy, and promised him that she would become his wife and that the pair would rule side by side. She also promised him the Tablets of Wisdom (the Meh).

According to a very influential Sumarian myth, Ershkigal was also the goddess of fertility and growth. This myth holds that when Nergal returned to the council of the gods, Ershkigal threatened to stop all growth on the face of the earth, causing all creatures to die of hunger. In the face of this threat the gods had no choice but to send Nergal back to her.

Nergal later appeared with the name Era, and seemed to be satisfied and happy in his marriage. He was described as tired and lacking enough sleep because of his riotous behavior in bed. He was indecisive and forgetful, and the world, in the absence of his intervention, experienced peace and tranquility. Soon, however, the world began to experience horrible droughts and epidemics. The land was not able to supply enough sustenance go support life, and everything suffered from exaggeration and lack of moderation.

Meanwhile, in the underworld, the Sibiti were the gods of the dead and the faithful servants of Era. During the days of quiet on earth, the Sibiti were bored from lack of activity. Spiders' webs were spun on their weapons which rusted from disuse. This lack of reason to fight depressed the Sibiti, and they appeared before the bed of Erra and awakened him. When Erra woke up he let out a shout which caused fear in the hearts of all gods and men. The mountains trembled, the forests shook, and the sea roared with tremendous waves. Erra conceived a broad plan for destruction and ruin. He wanted to remedy the situation where men and beasts multiplied with regularity, and return to former order where gods outnumbered men. He could not put his plan into action, however, without ousting Marduk, the great god, from his throne.

Era went to Marduk, and convinced him that he, Erra, could guard Marduk's kingdom while Marduk went down to the underworld to pick up some artifacts that he had been wanting. Marduk considered – he remembered that the last time he had arisen from his throne all mankind had suffered a horrible flood. He hesitated, and his hesitation gave Ea confidence to try another tact – he swore to Marduk that nothing would change. Everything would remain as it should. He would have Anu and Enlil stand guard at Marduk's shrine, to keep balance and order on earth and in the heavens and to prevent any demons of the underworld from taking control of the earth. Nothing would change, he promised, and all would continue to thrive. Slowly, Marduk began to relax and to believe Erra's words, until in the end he agreed, and left his shrine. He went out to the god's residence, leaving Erra to take care of things in his absence. At first Erra kept his word, and nothing changed and the earth remained tranquil.

Soon, however, Erra's evilness came to the fore. Temples were destroyed, communities turned to wastelands, and everything was in disarray. Sons hated their fathers, and mothers turned against their daughters. The lame ran faster than the healthy, and the handicapped became whole and strong. The young were buried by the old, and men began to consume the flesh of their brothers. All of society's values were turned on their heads, and nobody could escape certain death.

At last Erra got his temple back and all returned to its former order.

El

In the Canaanite pantheon, El was the father of the gods. He was the supreme deity, high above the others, and thus was called "god almighty". He was the father of all the great gods: Baal, Anat, Mot, and their siblings. All of his children respected him greatly, except for the aggressive Anat, who sometimes verbally attacked him with rudeness.

The Canaanites considered El the creator of the universe. The Canaanite faith in a supreme god was similar to the Arab belief in a single god who created everything, since the supreme deity ruled over al other gods and there was none who equaled his rank and power.

El lived in the Northern Mountain. He was called "the elder" or "lord of time", and was thought to be a good hearted and generous god. El knew all and saw all, and was always described and depicted as having horns of a bull – a symbol of strength and power.

According to one of the myths, El mated with two women, both of whom apparently represented goddesses of fertility – Ashera and Anat. With them he produced the Shahar (dawn) and Shalim (dusk), and the rest of the Ugaritic pantheon.

El helped his son Keret, a goodhearted king, to find a second wife, and he blessed his son with many male offspring. Later, El saved Keret from suffering from senility.

Apsu

The Babylonian deity, Apsu had Sumarian – Acadian roots. This deity personifies the ancient bodies of fresh water. According to Sumarian myth, Apsu is a place where Enki's palace of water and wisdom is built.

The Acadian-Canaanite creation myth holds that Apsu mated with Tihamat and produced three of the greatest gods – Anu, Ea (the Sumarian Enki) and Marduk.

Nikkal, Yarikh

Yarikh and Nikkal were the god and goddess of the moon according to Ugaritic (Canaanite) myth.

Kingu

Kingu was the son of Apsu – the deity of fresh water, and Tihamat – goddess of the salt water oceans. In the Babylonian creation myth, the god Ea killed Apsu, in order to gain control of the universe. Later, Marduk replaced Ea, and Tihamat sent Kingu to fight at the head of an army of demons in an effort to oust him.

Kingu was killed by Marduk and his blood mingled with the earth to form the human race.

Ashera/Astarte

Astarte was the Canaanite mythological fertility goddess, and wife of the supreme god, El. She was the mother of the entire Canaanite pantheon. Baal was one of her seven sons. She bore many similarities to Ishtar and to the Mesopotamian Inana. Astarte was sometimes called "queen of the heavens".

As "Ashtoret", Astarte appears often in the Bible where different forms of worship are described. This fact bears witness to the cult having reached even the Hebrews, during the periods of Judges and Kings.

Usually, Astarte was worshipped along with her Canaanite husband. Ashtoret was the goddess of sex, desire, and fertility. Some of her worshippers performed ceremonies consisting of orgies and licentiousness. As Astarte, she also had characteristics of a goddess of war.

The Canaanites considered Ashera their supreme goddess and called her "Ela" and "creator of gods". Her full name was Asherat-yam – she who walks by the sea, or goddess of the sea. Ashera, like the other fertility goddesses, was also the goddess of the concubines and prostitutes. An ancient drawing of a goddess called "prostitute" is apparently a depiction of Ashera. In it she appears as a naked young woman with braided hair, on the back of a lion. In one hand she holds a lily, and in the other a snake.

Trees were planted, usually near the shrine of El, in honor of the goddess Ashera.

The Ashera tree was the symbol of fertility, and under statues of Ashera stood additional statues of the Ashera tree.

Baal

Baal was the most influential god of the Canaanites. He was the son of El and Ashera, and the brother of Anat, Mot, and Zvul-yam (singer of the sea). He was identified with the Babylonian god, Adar.

Baal was the deity of fertility, the heavens, lightening, thunder, and rain. He was called "rider on the clouds", god of fertility, and also, lord of the north. He resided on the "north mountain" (Jabil el akra in our time). Baal had three wives: Padri -daughter of Or, Tali - daughter of Rav, and Artzi, - daughter of Yaavdar. These three symbolized the three powers of Baal himself – light, dew, and earth.

Statues of Baal attest to his being a proud figure wearing a pointed hat, and he was depicted with his right hand held high and his left held in a fist in front of his torso. This position calls forth a feeling of power and force – as if he is calling down the lightening from the heavens. Baal was the god of life, and held the powers of life in his limbs. He personified the opposite of his brother Mot, the god of death.

As the god of rain, who nourished the plants and the crops, he was also responsible for the propagation of humans and cattle. When the wife of Danel, the great judge, could not conceive a child, Danel turned to Baal for help. Baal presented Danel's request before El, father of the gods, asking him to cancel his order of barrenness where Danel's wife was concerned. Thus

Danel's wife bore a son. The name Baal, in Hebrew means "owner" and "lord" as well as having an older connection to the word meaning "carries out action".

Baal's first battle was against the ancient sea monster, Yam, who wanted to take over rule of the earth, and had announced himself as the new king. Yam represented the primordial forces of chaos and the great void, and by killing him Baal demonstrated his unmatched strength and the fact that he was the undisputed ruler of the seas, the skies, and the rain. In honor of Baal's victory over the monster, a huge feast was held – an awesome celebration. Afterwards, the worshippers of the aggressive and warlike Anat attacked the revelers and took part in a terrible massacre of Baal's believers!

In order to pacify Anat, Baal offered her a gift – the secret of the lightening. Baal then built himself a large temple, and as in other myths from the ancient East, he was forced to fight against his brother, Mot, god of the kingdom of the dead. While the temple was under construction, there were already rumblings of a coming conflict between the brothers. Baal was sensitive to Mot's actions and words, and during the building, Baal ordered the architects to build the temple without windows. That way Mot would be unable to penetrate the structure and kill his brother's wives, as Baal feared he would do.

The struggle between the brothers was long and protracted. It sometimes involved direct fighting between the two gods, and other times their proxies battled for them. Sometimes Mot had the upper hand, and then Baal would come back out on top. Baal was actually the instigator of the conflict. He had made a public announcement to the affect that only he, Baal, was lord of all the gods. Baal killed Zvul Yam, with the help of his trusty friend Kothar, god of the arts, who gave him two sticks with which to fight. This victory over the "singer of the sea" gave the sailors the courage to go out again in their boats. Kothar, Baal's talented helper, built him a magnificent castle.

The battle of the brothers was renewed after Baal's servant returned from Mot's palace having delivered a message to him (perhaps concerning Baal's higher status) and presented Baal with a threat from Mot. Mot's ambition was always to cause death, and in accordance with this, he wished to kill Baal, and all who were in his image, and to fill his belly with them. The servant was full of fear when he left Mot's presence and he described what he had experienced so graphically to Baal that the god too was filled with trepidation. The servant related Mot's suggestion that Baal become his slave forever. If he would do so, Mot would take pity on him. Baal's fear of the terrible underworld was so strong that he saw no choice and agreed to this suggestion! He went to Mot and told him that he surrendered to his demands. When Mot heard this he rejoiced in his victory. Baal was disappointed in his hopes of redemption however. Mot told him in a teasing manner that his fate would be life in the underworld – for him and all that was his.

Baal fell in love with a young cow, mated with her, and produced Mesh. Apparently, this mating with the cow was an attempt to free himself from the death sentence put upon him by Mot. The cow symbolized fertility, hope, and power.

In the end, however, Baal's efforts did no good. Mot and his helpers killed Baal and left his body in a field to be found by passing gods who brought the news to El, Baal's father. El grieved as a human would for a loved one. He came down from his throne, dressed himself in sack cloth and covered himself in dust. He scratched at his own flesh, and tore hairs from his head and beard.

Anat, the aggressive and angry goddess, decided to avenge the death of Baal, and went in search of his body in the field. She was able to recover it, and then set out on the trail after Mot. Finding him, she killed him and sent him on his final journey to the underworld.

The battles between Mot and Baal constituted a recurring

theme in the Canaanite mythology. The face-off between life, as personified by Baal, and death and decay as personified by Mot was a constant and never-ending struggle. At times death had the upper hand, and at other times life won out. In the end, on an optimistic mythological note, the forces of life had the final victory over the forces of death.

As in myths from other cultures, a period of drought followed the death of Baal. Similarly, a drought was caused when Osiris died, and when Persephone resided in the underworld.

According to one of the myths, El took it upon himself to make sure there was a balance between the two adversaries. In anther version, each year Baal would agree willingly to die. He would fall from his palace to the earth, and return again to the heavens later carried by a white deer driven by Anat.

Baal had several names, each afforded him in a different place. Some scholars believe he was known as Baal-Zebub, or "lord of the flies", but others thing that this may have actually been Baal-Zvul, an amalgamation of his name and his brother's, and that later Hebrews afforded the interpretation of Zebub, meaning fly in Hebrew.

The cult of Baal spread throughout the land of Canaan and beyond. It was practiced in Egypt, especially Lower Egypt, where Baal was the counterpart to the god Seth, or the war-god Monat, son of Nut. Shrines were built to Baal in Egypt, and his name was given to Egyptian citizens during the period of the twenty second dynasty.

When the Israelites conquered the land of Israel, the worship of Baal made inroads with them as well. We find mention in the bible of the fact that the father of the judge Gideon built a shrine to Baal, and Baal-Brit (another of Baal's names) was worshipped in Shechem.

Mot

The Canaanite god of the land of the dead, Mot was the arch-rival of Baal, who personified life and production. Mot wanted to take over rule of the universe, and to fill it with death and decay. The battles between the two are documented in the Epic of Baal, and in Ugaritic texts Mot is quoted as saying of himself: "my soul's ambition and longing is to kill, to kill...."

Mot was drawn to death and killing as a fish is drawn to water – it was his nature, his entire being. It was his wish to have piles and piles of corpses in his possession, and to swallow the dead and drink their blood from a large and heavy cup.

Baal's servant met with Mot at Baal's request, and on his return the servant delivered a threat from the god of death. Mot declared that if Baal chose to oppose him he would swallow him as a man swallows vegetables and olives.

Mot was death, the inevitable end to every life. He swallowed up every creature when its time had come. Animals, humans, and even gods – could not escape their fate, and descended eventually to Mot's domain.

Mot told Anat, Baal's sister, that in order to find Baal and put him to death, he had crossed every valley, forged every stream, and climbed every hill and mountain on earth.

Mot fulfilled his deathly purpose everywhere he went. Destruction of life and the causing of death was his only activity.

Mot's residence was the underworld, in the city of Mari. Like the Greek Hades, Mot's name too was used as a synonym for the land of the dead.

Death and the subsequent descent to the underworld were described by Mot in terms of eating. He said of Baal's death: I hunted Baal, I put him in my mouth, and he was like a goat-calf in my throat."

In the war against Baal, Mot was assisted by his mighty side-kicks Zvul-Yam, (Singer of the sea) and Tefet-Yam (Judge of the sea), and by two snakes and a seven headed serpent.

The battles between Baal and Mot were extensive and took place over a period of many years. Each had his period of mastery over his enemy, but the other would take precedence for a while. Some of the conflict was hand to hand between the adversaries and at other times the gods sent servants to fight in their place.

The war fought by Baal, the god who brought the rains and provided every living thing with the breath of life, and Anat, the goddess of love and fertility, against Mot, and their victories over him, symbolized in the eyes of the Canaanites, the victory of life over death.

Some researchers believe that as Baal represented the rainy season, the bodies of water, and the growth of vegetation, Mot was the deity of the heat and drought of summer. The war between them symbolized the cycle of the seasons of the year, each taking precedence in its proper time. This interpretation fits with Anat's killing of Mot after the latter killed her brother. As the goddess of growth and fertility, Anat spread Mot's flesh in the fields, fertilizing them and making them ready for new life. Researchers who dispute this interpretation assert that his was not an example of rebirth and continuation of life, since birds came and consumed what Anat had sown. They also point out the fact that often Mot and Baal were sometimes both strong at the same time, and not always in turn, as is true of the seasons. Also, when Baal came back to life it took him seven years to again regain dominance over his brother Mot. The seasons, of course, change over each year. One theory has it that this myth came about after the region suffered seven years of draught. Therefore it is possible that the original myth was based on the changing of the seasons, and that the myth of the seven years of Baal's death came after such an extended period of dryness.

Anat

Anat was the daughter of the principal god of the Babylonian myths, and the sister and wife of Baal. She was called Lady of the Mountains. Like Ishtar, Inana, and Ashtoret, with whom she was identified, Anat was the goddess of love, life, and fertility on the one hand, and at the same time she was the cruel goddess of war. Though she was called "the virgin" and "the lady", she was a blood-thirsty goddess, and ready to fight the enemies of Baal and murder her victims mercilessly.

The Ugaritic writings portray Anat as very aggressive and violent – even toward other gods. She was a loyal fighter alongside Baal in the battles against Mot. When Mot succeeded in causing her brother Baal's death, Anat went out to hunt the killer, and even the evil Mot trembled at her presence. In fact even her father, the highest and mightiest god in the Canaanite pantheon was not immune to her threats and would accede to her demands in the face of her wrath. El so feared his daughter's attacks that he would cry out in frustration and run to hide in his room to escape her tirades and her threats to tear out his beard by its roots! Of course El agreed readily to her request to build a shrine to Baal, by whose side she remained ever faithful.

Anat was known throughout ancient Asia, and was admired in Egypt as well. In ancient Egyptian art she is depicted with horns of Hathor on her head. In Anatolia and Cyprus she was identified with the goddess Athena.

Baal would bring down the rains in their season, and Anat would provide the morning dew and the water from the fresh underground springs. She was his sister, and apparently also his wife/lover. Together they were responsible for the growth and reproduction of everything that lived on the land, vegetation and animal life alike.

Shahar and Shalim

Shahar was the Ugaritic dawn, and Shalim was the dusk. They were the sons of the supreme deity, El, and Astarte, the goddess of fertility.

Dagon

God of crop growth and fertility, Dagon made sure that the fields gave forth the promise of their seeds. His name meant "grain". The Philistines built him a temple in Ashdod, and he appears in the bible as one of their national gods. An additional shrine to Dagon was built in Gaza. During the period of the Hasmoneans, Jonathan the Hasmonean enlarged and refurbished the shrine of Dagon in Ashdod.

The cult of Dagon had influence in Sumaria as well, during the third dynasty of Ur (The twentieth and twenty-first centuries B.C.) where his was identified with the cult of Enlil.

In the Sumarian language, Dagon meant "god of all". In Mari, where a large temple to Dagon stood, a large staff of "messengers" or "prophets" would hear the words of Dagon and interpret them for the monarchs.

Dagon was also identified with Greek god, Kronos.

Ashur

The highest god of the Assyrians, they named their country and a city after him. He fulfilled the same roles as Enlil and Marduk, but as might be expected when concerning a warlike society such as the Assyrians, he was also the god of battle.

At first, it seems, Ashur was a god of fertility, growth, and renewal, and like Tamuz, he died at the end of every summer and "lived" in the winter in the underworld. The Assyrians depicted him in the form of the tree of life, and they put statues of him next to streams in the spring. In later periods, the character of Ashur was affected by that of the Babylonian Marduk, and Ashur became the father of all the gods and kings. According to Assyrian myth, Ashur created himself and afterward stood at the head of the gods that fought against Tihamat. As creator of the heavens and all the heavenly bodies, he was considered the creator of the entire universe. It was Ashur that made the human race, and the Assyrian people as his chosen group. Ashur himself was a war hero who helped the Assyrians in their conquering battles.

A ceremony full of pomp and circumstance was held in honor of Ashur in the city of Ashur, during which the Assyrians would cruelly torture and execute prisoners of war. Ashur's figure appeared on monuments as a bearded war hero within a wheel, grasping a drawn bow. Around this figure a great pair of wings was spread.

Ashur's mate was Ishtar, who matched her husband as a warrior personality, and she too was often depicted with a flowing beard!

Asmun/Ashmun

The Phoenician god of medicine, Asmun was identified with the Greek-Roman Asclepius and with Melkart – the Phoenician-Assyrian god of the dead. He also had similar characteristics to the goddess Ashtoret.

The great herbal healer Dioscorides relates the name Asmun to the healing plant, solanum.

Ashmun was young and handsome, according to myth, and the mother of the gods, Ashtoret fell in love with him. Trying to escape her affections, Ashmun castrated himself and died. Ashtoret brought him back to life with her vital heat, and made him a god.

The cult of Ashmun was practiced mostly in Sidon, where he was one of the trio of gods that included Baal, Ashtoret, and himself. The senate would meat at his temple in times of emergency. In places where he was worshipped coins were minted bearing the likeness of a snake wound around a staff – the symbol for medicine and healing.

Adonis

Adonis was a Canaanite deity whose worship spread to Cyprus, and from their to Asia Minor and to Greece. The source of the name Adonis is apparently the Hebrew "adon" meaning "lord".

Adonis represented vegetation, flowering and the renewal of life which took place in certain seasons and withdrew in others, much like Tamuz in the Sumarian-Acadian myths and Baal in the Ugaritic myths as well as the Aramaic Hadad Ramon.

The major part of the worship of Adonis consisted of funeral songs and elegies. In Athens, women would mourn Adonis on the rooftops of their houses, especially in late summertime. A wooden figure representing the body of the god would be displayed, and the songs of grief would be sung to it. The mourning custom ended with the burial of the doll-body. In the springtime the holiday of awakening of Adonis was observed and celebrated. Grains of wheat would be sprinkled into pieces of pottery, and the subsequent growth was called "garden of Adonis".

Attis

Attis was an Eastern, perhaps Syrian god, whose cult was practiced from Asia Minor all the way to Greece. The cult of Attis seems to have been connected to that of Cybele "the great mother of the gods". Myths concerning Attis abound and while they all have a common thread, there are serious differences between them. According to one of the legends, Attis was a shepherd with whom Cybele fell in love and made him a high priest after he vowed never to take a wife for the rest of his life. When Attis broke his vow, Cybele beat him viciously until Attis castrated himself in desperation, causing his own death. One of the versions of this myth holds that the castration took place on the eve of Attis' wedding. Cybele lamented his death, however, and brought him back to life. According to another myth, it was a monster, and not Cybele that fell in love with Attis, and he castrated himself to deter the monster's sexual advances. In still another version, Attis was Cybele's son, and another tells that it was Attis that fell in love with Cybele, and not the other way around! One of the legends describes Attis as a shepherd who noticed Cybele as she wandered in the forests and mountains along with her wild animal companions. He fell in love with her, and knowing he could never have her, he castrated himself out of frustration. Cybele found him and put his body into her chariot drawn by lions.

Another tradition tells that Attis was the son of Nana, who became pregnant after eating from the fruit of an almond tree. Cybele (or her monster counterpart) fell in love with Attis. When he was about to marry another woman, she burst in and attacked the wedding party and the guests. The worst beating was suffered by Attis himself, whom she hit mercilessly. So crazed was he by what had occurred, Attis castrated himself under a tree, and died. Zeus hears Cybele's cries but does not honor her request to bring him completely back to life. Instead, he agrees to let Attis' hair continue to grow, and for one of his fingers always to have movement as in life.

The worship of Attis was accompanied by wild orgies, and some of his priests castrated themselves. The ancients thought of Attis as a symbol of the rise and fall of nature in its cycles. (Like Adonis, Tamuz, and others)

A spring festival was held yearly in honor of Attis. His death and rebirth were retold by his followers and in identification with him they would enter states of ecstasy and joy which symbolized the joy awaiting every man upon his death. They reached these ecstatic heights by performing consecrated wedding ceremonies or by self-mutilation.

In the spring, the Romans who worshipped Cybele would celebrate for eight days, behaving in various licentious manners. Then would come the blood ceremonies, in which the believers would cut their own flesh, and the priests would emasculate themselves, either actually or symbolically. A very noisy funeral procession would then be staged in memory of Attis, after which they would celebrate his subsequent return to the living. A further ceremony was performed around the statue of Cybele and the black stone that was consecrated to her, which they carried around the city in a chariot drawn by cattle. From the third century B.C. an additional custom was added. The blood of a slaughtered bull was sprinkled on the believing celebrants.

Cybele

Cybele was the Asiatic goddess of the mountains. The center for her worship was in Phrygia. She bore resemblance to the goddess Inana, and was sometimes called Agdistis. Cybele was a hermaphrodite monster (having both female and male characteristics). She was born from a stone that was fertilized by the sperm of Zeus. The gods decided to castrate the androgynous creature and turned it into the goddess Cybele. Cybele lived in the mountains and forests along with the wild animals and with her priestesses.

Cybele was apparently of Hittite origin. The Hittites worshipped her in the second century B.C. and called her Kapapas or Cobaba. They considered her the most important Neo-Hittite goddess. A mythological figure with a similar name was worshiped by the Sumarians as well.

Cybele's cult was found throughout Greece and the Hellenistic world. She was identified with Raya, the mother of Zeus, and called the Mother Goddess. She was depicted wearing a crown shaped like a tower, and sitting on a thrown flanked by two lions, or riding a chariot drawn by lions. At her side, as a secondary god, Attis appeared. Worship of Cybele was often accompanied by ecstasy and wild music and dance.

The cult of Cybele was introduced into Rome in the year 204 B.C. as a protection against Hannibal. In Rome she was called Magana Matar (The Great Mother). Every April a festival lasting seven days and nights was held in her honor. An additional holiday was celebrated on the fifteenth of March. This day commemorated Attis as a child who had been found on a cliff over a river bank. On the twenty-fourth of March the "Day of Blood" was observed and priests often symbolically castrated themselves on this day. The twenty-fifth of March was the day of Attis' resurrection. One of the strangest ceremonies in relations to this celebration was the slaughtering of a bull and subsequent baptism in its blood to "wash away the sins" of those who endured this rite.

The Phrygian city of Pessinus was the center for the worship of Cybele. There her cult rallied around a black stone which was holy and consecrated to her name. Her cult spread also to Rome and Greece, where she was officially received in 404 B.C.

Cybele's priests, dressed in women's clothing and made up like prostitutes, danced in a trancelike state. At first the Roman leaders were suspect of the cult, and forbade Romans to enter Cybele's priesthood. However in time the Caesars stood with the head of Cybele's priests at the yearly festivals.

Molech

The Ammonite god of knowledge, evil, and magic, Molech was also the god of human sacrifice. During the days of the kings of Judah babies were passed through fire as a sacrifice to Molech.

Melqart

Melqart was the son of El and Astarte, and he symbolized the changing of the seasons. He was also known earlier as the god of the sun. Melqart was a hunter and warrior, and controlled the seas, making them safe for the travelers and sailors. Melqart was responsible for the bountiful agricultural crops which were so vital to the region. Tyre was the center for his worship. The Greek historian Herodotus tells that Melqart's temple had two tall pillars – one of pure gold and the other of agate. These pillars shone clearly in the night. Melqart was killed by fire, but his yearly rebirth was celebrated with an annual festival.

Illuyankas

According to Hittite tradition, Illuyankas was a dragon that personified the forces of evil. In character he resembled Tihamat of the Babylonian mythology. Just as Marduk killed Tihamat, Illuyankas was murdered by the Hittite god of air, thunder, and storms.

There are two versions to this ancient story. According to the oldest one, the dragon Illuyankas succeeded in overcoming the storms sent by the god. The goddess Inaras intervened however, and set a trap for him. She prepared a large feast with huge barrels of wine and fruit juice and other drinks, and invited the dragon and the members of his household. The dragon and his children ate so much that they could not return to their home at the end of the festivities. At this point, the goddess's lover, Hupasiays, came to assist in the plan. He tied a strong rope around the dragon's limbs, making it impossible for him to move. The god of storms caused a huge wind to tear at Illuyanka's eyes, and the god them killed the dragon.

Inaras rewarded Hupasiays, but the reward later turned into a punishment. She built a special house in his honor and he went to live there, but she forbade him to look out of the windows for fear he would catch sight of his wife and children. When Hupasiays disobeyed and indeed saw his family, he wanted more than anything to return to them and abandon his "reward". He asked Inaras to let him return to his mortal home, but she not only denied his request – she put him to death.

A later version of this myth tells of a battle between the storm god and the dragon during which the dragon Illuyankas snatched the eyes and heart of the god. As in the Egyptian myth of Osiris and Horus, the murdered god fathered a son whose task it was to bring his father back to life. One of the dragon's daughters married the storm god's son, and she indeed loved him. The son asked his wife to bring him his father's stolen organs. When he had them in hand, he brought them to his father who was then strengthened and whole and went out to battle the dragon. The storm god this time killed the dragon, and in addition he killed his son, and returned to his place of power.

Both versions of this legend have similarities to the western Asian myths about the death of the fertility god (who brings the rain, as does the storm god), and his subsequent return to life and power.

Kumbari

Kumarbi was as important to Hittite and Hurrite mythology as was Enlil to the Sumarian. Kumarbi, according to the Hurrites, was the god responsible for the creation of the human race. He was called "the father of humanity". Hurrite myth tells that for nine years ruled all that occurred on earth. However, the god Anu saw himself as above Kumarbi, and attacked him, taking away his kingdom. Kumarbi bowed down to Anu and placed himself in his service, but he had hidden plans. Since Anu sensed that Kumarbi had ulterior motives, and since he could no longer stand to have a servant whom he mistrusted, Anu sprouted wings and flew off to the heavens to get away from Kumarbi. Kumarbi followed close behind him, however, and bit his ankles and chewed off his sexual organs. Kumarbi then took over for a time as the supreme god, but not for long. Anu's injuries healed, and he taunted Kumarbi, saying he'd taken a heavy load upon himself. Anu spilled his semen and declared that he would bring forth three sons. These three were Teshub– god of storms, Aranzach – the tiger, and Tashmishu. The three may actually have been three aspects of the one storm god, Teshub. In response to Anu's threat, Kumarbi spit, and his saliva landed in Anu's semen. This caused the birth of the three. Teshub took over Kumarbi's place of power, but Kumarbi could not make peace with his loss of status, and plotted to return to his former glory. He took his staff and attached the wind to his feet. He left his city and marched to a giant boulder three thousand long and three thousand wide. He slept on the boulder and dreamed of creating a monster that could beat his enemies. The stone moved beneath him as if he were making love to a woman. Kumarbi's mating with the stone brought forth a son, and Kumarbi named him Ullikummi. Kumarbi declared that he would overcome the storm and turn him into grains of salt and trample him as if he were an ant under his shoes. Kumarbi's son was a stone monster of great proportions and he did not stop growing! The gods, and particularly Teshub, were desperate to stop his growth, and the only solution they could find was to cut off his legs. This indeed stopped Ullikummi's growth, and also killed Kumarbi's hopes of getting his kingdom back. Kumarbi remained in the Hurrite pantheon, and the Hurrites and Hittites continued to worship him for quite a while even after the cult of Teshub was established.

Ullikummi

Kumarbi had a sexual encounter with a boulder which resulted in the birth of his son, Ullikummi, a man of gigantic strength and proportions. Another version holds that Kumarbi mated with the sea to produce Ullikummi. Either way, Kumarbi wanted a child with the wherewithal to destroy his enemy, Teshub, who had stolen his kingdom. Ullikummi's body was made of green rock and he shared many characteristics with his parent boulder. Kumarbi and the goddess who served him, Irshira, drove Ullikummi into the earth like a spear. Ullikummi began to grow, and grow… until he was taller than any of the buildings on earth and even touched the dwelling place of the gods.

The storm god, Teshub and the sun, looked with alarm at the enormous growing intruder, and tried to recruit help in stopping it. Ishtar, the goddess of love, tried to tempt him with her seductive ways, but to no avail. The stone monster was not impressed. Teshub tried to fight Ullikummi, but the boulder was too strong for him, and Ullikummi continued to grow. The heavens shook with his presence, until Hebat, Teshub's wife, ran away from her heavenly shrine in fright. The gods gathered to discuss what could be done, and could come to no solution but to cut off the legs of the enormous Ullikummi in order to stop his growth. This indeed stopped Ullikummi's climb heavenward, and when he stopped growing Teshub killed him, thus winning his final victory over Ullikummi's father, Kumarbi.

Telepinu

Son of Teshub, god of storms and thunder, Telepinu was the god of agriculture. According to myth, the desserts were created when Telepinu was angry about something and ran away. Telepinu had been so caught up in his rage that he put his left boot on his right foot, and vice versa. His leaving left human kind as well as the gods to suffer from a terrible draught. All vegetation shriveled, the streams ran dry, and the forests and fields lay barren. Women stopped having babies and cattle as well stopped reproducing. The myth goes on to relate the steps taken in effort to appease Telepinu and bring him back so that the land could thrive again.

AT first, the sun god sent an eagle out to find Telepinu and bring him home. The eagle returned with nothing to show for its search. The Mother Goddess Hanahana then called to a bee to seek out Telepinu. She told the bee that when he found Telepinu he was to sting him on his hands and feet, and then to spread wax all over his body and bring him home. The bee found Telepinu and stung him, but the bee stings only served to further anger the god, and he brought a great flood on the earth, washing away people, homes, and animals.

Kamrusepas, the goddess of healing and magic then performed a ceremony that succeeded in assuaging Telepinu's temper, and he agreed to return. He arrived back home on the back of an eagle, and again the fields bloomed and the streams filled with flowing water.

Teshub

Teshub was the Hittite god of weather, storms, and thunder. He was one of the most important gods in the Hittite pantheon. Alulu was at one time the ruler of the heavens, but he was taken over by Anu. The god Kumarbi, in his turn, thrust Anu from his throne when he bit off his genitals. Anu's sperm fertilized Kumarbi, thus producing the "three terrible gods", which apparently each represented one of the three aspects of Teshub. Teshub then toppled Kumarbi from power and became Kumarbi's enemy. Kumarbi mated with a rock (or the sea, according to one version) and produced a son – a huge boulder named Ullikummi.

Ullikummi threatened Teshub's supremacy as well as the security of all the gods who greatly feared the fast-growing boulder. Ishtar ran frightened from her palace, and Teshub made his escape as well. Teshub understood that drastic measures would be needed to thwart Ullikummi and he girded himself for battle. He brought about a fierce thunderstorm, with lightening cracks, raging winds and blinding rain. The brave and solid Ullikummi was not in the least deterred by such weather, however, and continued to grow unabated. His size threatened to swallow up the entire universe if a solution could not be found. He threatened man and god alike.

Teshub consulted Ea and asked for his help. Ea cut Ullikummi's legs off, which finally caused him to stop growing and weakened him so that Teshub was able to do him in.

Teshub remained supreme, and his cult spread during the second millennium B.C. to all countries that spoke the Hurrite language. Temples were built in his honor all over the Hittite Empire, in Babylonia, Sumaria, and even Syria and Anatalia. Teshub was identified with other gods of thunder, such as the Canaanite Baal, and the Assyrian Adar.

The Great Celtic Epics

The Celts

The ancient Celtic culture was made up of a mixture of peoples and traditions. It penetrated into most of Western Europe, from southern France and part of Spain to Northern Germany, Britain, and Ireland. At its height it extended from the British Isles all the way to Turkey.

In ancient times, the British islands were invaded by many peoples, European, Greek, and even African. Before the Celts invaded Ireland, it was already populated by the offspring of invaders from Spain, Greece, and as far off as Egypt.

The Celts burst on the scene from the East in the ninth century B.C. (Proto-Celtic culture, however, predates this – 3500-1500 B.C.) The Celts intermingled with the Iberian inhabitants of the British Isles.

The influence of these many and varied cultures was felt in the Celtic myths. It must be remembered that the Para-Celtic culture was greatly affected by the ancient Phoenician and Babylonians as well.

Roman culture also played a part in Celtic myths. Relations between the Celts and the dominant Roman culture took many a different turn over the years. During the third and fourth centuries B.C., the Celts, a people of brave and adventurous warriors, constituted quite an annoying threat to the Roman Empire. The Celts sent bands of robbers and plunderers into Rome and managed to do quite extensive damage. At times these bandits even desecrated temples, altars, and sites holy to the

Empire. But during the first century of the Common Era, Julius Caesar turned this situation around. Soon the Celts were no longer any threat to the Roman Empire, and in fact had become a conquered people totally under its control. Under Julius Caesar, the Celtic cities in northern Italy were taken over quickly, and soon the whole of Gallia was taken as well. After the Romans took Northern England and Wales, the pure Celtic tradition could be found only in Ireland, central and northern Scotland, and the far northern Islands. Since the Romans never got to Ireland, the Celtic and Druid cultures thrived unhindered until the onset of the Christian period.

The influence of the Roman culture during the fourth and fifth centuries made inroads with the Celts. A certain blending of cultures took place and worship of Celtic and Roman gods often took place side by side. From the fifth to the eighth centuries, following the Anglo-Saxon invasion, Roman philosophy blended with that of the Christians and the Celts. During the same period many pagan Celts converted to Christianity. From the eighth to the eleventh centuries the Normans invaded the Celtic cities and under the rule of the French Normans the Celts were segmented into small areas which were sometimes quite isolated from one another.

The Celtic traditions, legends and customs, were passed verbally from father to son in an almost completely oral tradition. The earliest written Celtic literature dates from around the year 1300 and shows the influence of the Norman conquerors. In the twelfth century, the Troubadours (wandering singers) introduced Celtic folk stories and legends to the Christian world. Some of those stories – notably those about King Arthur and the Round Table, and Merlin the Magician, are popular still today throughout the world.

The period between the thirteen and fifteenth centuries was a difficult and cruel one for anyone in Europe who was not Catholic. Harsh religious laws caused the minority of Druids and

Celts who had not yet converted to Christianity to leave or be expelled from their homes. However it was during this period that traveling poets and songwriters wrote many of the most important collections of Celtic folk stories and legends, and it is through these that we can learn about the faith and belief of the Celtic people. The most famous of these works is "The Death of Arthur", which was written in 1470 by Sir Thomas Mallory, an English knight. During the Renaissance, when the printing press was invented the King Arthur legends were widely distributed.

The Celtic Social Structure

The culture of the Celts was founded on the basis of traditions and faiths from many nations and was affected by places geographically as far removed as India, Egypt and Siberia, The pagan Celts were a blend of local residents and newcomers that was united by common language (though there were many dialects) and spirituality despite their diverse cultural roots.

The basic social unit was the tribe, which developed out of the family and widened by way of marriage, adoption, subjection, absorption, and even rape. A tribe made its home on a certain piece of land and its members did not generally wander far from the area. They were fiercely loyal to the tribe and to its locale. Members of the tribe shared a name, and each tribe had a totem – usually a flower or animal.

The head of the tribe (called king or queen) was chosen and anointed by the Druids and was thought of as a direct descendant of the god or goddess of the tribe.

Celtic worship ceremonies were associated with the cycles of the sun and moon, as well as the changing of the seasons and the agricultural year. The Celts believed that the gods and goddesses had many forms and could appear at any time and any place. Humans could therefore always turn to them for help and assistance. The men and women of the tribe were considered social and religious equals. Every member had the same opportunity to achieve "godliness" and was afforded every encouragement in doing so.

The cultural hierarchy was simple – it was made up of a leader, an aristocracy, free landowners, artisans, and common citizens. The commoners dwelled within the boundaries of the tribe's land, and had to remain loyal to one of the nobles. They served their noble by raising his cattle, fighting his battles, and protecting him from possible outside invaders. In return, they received a small plot of land on which to live and raise crops.

The Celts were known as great metal artisans (and makers of weapons) and skilled road pavers as well as salt refiners. The last was particularly important due to the vital necessity to preserve food, especially fish. In addition they were excellent farmers and tenders of livestock.

The Celts were reputed far and wide as expert horsemen who exhibited the utmost bravery in battle. While they loved extreme sport and competition involving bodily risk, they also invented several board games, many having spiritual themes.

The Druids

The Priests of the Celtic religion, the Druids were magicians, soothsayers, and the go-betweens that connected the worldly with the invisible, spiritual realm.

The Druids were central to Celtic life and had a large impact on all things religious and cultural. They were the judges, ministers, and lawmakers, as well as the medicine men, healers, prophets, and astronomers.

Before the Roman invasion, Druidism thrived in Britain and Europe, free of outside influences. Under the Roman Empire, however, Druidism began to recede – Roman soldiers did not hesitate to execute anyone who showed obvious tendencies toward the Celtic religion. In the Celtic areas conquered by the Romans, the Celts practiced their beliefs in hiding and passed along their traditions orally.

Fortune telling was a vital part of the Celtic religious tradition, and the Druids were the soothsayers of the people. The connection between man and nature and between heaven and earth made up the foundations of their faith.

There are several theories as to the origin of the Druids. One of these holds that the Druids came to the West from Siberia and that their spiritual traditions were based on Siberian shamanism. Other possibilities include the Druids being descendents of the Hebrew Abraham, their being of Tibetan origin, or even that they were directly descendant from the people of Atlantis, the lost continent.

Most researchers agree, however, that the Druids' ancestors were Phoenician, and that they came to the shores of Gallia and Britain on sea vessels. In fact, there is much similarity between the British and the Phoenician traditions, customs, religion, and deities. Among the most notable examples we find the British god of the son – Bel, the parallel god to the Babylonian and Phoenician Baal.

Merlin, the right hand man to King Arthur, is undoubtedly the most famous of the Druid magicians. Merlin's position was not an unusual one, as the Druids had important tasks and were in some ways considered no less powerful than the King. The first right of speech in meetings was always given to the Druid, and many kings were chosen and anointed at the say-so of a Druid.

Unlike the common people, whose homes had to be within the boundaries of the tribe's land, a Druid could live anywhere he chose. He was exempt from payment of taxes in return for the rendering of his services and also received recompense in the form of precious metals, jewels, and food. The Druids were not required to work the land to bring forth their sustenance as were the commoners.

There were Druids of both genders, and the status of the women was no lower than that of the men. The best known among the women were Morgan la Fey and Viviana, students of the Merlin the Magician.

The Druids worked with energies: cosmic, heavenly, and earthly. They believed in the reincarnation of souls and in the existence of parallel lives – that is, that man lives more than one life simultaneously. Each life was thought to be just one of many that the soul had experienced and was experiencing.

It was believed that the Druids could change their form at will. They could become animals, such as wolves, eagles, or ravens; they could change from one human body to another; they could even become invisible. In order to achieve these abilities, the Druid would undergo long and arduous training at special institutions of learning in holy buildings constructed for that purpose. Many of these places were confiscated by the Romans, who massacred without mercy those who took part in studies or ceremonies connected with Druid beliefs and practices.

The Great Celtic Epics

Celtic mythology consists of various epic stories called Cycles. All of the stories in a particular cycle are arranged according to the major people and places mentioned in the tales.

The Mythological Cycle

The Mythological Cycle includes historical myths and legends which tell of five invasions of Ireland, the mythical battles, and the gods of the Tuatha De Danan. The five invasions in the cycle are as follows, in chronological order:

The grandson of Noah, Cessair, led the first group of settlers to Ireland. This group was completely wiped out in the flood, Cessair's wife being the only survivor.

Partholan, leader of the second race to conquer Ireland, was also a descendant of Noah. His race began to work the Irish land. Partholan and his people had to deal with the Fomorians, but it was not they who wiped them out, but rather a harsh epidemic which did in the entire tribe save one person.

Nemed and his Nemedians were the third group to invade Ireland. Nemed and his people arrived thirty years after the Partholans perished. The Nemedians continued to work the land as had the Partholans. They too suffered under the Fomorians, fought them, and won, but in the end the epidemic took them. The few that survived were forced to live under Fomorian rule. After the last battle took place between the Nemedians and the Fomorians the Nemedians exited Ireland.

The fourth invasion was by the Fir Bolg, offspring of the Nemedians who had settled in Greece. They ruled Ireland for thirty seven years. They divided the country into five territories, and created a system of law and order. The Fir Bolg were overrun by the fifth wave of invaders – the Tuatha De Danan, in the battle of Magh Tuiredh.

Tuatha De Danan, the fifth group to invade Ireland, was made up of offspring of the Nemedim that had settled on the Northern Islands. They were considered sons of gods. The Milasians (who were not included in the five conquering races) invaded Ireland in 1500 B.C. and caused the people of Tuatha De Danan to go underground and build a separate kingdom in the lakes and the caves.

The Ulster Cycle

A manuscript circa the seventh and eight centuries contains the Ulster Cycle – the most famous of the Irish cycles of folk stories, handed down, as most were, by mouth.

The Ulster Cycle describes the life, customs, and cultural practices of the ancient Celts. Most of the stories took place around the first century B.C., when Conchobar was king of Ulster.

The longest and most important epic in the Ulster cycle was the Tain Bo Cuailnge, also known as the Cattle Raid of Cooley.

The Tain Bo Cuailnge

The Tain Bo Cuailnge – the Cattle Raid of Cooley – is the central piece in the great cycle of Irish myths, the Ulster Cycle. It focuses on the war between Maeve of Connacht and Conchobar from Ulster, and on other Ulster heroes. The spark that escalated the conflict between Maeve and Ulster into a war was the theft of a bull from Cooley of Ulster. The crime was organized and instigated by Queen Maeve. The main character in this epic was Cu Chulainn, the greatest of the Ulster heroes.

The personalities of the two warring monarchs, Conchobar and Maeve greatly influenced their forces. Conchobar was much loved by his people and a highly regarded king. However, in several instances he betrayed his adopted daughter Deirdre, and lost two of his heroes by the breaking of the knights' code of honor. In this manner he lost Fergus, the king previous to Conchobar who had given up his throne for him. Fergus had been in love with Conchobar's mother who demanded that in return for her affections, Fergus allow Conchobar to rule in his stead for one year. Fergus did not hesitate, even though this ended up costing him his kingship. Conchobar remained on the throne because the people admired him and wanted him to permanently replace the real king. Regardless of all this, Fergus remained Conchobar's right hand, and his great strength, along with his inhumanly large size, made him a most important warrior for Ulster.

Conchobar adopted a daughter, Deirdre, planning to take her as a wife when she became of age. She later ran away from Ulster to escape Conchobar, but he promised to allow her to return, along with her lover. Fergus, himself an honorable man of his word, expected Conchobar to hold to this promise, but alas, Conchobar reneged and murdered his daughter's lover and put Deirdre in chains. Fergus had remained ever faithful to Ulster and the kingdom, and never tried to harm Conchobar even after he ousted him from his reign. After witnessing this treatment of

Deirdre however, he defected from Ulster, and in the ultimate anti-Conchobar act, he became the lover of Maeve, the enemy queen. This move strengthened the position of Connacht in the conflict.

An additional legendary hero moved over to the forced of Maeve – the step brother of Cu Chulainn, a great warrior who had studied at the knees of Conchobar. The brothers faced an impossible mission, as they faced off on opposite sides, not wishing to harm one another. They managed to avoid direct combat with one another until at last Maeve ordered Per to fight against his brother.

The decisive moment in the battle came about when Fergus, fighting for Maeve, stood face to face with the king that had so disappointed him – Conchobar. Fergus managed to neutralize Conchobar, and was about to kill him when Conchobar's son, Cormak intervened and begged for his fathers life. Fergus could have ended Conchobar's life with one swipe of his sword and thus declare victory for Maeve and for Connacht, but he decided to heed Cormak's pleas. A few moments later Cu Chulainn, the Knight of Ulster, arrived and brought a swift victory over Maeve for Conchobar.

Cu Chulainn himself was beaten by Queen Maeve after he was forced to eat dog meat, a transgression which led to further crimes and which weakened Cu Chulainn's powers until eventually he could no longer stand against the enemy.

The Arthurian Cycle

The Arthurian Cycle is a collection of myths concerning King Arthur, who according to tradition, lived during the 5th century. The stories take place mostly in Camelot and describe the adventures of the Knights of the Round Table.

The legends of King Arthur give expression to Celtic art, spirituality, and belief in the sacredness of the land.

The Finian Cycle

Fin McCumail and his son, Oscar are the main heroes of the collection of legends called the Finian Cycle. Fin McCumail was active around the third century and the stories were written down during the twelfth through the seventeenth centuries. The stories stress Celtic values such as honor and generosity, and describe the bravery of the ancient Celts. Most of the myths in the cycle appear as traditional ballads.

The Prophecies of Merlin

Hidden secret prophetic meanings are contained within the poems and stories of manuscript called the Prophecies of Merlin. They were recorded in the twelfth century by the Welsh scholar Geoffrey Monmouth. The stories are full of magical acts and sorcery.

The Mabinogion

A collection of Welsh myths, the Mabinogion is the main source of Welsh and British legends available. The text of the Mabinogion has four parts, called "wings" containing stories about the families of Pavil, Lear, and Don. Many of the heroes appear more in one wing than another, but there are many common characters to all of the wings.

Many legends sprang as offshoots of the Mabinogion and there are quite a few parallels between its stories and other Irish myths.

Gods and Heroes

Eochaidh mac Eric

Eochaidh mac Eric was the ninth king of the Fir Bolg – the fourth wave of conquerors of Ireland. According to the myth, Eochaidh was an exemplary king. During his rule, the wet country of Ireland enjoyed a respite from constant rainfall, and the dew provided enough moisture for the people to bring forth bountiful crops. Eochaidh was the first Irish King to found a system of law and order and cheating and crime was almost unknown in his realm.

Eochaidh was killed in the first battle against the Tuatha De Danon, the fifth wave of conquerors that caused the end of the Fir Bolg period. The death of such a king – one who had brought a period of joy and prosperity to Ireland – did not occur on the battlefield itself. Eochaidh had left the fighting momentarily to search for a source of water, when three of the enemy's troops appeared before him. In the end all four lost their lives.

Edain/Etain

Edain was the second wife of King Mider. According to Celtic tradition she was the goddess of beauty and benevolence, and she was famous for her ability to change forms. She was one of the White Ladies of the Faery. Edain is connected to the underworld and to horses. She had a herd of white horses with blue eyes.

Oisin/Ossian

The poet and fighter Oisin was the son of Sadv, goddess of nature, forests and armies, and his father was the famous hero

Fin McCumail. The name Oisin means foal, and Oisin shared with his mother the ability to change at will from human to deer. Oisin was raised by Sadv in the forests and open fields, until Fin, the leader of the elite fighting unit "Fiana" found him and taught him the ways of war. Oisin later became one of the Fiana's most outstanding warriors.

One of the best known myths of Fin is reminiscent of the story of Conla, one of the fighters of the Fiana. Like Conla, Fin two was bewitched by a woman from another world who promised to take him into another reality.

IN the case of Oisin, it was the goddess Niam who put him under her spell and took him with her to another world – the "land of youth". According to another version, a mysterious woman found Oisin in the forest. She had a beautiful human body but her head was that of a pig. This woman told Oisin that the state of her head was the result of a spell put on her by a Druid, and that she would turn back into a beautiful woman is only Oisin would marry her. They wed, and the pig's head indeed turned into that of a beauty. Oisin lived with his wife (who was a goddess according to one version) in the Land of Youth for a long period, but he began at some point to pine for his native Ireland. His wife agreed that he should pay a visit his homeland and sent him to Ireland on the back of a horse, but there was one condition to the trip. Oisin must not allow his foot to tread on the ground of Ireland. When Oisin arrived on horseback and looked around he was shocked to discover that nothing in Ireland looked familiar! He had spent three centuries in the Land of the Young, and while he had not aged a day, his homeland had undergone the immense changes that three hundred years had wrought. Once he acclimated to the new reality, Oisin fell from his horse and his foot touched the ground. In a moment he aged three hundred years. Before he died, Oisin visited St. Patrick, and related to him all the legends of Fiana so that they could be passed on for future generations.

Oenghus/Angus/Angus Og

Angus, one of the Tuatha De Danan, was the Irish god of love, courting, and youth. He was the son of Boann, goddess of the river and mother of the herds of Dagda, father of the gods. Angus' modern description as the god of love stems from the help he afforded couples, most importantly to Diarmair and Grainne. Another myth tells of Angus himself falling in love with a beautiful swan maiden named Cair. Every two years, Cair would turn into a swan during the festival of the First of November. On one of these occasions, Angus dressed as a swan, and flew with her to her palace.

The title "young son" was sometimes attached to the name of Angus, since the British god of love was called the "heavenly son". Some believe that the two gods were actually one and the same.

Ogmios/Ogma

Ogma, son of Dagda, was one of the most famous of the Tuatha De Danan. He was the god of knowledge, song, and speech according to the Celtic tradition. He was also the god of sexuality and verbal communication, and thought to be a particularly handsome god. In addition to all of these attributes, Ogma was a warrior and had tremendous physical strength. Ogma was credited with inventing the holy Druid alphabet, called the Ogham, which was used by the Celts during the seventh century. The characters of this special kind of writing were thought to have powers, and were sometimes used to paralyze enemies.

During times of war, Ogma encouraged the fighters of the battle of Mag Tuireadh and was himself an important warrior. Ogma carried a bow and a stick,

In Gaelic myths, there is a hero names Ogmios who shares many attributes with the Roman Hercules (and the Greek Heracles) - some exceptions being that Ogmios was a wrinkled old man and known as the god of eloquence. The Gaelic Ogmios was almost certainly the Irish Ogma. Ogmios wore a lion skin and carried a staff, bow, and quiver. Ogmios was able to drag several men, all attached to a golden chain by their ears. The chain ran through Ogmios' tongue. He was able to charm his believers by using magic as well as the eloquence of his speech. Ogmios symbolized the importance and centrality of words – especially religious and ritual words. The name Ogmios was thought to be one of great power, and was used in curses, spells, and blessings.

Aine

The Irish goddess of earth and sun, Aine was also a queen and a magician. She was the goddess that brought the summer solstice. Aine was associated with dawn, fertility, and the wildness of nature.

Aife/Aoife

Aife, the wife of the sea god, Mananan, was a Scottish queen, associated with the alphabet, the swan, and the crane.

Elayne/Elen/Elen Lwyddawg

Elen was an Irish goddess of particular power and strength, especially in times of war.

Goddess of leadership and battle, Elen would shield the army's generals and the leaders' abilities to guide. She gave the soldiers their bravery and watched over them as they marched into the fray.

Amaethin

Called the "king of the harvest", Amaethin was the god of agriculture and reaping. He was responsible for the growth of fruits and vegetables, and the Celts believed that by worshipping him their fields would yield abundance.

The hoe, the thresher, and the plow were his symbols.

Andraste/Andrasta

Andraste was the goddess of fertility. Like goddesses of productivity in other traditions, Andraste was responsible for the reproduction as well as for war and death. Her cult was practiced in the holy forests where her temples were built.

Anu

Anu was an Irish goddess of fertility and thought of as the Mother Goddess. She seems to have been related to Danu, the mother of the Tuatha De Danan (or they may have been one and the same).

Esus

The god of the forest, Esus was able to change form at will. He guided and watched over the hunters, and at the same time protected the forests. Esus was associated with bows and arrows, spears, hunting and the bull with three skulls.

Epona

The ancient inhabitants of north-eastern Gallia worshipped Epona, the horse-goddess. Epona was usually depicted sitting side-saddle on a white horse and surrounded by other horses.

Epona was the only Celtic goddess to appear in the Roman pantheon and to attain a high level of popularity among the Romans. Her identification with horses may have had something to do with this, since the animal was highly regarded by the Romans. The Roman festival of the 18th of December was in honor of the horse-goddess.

Arawn

King of the underworld, Arawn was considered the god of death and of war. The legends about Arawn relate that he owned magical animals and that he was able to change his own form to that of an animal in the blink of an eye.

Arianrhod

The goddess of the moon, Arianrhod's name meant "silver wheel". She was the daughter of Dano, and the sister of Gwydion.

Arianrhod volunteered to help Math, who required a virgin that would allow him to rest his feet in her lap at all times when he was not needed in battle. To make sure she was a virgin, Math tested Arianrhod by requiring her to pass over a magic stick. Arianrhod failed this test – and immediately gave birth to two offspring – Dylan and Llew Llaw. Llew Llaw was forbidden to receive the usual male rights of passage – he was not given his name until much later, he was not to be armed for war, and he was never to have a wife. When he came of age, Math and Gwydion helped him defy these rules and fashioned him a wife, Blodenwedd, who sprang from a flower.

Arianrhod was associated with the moon, stars, reincarnation, and the three aspects of death.

Erin/Eriu

The Irish Earth goddess, Erin was the queen of the Tuatha de Danan. Erin was known for her ability to change forms and was connected with the powers that existed in the depths and the bowels of the earth. She was also the goddess of creativity.

Arthur/Artus

Arthur was the most famous of the Celtic heroes. He was born to the King of Britain and his wife the Duchess of Cornwall. As a child born out of wedlock, Arthur was not raised by his parents. It was Merlin, the famous and powerful magician, who educated and cared for the future king. Arthur attained the throne of Britain when he was only fifteen years old, after he succeeded in freeing the proverbial sword, Excalibur, from the stone in which it had been stuck for years. No man had been able to move the sword even a bit, but according to myth, Arthur did not even have to try hard at this feat – he simply saw the sword in the stone, approached it and drew it out effortlessly, making it clear to all who witnessed this amazing occurrence that Arthur was destined to be king.

Armed with the magical sword, Excalibur, Arthur rid the land of all manner of pesky monsters and giants, to the great relief of the populace. Arthur pushed out invaders, and then pushed on until he had conquered the entire continent, all the way to Rome. He even got as far as the land of Israel, according to some versions, and brought the cross of Jesus back to Britain.

Arthur was a brave and intelligent king, but he was not immune to the double betrayal by his most trusted knight, Lancelot, and his wife, Genevieve. Arthur had wed Genevieve against the advice of Merlin, and indeed this choice caused Arthur much suffering and sorrow. There were other betrayals as well. Arthur's nephew, Mordred, took advantage of the fact that the king was absent on his conquering journeys abroad, and took control of the crown for himself. Arthur tried to oust Mordred from power but the latter held fast, causing a bloody and protracted battle to ensue in which many of the Knights of the Round Table perished. Arthur himself was mortally wounded, and thus his reign came to a decisive end. After Arthur's death, the legendary sword, Excalibur, sank to the bottom of a lake, where according to legend it remains to this day, kept by the

Lady of the Lake. Morgan la Fay, the great magician, and three of her fairies, floated the wounded king on a raft to Avalon, and from there, the myth goes on, he will someday return to take over the kingdom and redeem his people. This belief was very popular in the middle ages.

Camelot, Arthur's stomping ground, was known for its uncompromising code of valor (which was broken by Lancelot's betrayal with the wife of the honorable one himself). Arthur founded the "Order of the Knights of the Round Table", the round table being a symbol of equality among the participants. They all enjoyed the same importance, rank, and stand, and each knight kept the code of honor, though each went his individual way in search of adventure. Above all, the knights honored the brotherhood of arms, and their obligation to protect the weak, and to guard the church.

The knights endured many hardships and varied adventures, but one desire united them all and ignited the imagination and motivation of each of them – the search for the Holy Grail. This vessel was believed to be the cup which Joseph used to collect the blood of Jesus as he died on the cross. Alternatively, it was thought to be used by Pontius Pilate, the Roman commissioner who ordered the execution of Jesus. The search for the Holy Grail could be undertaken only by a "pure" knight. Galahad, son of Lancelot, was the only knight found fit for the undertaking. He was considered a true knight – the chosen – the only offspring of the kingly dynasty of Solomon and Joseph, and the only one who might succeed in finding the Holy Grail and bring an end to a long period of searching.

Arthur was by far the most important character in the late Celtic mythology. Proof of his actual existence has never been demonstrated. Most of the stories about King Arthur, such as those concerning the Knights of the Round Table and the search for the Holy Grail, are part of a European literary tradition which began with a group of legends called "The History of the Kings of Britain" by the Welsh-Norman scholar, Geoffrey of Monmouth, which was published around the year 1150. One of the first known mentions of Arthur describes him as a British military leader who fought against the Saxon conquerors. Certain texts from the 12th century depict Arthur as the ruler of an underground community, and in other legends he was a giant.

In the majority of the legends, Arthur was a fighter of monsters and giants, as were the heroes of many other mythological and folklore traditions.

Today, the Arthurian stories have been given psychological connotations, according to which their source is the conflict between man (the ambitious knights) and the darker side of his personality and deep inner urges (the monsters).

Badb/Badhbh/Badb Catha

Badb was the goddess of war, as well as the goddess of inspiration and understanding. Like the Greek goddess war, Athena, Badb too had two aspects – the spirit of battle, and wisdom. Badb was nicknamed the "raven of the battlefield" and was known for her abilities at sorcery. She was the sister of Lanu, Morigu, and Mackne.

Badb's battle cries would cause confusion and terror among the fighters and often she would fly over them in the form of a raven, which was taken as a symbol for impending death.

Balar

Balar was the leader of the Fomorians, a tribe of monstrous humans considered the offspring of Ham, the cursed son of Noah. Some myths describe them as people with only one leg and one arm.

Balar was known as "Balar of the Evil Eye". He had only one eye – oversized and with a poisonous gaze. One look from Balar could cause a person to become paralyzed.

It was prophesied that Balar would be killed by one of his grandchildren. Hearing this, Balar locked his daughter Eithne, into a cave to prevent her from bringing forth any potential murderers. Cain, one of Tuatha de Danan, and enemy of the Fomorians, managed to find and lure the young woman with his charms, and she bore triplets. Balar drowned them all, but one of them, Lug, was saved and grew up. Years later, when Llew had become an intelligent and talented musician, magician, and fighter who was proficient at handicrafts, he impressed Noada, King of the Tuatha de Danan, and became one of his military leaders against the Fomorians and thus he fought against his grandfather's army. He led the Tuatha de Danan into the second battle of the Mag Tuiard. Llew was such a good shot that he was able to land an arrow directly in Balar's only eye. The eye retreated and came out the other side of Balar's head, killing him with the very paralyzing gaze he had formerly used on his adversaries.

Boann/Boi/Boanna

Boann was the goddess of the river and considered mother of the cattle herds. Her symbol was a white cow. She was also a fertility and productivity goddess. Boann was the wife of the water god, Nechtan, but she had intimate relations with Dagda, Father of the Gods, with whom she conceived Aengus, the god of love. Boann had violated a most important prohibition, and when she came to the well of Nechtan she was enclosed by banks of earth and turned into the River Boyne. Boann's name is associated with salmon and almonds.

Bormo/Borvo/Bormanus

Bormanus was the god of the "truth that can't be seen". He had the ability to heal through the inspiration of dreams. Bormanus was the Celtic version of Apollo, and he too was associated with a golden harp, the flute, and the sun. Bormanus was also the god of healing and of the hot springs which were believed to have had medicinal properties.

Blodenwedd

The goddess of the sun and moon, Blodenwedd possessed a rare beauty, but she was the most disloyal of the goddesses.

Blodenwedd burst forth from a flower as a result of the magic of Math, who created her to be the wife of the hero Llew Llaw, whose mother, Arianrhod, swore that he should never marry. She was called sometimes called "white flower" and "flower aspect".

Blodenwedd was unfaithful to the husband for whom she had been given life. With her lover, she plotted to kill Llew. The pair managed to turn him into an eagle, but he was promptly returned to human form by Gwydion. Gwydion then killed Blodenwedd's lover and turned the goddess herself into an owl.

Blodenwedd's symbols are the white owl, the dawn, and the broom.

Belisama

This young fire goddess was connected with the rising sun. Her name meant "the shining and clear".

Belisana

Goddess of the forests, laughter, and healing, Belisana was related to the sun's heat as well as the wild animals and plants.

Belenus/Bel/Belanos/Beli

A god of fire and light, healing, inspiration, music, and truth, Bel was a powerful god indeed and considered the father of several early royal Welsh families. His name meant "light" and he may have been connected to the Celtic festival of light which was celebrated on the first of May. Bel carried a sword, harp, and javelin, all of which were made of gold.

Bran the Blessed/ Bendigeidfran

The son of Leer and the brother of Branwen and Manawydan, Bran was a giant fighter. His Welsh name was Bendigeidfran. Bran gave his sister, Branwen, the Welsh goddess of love, in marriage to Matholwych, King of Ireland, who treated her horridly.

To avenge the abuse of his sister, Bran, who was so large that no building could contain him, marched a Briton army against the Irish. The Britons won the battle, but only seven of Bran's soldiers were left alive. Bran himself was stabbed by a poison sword and mortally wounded. As his life ebbed away, Bran ordered his men to decapitate his body and to bury his head in the white mountain of London where it would protect the people from conquering enemies.

The seven remaining soldiers made set off to London with the giant's head, a journey which took eighty seven years. On the way, they stopped and enjoyed seven years of feasting in Harlech, and eighty years of joy in Gwales. During all this time, the head of Bran continued to speak and communicate as it did when Bran had a living body.

Branwen

One of the Welsh love goddesses, Branwen's name meant "white raven". She was also called "White Breast" and "Venus of the Northern Sea". Branwen's brothers were Bran, the giant fighter, and Manawydan the magician. Branwen was paired off with the King of Ireland, Matholwych, who behaved crudely toward her. This led to a protracted war with Bran, who hurried to punish his brother in law for his treatment of his sister. The beautiful Branwen's symbol was the white raven.

Bres

Bres was the son of the Fomorian prince Elatha. The Fomorians were a race of robbers or as others have put it, of evil-doers. Some have called the Fomorians a race of people having only one hand and foot each. Bres' mother, Erin, however, came from the Tuatha De Danan. Bres therefore had double loyalties. He was nicknamed "Gormack" – Full of a feeling of duty – he never did live up to this name.

Bres grew up twice as fast as was normal. He was appointed ruler of Ireland after Noada, the Tuatha De Danan king, lost his arm in a battle with the Fomorians and was unable to continue to his reign. According to the law of the Tuatha De Danan, only a man of perfect physical form could sit on the throne. Bres was chosen by the Tuatha De Danan to take the kings place and it was hoped that he would bring about an accord with the Fomorians that inhabited Ireland. It soon became apparent however that Bres was a ruler of evil intent and purposes who took advantage of his position for his own ends.

When the god of healing, Diansecht, created a prosthetic arm made of silver for Noada, making his body perfect once more, Bres escaped to his father, King of the Fomorians, and raised a large army. He marched this force into Ireland. At the same time Llew had beaten Noada in a chess game, and Noada gave him his kingship as a prize – for a period of thirteen days. Lug's responsibilities during this period included the commanding of the army in their battle against the invading Fomorians.

And so, in the second battle of Mag Tuaird, a particularly gory and bloody debacle, ateh Tuartha De Danan were victorious, due to the leadership of Lug, the god of such wisdom, and Bres himself was taken prisoner and jailed until he agreed to reveal to Llew the secret of his great strength and power.

Brigantia

The Welsh-Briton goddess of nature and the sun, Brigantia was also associated with the mountains, rivers, and valleys in the rural areas.

Bridget/Brede

An Irish goddess, Bridget was the daughter of Dadga. Like Minerva, the Celtic Bridget was the goddess of the hearth and the fireplace in the home.

Bridget was responsible for the holy flame and was associated with the sun. She brought inspiration and healing and aided poets and smiths in their crafts. She was the patroness of the prophets and fortune-tellers. Pregnant and birthing women would turn to this goddess for help and protection.

Bridget was said to have two sisters having the same name that wee associated with the art of healing. Actually however, these were two additional aspects of the trinity that made up the goddess Bridget. Bridget did not disappear with the spread of Christianity in Ireland. She was adopted into the Christian tradition as Saint Bridget of Kildare, where Bridget was associated with the foundation of the first convent in Ireland. Saint Bridget was said to have given all of her family's possessions to the poor and needy.

Saint Bridget retained many of the characteristics of the goddess Bridget, and fertility rites were an important part of her cult. The first of February, which was the sacred day of the Goddess Bridget, became the Christian holy day of St. Bridget.

Gaba/Gabis

The name Gaba meant "crystal". Gaba was the queen of darkness, as well as the elderly aspect of the 'mother of darkness'.

Gobannon/Govannon/Goibhniu

Gobannan, like the Greek Hephaestus was the heavenly metal worker. He was the god that forged a connection between the metals and sorcery or magic. Like Dagda, the father of the gods, Gobannon was a cross between a magician and a god. Fire changes the form of substances and also purifies them. The transformative fire was one of Gobannon's symbols. According to Irish myth, Gobannon invented the craft of ironworking, and he stood at the head of the three gods of metal working, and forging of weapons of the Tuatha De Danan. The others were Luchta and Kraiden. According to the belief, weaponry prepared by Gobannon would always hit its mark and kill the enemy. It was said of Gobannon that he was able to fashion a weapon with no more than three strikes of his hammer.

Gwalchmei

The son of Mei, Gwalchmei was a god of music and love. He was also strongly associated with hunting, with the fields, and with the times of day most appropriate for hunting – the early morning and the late afternoon.

Gwydion

Gwydion was the god of the arts. He represented generosity, eloquence, and also sorcery. He was considered a magician and the prince of the powers of the air. He could change his form at will. Gwydion was the son of Danu, and the brother of Amaethin, Gobannon, and Arianrhod. He was the nephew of Math. Gwydion was one of the twelve who brought the swan to the Celts.

One of the most famous Celtic myths relates that all the while that Math was not actually involved in war, he had to sit with his feet resting in the lap of a virgin. Gwydion's brother fancied the virgin who was thus serving Math. To help his brother, Gwydion stirred up a conflict which led to war, so that Math would abandon the maiden. When Math returned from battle and discovered the plot, he turned the virgin and Gwydion into animals for a period of three years.

When the three years were up and Gwydion returned to his original form, he helped Math create a beautiful woman from a flower for the hero Llew Llaw. The women that resulted from their efforts was the lovely Blodenwedd. She turned out to be unfaithful to her husband and with her lover plotted his death. Llew Llaw turned himself into an eagle and escaped their trap. Gwydion then turned him back into a human and killed the treacherous Blodenwedd and her lover.

Gwydion is associated with the harp, healing, and magic.

Gwyn ap Nudd

Gwyn ap Nudd was the all-powerful god of the "other world" as well as the wild god of hunting. Gwyn ap Nudd was associated with the souls of the dead, and was always accompanied by his faithful friend Dormart, the white dog with red ears.

Dagda

The name Dagda meant "the good god". He was also called "the good hand". Dagda was the Irish god responsible for life and death. He carried a huge staff with one end of which he could kill nine men at a blow, and with the other end he could bring them back to life.

Dagda was also the god of wisdom, abundance, and knowledge. He was the son of Danu, and he fathered Bridget and Angus. His wife was Morrigan. Dagda was the supreme god of the Tuatha De Danan. He was called "fire", "father of all", and "the lord of great wisdom". He was associated with abundant fruit trees and a pig that was always roasting while an additional swine was being raised.

Danu

Danu originated with the ever-changing Nemed. She was the Welsh mother goddess of the Tuatha De Danan – the people of Danu.

Danu was associated with wisdom and with control of all that existed. She was goddess of the air, of abundance, and of the groves. Some researchers associate her with the many rivers in Europe which bear her name or similar names.

Dwyn

The brave hearted Dwyn was the god of love and mischief. He was known as the tactician of the Celtic myths.

Dumiatis/Dumeatis

God of creative thought and study, Dumiatis was associated with children, children's stories, and the study of folklore. Ink and books were his symbols.

Donn

Nicknamed "the gloomy", Donn was the Irish god of death. Don was the god of the Gauls, offspring of Mil, the last race to conquer Ireland according to the Book of Invasions. Donn and his people arrived in Ireland during the celebration of the first of May, and beat the fifth group of conquerors, the Tuatha De Danan. However, Donn insulted the goddess of man, Erin, and she drowned him in the sea as punishment. According to the myth, the point at which Erin drowned Donn is now an island called Duin (House of Donn) and Donn dwells there still as the god of the dead. Myth held that all the dead went to this island on their way to the other world.

Diancecht

Physician to the gods, Diancecht was symbolized by the mortar and pestle with which dried herbs were ground into medicines in ancient times. In the Book of Invasions, it is told that Nuada, king of the Tuatha De Danan, lost his right arm in battle and was forced to give up his throne because of the law forbidding a handicapped person from ruling. Diancecht fashioned Nuada a silver arm and thus he was able to recover his kingship. After the second battle, Diancecht sang various incantations over a well, imbuing its waters with powers to heal the wounds of the injured fighters.

Deirdre/Deirdriu

The beautiful heroine Deirdre had a tragic life, followed by a tragic death. She was the daughter of Feidlimid, the poet of King Conchobar of Ulster. When Deirdre was an infant, the Druid Cathbad prophesied that she would grow to be a woman of unusual beauty but that she would bring death and destruction to Ulster.

Conchobar secretly adopted Deirdre with the intention of marrying her when she became of age. Before the marriage could take place, however, Deirdre fell in love with Naoise, and ran away with him to Scotland. Conchobar pressed the couple to return to Ulster, promising that they would come to no harm, and that he would send Fergus to accompany and guard them on their journey home. Conchobar did not keep these promises, of course, and instead of Fergus he sent his warrior, Eoghan, who killed Naoise and brought Deirdre to Conchobar in chains.

This action against Deirdre and her lover was a direct transgression of the Celtic code of honor. Fergus, shocked and angered at Conchobar's behavior, ordered his fighters to wreak havoc on Ulster, and breaking his bond with Conchobar, he defected to the enemy – Queen Madb of Conacht. A major war then broke out between Ulster and Conacht, and the second part of the Druid's prophecy came true.

This was not the end of the tribulations of Deirdre however. For an entire year she did not smile as she mourned her beloved, and not once did she even life her head. Conchobar, who was actually considered a kindhearted king and admired by his subjects, again showed the evil side of his nature. He asked her who among men she most despised. Deirdre answered, "Eoghan", the fighter who had killed her lover. Out of pure spite and meanness, Conchobar ordered Deirdre to live with Eoghan. The next day, two men came and dragged Deirdre to a carriage which was to bring her to Eoghan. As they drove, the carriage drew up next to a cliff, and Deirdre threw herself out of the carriage to her death.

Hellith

Goddess of the setting sun, Hellith was the keeper of the souls of the dead. The flute, with its relaxing and harmonic sound are associated with this goddess.

Hertha/Herdda

Hertha was the goddess of healing, earth, and rebirth. Her symbols were those of birth, renewal, and fertility, such as the cow and the calf, the milking pail, and the springtime.

Viviana/Vivian/Vivien

Viviana was the wife of Merlin, the famous Druid. This goddess was considered the goddess of birth, love, and motherhood. Women turned to her for assistance with the raising of their offspring and protection during childbirth and pregnancy. Viviana's symbol was a five-petalled red rose.

Tautha de Danan

According to ancient Irish mythology, the Tautha de Danan were a divine race of people that received knowledge, wisdom and strength, and lived on the northern islands of Greece and the Middle East. Some say they got to Ireland by way of Egypt and Asia. The Tautha de Danan were said to be the offspring of Nemed, son of Agnoman from Scythia. The name Tautha de Danan meant "children of Danu" or "family of Danu". Danu was the goddess of the race. The Tautha conquered what is today known as Britain. According to myth, when the Tautha arrived in Britain they brought with them the knowledge of the Druids – sorcery, arts, and sciences. According to Irish myths, astrology also numbered among their skills.

The Tautha de Danan were described in the myths and legends as a good looking race of strong, intelligent, and talented fighters. They were a mixture of mortal man and god. They often fell in love and married ordinary mortals. The Tautha de Danan were able to change form and to become invisible. They assisted their mortal admirers by giving them supernatural help, and brought death to their enemies.

The Tautha de Danan brought four magic objects to Ireland. These objects, ordered according to the direction of the clock, symbolize the four foundations of life: air, water, fire, and land – and the balance between them. At the northernmost point was placed the stone of Pal, and the unbeatable javelin of Log was at the eastern point. The sword that never missed its mark was put at the southern point, and Dagda's cooking pot that never empty was in the western spot. The Tautha de Danan were threatened by the invasion of the Milesians, the last race to overrun Ireland, and their king Dagda, decided to go underground and build a community below the earth's surface in caves and man-made lakes. The Celtic belief was that the Tautha de Danan dwelled forever in this other world, and will remain there until called forth again.

Taillte

The Irish goddess of the earth was the adoptive mother of Lug. The Tailtian games (the Irish answer to the Olympics) were named after her.

Taliesin

A Welsh poet, sorcerer, and musician, Taliesin was a prophet, and a wandering songster. He was nicknamed the "hands of the gods". He was lord of metamorphosis and his symbol was the harp. He may have lived in the sixth century, during the period of the leader who became "King Arthur" of the later legends. The myths about Taliesin and his songs are contained in the epic Mabinogion. Taliesin said of himself, "I sleep I am renewed, I was dead, and now I live, I was alive.... I am Taliesin".

Taranis

The Celtic god of thunderstorms, Taranis made the seasons appear in their cycles. He was identified with Jupiter, but apparently only the thunderous aspect of the Roman god. The symbol of Taranis was a wheel with eight spokes.

Tarvos/Trigaranos

Trigaranos was the Celtic god of growth and virility, and he was symbolized by the traditional upstanding oak and the potent bull.

Twrch Trwyth

A bewitched wild boar of huge proportions, Twrch Trwyth was an evil king whom the gods punished by turning him into a beast. According to the myth, the boar was hunted by King Arthur and by Mabon, son of Modoron.

Triana

Triana had three aspects to her character: Sun, earth, and moon. She was a goddess of healing, knowledge, and mental arts. She also oversaw life and death. Triana was an example of three within one, which characterized several gods in the Celtic tradition. As Ana-Sun Triana was a maiden. As Ana-Earth, she was a mother and the goddess of nature, life and death. As Ana-Moon she was an elderly goddess of love and wisdom.

Tethra

Goddess of the sea, magic, and sorcery, Tethra represented the airy aspect of water. Her symbols were the albatross, the seagull, and the rays of the moon.

Lancelot

Lancelot of the lake – was one of the best known Knights of the Round Table. He was considered the most handsome and desirable of all of King Arthur's knights, even considering the fact that he stained the knight's code of honor by betraying his king by his love and desire for the queen, Arthur's wife, Genevieve. Lancelot's affair with Genevieve made him "impure" and therefore unfit for the search for the Holy Grail, but it did little to change his legendary reputation and the admiration felt for him even to this day.

Lancelot was stolen from his parents when he was a year old by the Lady of the Lakes, Nimoi, the same Lady that had given Arthur the magic sword, Excalibur. Nimoi was also took Excalibur back into the lake after Arthur's death.

From the feminine point of view, Lancelot was the ideal Knight. His love for Genevieve sealed his fate. After the disappearance of Arthur, who had been taken by Morigan and his fairies to the island of Avalon, Lancelot became a priest and took care of the king's grave.

Lugh/Lug/Lleu/Llaw/ Gyffes

Lug, also called the "clear" or the "light" was a fighter-hero and the god that stood at the head of the Tautha De Danan. Llew was unusual in that he was not given a definitive job, and he fulfilled a wider variety of tasks than the other gods, each of whom usually had just one assignment. Llew was lord of all the arts and crafts, as well as god of the poets, singers, metalworkers, and even warriors. He was a powerful magician, and was known for his very generous ways. He as a fighter, but and also an artist skilled in music and all the crafts.

Lug was connected to the setting sun and the moon, the goat, the chicken, the turtle, and with sacks of coins and the magic sword. Llew was the son of Delbit. – the evil wind, and Eri. He was the grandson of Balar "the evil eye", leader of the monstrous Fomorians. According to a different version of the myth, his mother was Eithne who was trapped in a cave after Balar, leader of the Fomorians heard a prophesy by which his grandchild would grow up to murder him. In this version, Llew's father was Cain, one of the Tautha De Danan, who secretly mated with Eithne causing her to give birth to triplets. Balar destroyed two of the infants, but the third, Llew, survived.

Llew's rise to the leadership of the Tautha De Danan occurred due to the war between the Tautha and the evil robber Fomorians. Nuada, king of the Tautha De Danan, went to war with the monstrous race after they tormented the people of Ireland for quite a while. Nuada himself took part in combat, and lost an arm in battle. Tautha De Danan law would not allow an "imperfect" physical specimen of a man be king, so Nuada had to be replaced. In hopes of making peace with the Fomorians, Bres was chosen as Nuada's successor. Bres later had to give rule back to Nuada, when Diancecht, the physician, made Nuada a silver prosthesis to replace his lost limb. Bres was incensed by this upset and ran off to his father, king of the Fomorians. He gathered a large army and marched with it on Ireland.

Llew, the young hero, presented himself as a man of many talents and skills, and went out to prove his claims. At first, he called himself a musician. On the harp he played three Irish tunes – one that brought tears to the eyes, one that put listeners to sleep, and one that brought joy. Llew's immense strength was evident in his ability to return the stone of Pal – the same stone that took eighty oxen to move it – to its rightful place, and he proved his cleverness when he beat the king at a game of chess. Nuada, after he lost the chess game, announced to everyone that Llew was the smartest of them all. He awarded Llew his crown and rule for a period of thirteen days, during which the battle against the Fomorians took place.

Llew divided the various tasks among the groups participating in the war against the Fomorians. The Druids were assigned the gathering of the waters to hold back the Fomorian forces. The sorcerers were to cast spells on the enemy armies. The craftsmen went to work forging new weapons, and the fighters prepared for combat, and the healers who would care for the wounded gathered their supplies. Llew himself played only a small role in the actual battle, as he was of too much value to risk loss of life or limb. He did, however manage to cut out Balar's eye – the eye with which Balar could paralyze any man he gazed on – by hitting him with a well-aimed stone. Llew placed the Fomorians under the "supreme curse" – and victory was had. Llew's exemplary planning and organization brought about a decisive win for his armies. Bres was taken prisoner but was kept alive, pending his giving up of the secret of abundance.

Another version of this story concentrates on the conflict between Llew and Nuada, the Tautha De Danan leader. According to this account, Nuada chained Llew to a post, in order that he might claim for himself the glory of the victory. However, Llew, with his awesome bodily strength, managed to free himself from the chains and won the battle using his own might.

The cult of Llew spread far beyond Ireland, as we can see by the names of cities all around Europe. The ancient festival of Llewnasad was celebrated on the first of August was in honor of Llew.

It is possible that the ancient Celtic god Lugus and the Welsh Lau are actually identified with Llew.

Lugus

Lugus was a very popular god in the ancient Celtic countries. His name meant "shining" or "clear", and he may be the same as the Welsh and Irish hero Llew. Some say that when Julius Caesar spoke of the god Mercury (Gaelic god who invented art), that he was actually referring to Lugus.

Caesar Augustus started the August first festivals in honor of Lugus.

Luchta/Lucta/Luchtaine

An additional god of arts and crafts, Luchta was also the god of the carpenters and of the artisans who fashioned the shields used in battle by the Tautha de Danan. The shield was one of his symbols.

Llyr/Ler

God of the sea and king of the oceans, Llyr was known as a shy god. Llyr was half man and half fish, and could change his form at sill. Llyr was connected to the sea mammals, the sea serpents, shells, and sharks. He played a harp made of silver, pearls, corral and shell.

Mabon/Mapon/Maponus

Mabon was nicknamed "the heavenly son" and "the son of light". In the Celtic mythology Mabon was the god of sex, beauty, love, magic, as well as prophesy and power. In Gallia and Britain, where his cult was quite widespread, Mabon was called "Maponus" (heavenly son or heavenly youth), and the Welsh called him Mabon (son).

Mabon affected the youth of all in his surroundings. His symbol was the wild boar (which stood for power and the wild), and the lyre – a musical instrument which resembled the harp and stood for musicians and poets. He was also connected with mineral springs and their healing properties.

Medb/Maeve/Mab

Queen of Conacht, Maeve was a divine magician as well as goddess of earth. She was considered the most generous of her sisters and excelled in running races in which she was faster than a horse. She would compete in running while carrying a sword and shield in her hands and animals rode along on her back.

Maeve was the lover of many kings, and the only woman who succeeded in satisfying the sexual urges of the hero Fergus, urges which were seven times stronger than those of ordinary males. Maeve's daughter was Pindabaier, goddess of the underworld, who became pregnant from a mortal man. Maeve died from a piece of hard cheese which was shot from her nephew's slingshot in revenge for Maeve's murder of his mother.

Mei/Mai/Meia

Goddess of the sun and earth, mother of Gualchmi, and Mei was connected with the green fields and new grass.

Macha

Macha was an Irish queen, goddess of the sun, fertility and war. Like so many goddesses of fertility and war in the various mythological traditions, Macha represented the aspects of life that brought life (fertility) and death (war). Macha was the wife of Nemed and also of Nuada. She was nicknamed "woman of the sun". Macha was the daughter of Arnmas and the granddaughter of Nat. The red wing dynasty originated with Macha. Her major symbols were the raven (the classic Celtic symbol for war) and the horse, a symbol of strength and fertility as well as battle.

Mael Duin

A mythological Irish hero, Mael Duin went in search of the murderer of his father in order to avenge the death. He brought a large number of people on his journey – too many, according to the advice he was given be a Druid before setting out. When he neared the island where the murderer had taken refuge, a huge storm suddenly surged up and pushed his boat off course and away from the island. Mael Duin and his entourage wandered to many places where they met various wondrous and monstrous beings. They encountered ants the size of human beings, maidens who could make themselves invisible, wild pigs that gave off tremendous heat, and a "land of women" where an endless celebration was always at its height and aging was unknown. In the end, Mael Duin and his group returned to Ireland.

Manawyddan

A Welsh sorcerer-hero, Manawyddan was the son of Llyr. When Rhiannon's husband died, her son married her off to his good friend Manawyddan, hero of the third branch of Mabinogion legends.

Manawyddan's homeland was under a spell of some kind which caused the people and animals to disappear suddenly. Manawyddan and his wife, along with Rhiannon's son Pryderi and Pryder's wife Sigfa, came to England. After many magical adventures, Manawyddan discovered that the spell had been cast by a priest as revenge for the unjust way Pryderi's father, Pwyll, had behaved toward the priest's friend, Gwawl. Many years beforehand, Gwawl had been promised by Pwyll that he would received anything he requested. Gwawl asked for Pwyll's lover, Rhiannon, who had anyway already been promised him by her parents. Pwyll did give Rhiannon to him, but he then trapped Gwawl in an enchanted sack and forced him to return Rhiannon to him. The priest was now exacting revenge. When Manawyddan discovered the source of the enchantment of his homeland he returned there with his wife and her son, and managed to convince the priest to lift the spell.

Manannan/Manannan Mac Llyr

Manannan was the son of Llyr, the sea god and was himself an Irish sea deity in the Tautha De Danan. He was considered the guardian of Ireland, a country surrounded by the comforting presence of the sea. Manannan was known for his ability to change his form, and in addition to his dominion over the sea, he was god of sorcery and magic, and of travel. He was a teacher of other gods. With the help of his vast knowledge of sorcery, Manannan assisted Llew in the victory over the evil Fomorians. He provided Llew with an enchanted boat, horse, and sword. He also gave the king of Cormac a golden cup which cracked when lies were told in its presence and mended itself when truth was spoken. Manannan's home was the island called the "land of promise" and his wife was Rhiannon. Manannon carried a magic staff and an enchanted red javelin. He also had three magical swords called "Little Fury", "Great Fury", and "Retaliator". His helmet and cloak made their wearer invisible.

Math

The son of Mathonwy and the uncle and teacher of Gwydion, Math was a Welsh god of magic, wisdom, and sorcery. He was a well-known instructor and trainer of the Druids.

Math had an unusual attribute – whenever a war was not in progress, he was required to sit with his feet resting in the lap of a virgin who provided a source of energy for the god. Math's nephew Gilvaethwy fell in love with the Goewin, the virgin who was thus serving Math while the land was at peace, and needed a distraction for Math so that he could woo her. Gwydion, Gilvaethwy's older brother, stirred up a war with the neighboring country so that Math would be forced to release the virgin temporarily. When Math returned, he immediately understood that Gwydion had manipulated him, and he turned him and Goewin into animals for three years.

Math was now in need of a replacement virgin on whom to rest his feet. Arianrhod, sister of Gilvaethwy and Gwydion, volunteered for the task. In order to be sure of her viginity, Arianrhod had to undergo a test in which she passed over Math's magic staff. Not only did Arianrhod fail the test, but she immediately birthed twin children, Dylan and Llew. She forbade Llew ever to marry a human woman. Later, Math and Gwydion, both excellent sorcerers, created a gorgeous wife for Llew from a flower.

Modorona/Modoron/Madorna

Queen of death and goddess of magic, Modorna was also the deity of sexuality and fertility. She was the daughter of Llyr the sea god. The cypress tree (which was often planted in cemeteries) was her symbol.

Morrigan/Morrigana/Morrigu

A powerful sea goddess called "the great queen", and "mother of the great sea" Morrigan was the deity of life, death, and the seashore.

Morrigan was the patroness and guardian of the seafarers off the coast of Ireland. She was pleasant and gentle, but could become violent and dangerous when angered. Morrigan was also known as a goddess of beauty and knowledge and she was greatly endowed with both. Morrigan's lover was Dadga, with whom she would mate during the festival of Samhain.

Morrigan's symbols were the whale, the silver harp, pearls, and shells.

Mider/Midir

God of the underworld, husband of Etain, Mider was the Fairy King. Mider was known as a poet – singer and expert chess player. His symbols were the chessboard and its pieces.

Myrddin/Merddin

God of nature and the forests, laughter, the earth, and the heavens, Merddin was also a deity of healing and sorcery. Merddin expressed the fire aspect of the foundations of earth. He had a flute that made people get up and dance, and he worked with healing crystals and herbs.

Merlin

Merlin was the most famous of the Druid magicians and sorcerers and a most important character in the stories of King Arthur. Merlin was said to be a prophet that lived in the enchanted forest of Brittany, called Broceiand, in Scotland.

He was said to have lost his mind after witnessing horrible battle scenes. Geoffrey of Monmouth described the Merlin we are familiar with today in his "History of the British Kings" which he wrote in the year 1136. He described a magician-prophet who was responsible for bringing together Arthur's parents – King Uther and Queen Igraine, as lovers. Igraine was the wife of the Duke of Cornwall, but Merlin used enchantment to couple her with the king. When their son Arthur was born out of wedlock, Merlin educated and cared for him, secretly preparing him for his future as monarch.

According to the traditional stories, Merlin himself was born to the daughter of a king when a mysterious youth stole into her cloistered room. Geoffrey of Monmouth wrote in the twelfth century that Merlin's father was a robber.

Merlin's prophesies had great impact on many European scholars of the middle Ages. The building of Stonehenge is thought by many to have been connected to Merlin's magic – the huge stones having been brought from Ireland and erected as a monument to the British lords who perished at the hands of the Scots. The Round Table, around which the Knights of King Arthur sat, was also designed by Merlin.

Merlin's tragic end attests to the great power of the fairy world. Merlin fell deeply in love with Niviane, daughter of a Sicilian siren. Merlin shared with Niviane the depth of his knowledge of sorcery, until she rivaled the master himself in her magical abilities. When Niviane turned against her lover and teacher, she was able to trap him in an enchanted pine tree forever.

When the Knight Gowen passed the pine one day, Merlin spoke to him. His words were full of psychological relevance even for our day: "I am the biggest fool of them all. I loved another more than I loved myself, and I taught my love how to keep me dependent on her. Now nobody can free me."

Nantosuelta

Nantosuelta was a goddess of rivers and of abundance. Her name meant "winding stream". An ancient Gaelic stone tablet was found on which Nantosuelta is named as the wife of Sucellos, the hammer god. She always held a container of some sort in her right hand, and in her left she had a long staff on top of which was a sort of house. This house held up by a stick came to symbolize success and abundance. Nantosuelta was associated with ravens and with the dark months of the year.

Nehalennia

Nehalennia was the ancient goddess who assured safe passage across the North Sea. Her worshippers practiced sacrifice before setting off to sail the seas, and many of altars for this purpose have been found. The original source of the belief in Nehalennia is obscure. She may have been a Celtic or a Germanic goddess and it is known that her cult was practiced extensively in the third century.

Nuada

Nuada was the Father of the gods. He was the husband of the war goddess, Fea. A powerful leader, god of thunder, Nuada was also the god of rulers, rebirth, war, and wealth. He was called "Nuada the silver-handed" due to the prosthetic arm which the physician Diancecht made for him after he lost his own arm in battle. Nuada was the King of the Tuatha De Danan, the celestial race which was the fifth to conquer Ireland according to the Book of Invasions. Nuada led the Tuatha De Danan to victory over the Fir Bolg in the first battle of the Mag Tured, during which his arm was severed. Since according to law, only a man with no physical defect was allowed to be king of the Tuatha De Danan, Nuada had to step down. His replacement was Bres, "the handsome" whose father was king of the Fomorian enemies of the Tautha De Danan. It was thought that with Bres as king, peace could be achieved with their adversaries.

According to one version of the story, Bres was a careless king, and the land became desolate under his rule. Bres became fat and his face sprouted pimples, and he was forced off the throne. As revenge Bres went back to the Fomorians and raised an army to march with him against the Tautha De Danan. Meanwhile, Diancecht, physician to the gods, fashioned a silver prosthetic arm so realistic that it allowed Nuada to return to the kingship just in time for the impending war. However, when

Llew defeated Nuada in a chess match, Nuada saw that he was the better strategist, and gave him control of the armies of the Tautha for thirteen days. Thus it was Llew who led them to victory in battle against Bres and the Fomorians. In this battle (the second battle of the Mag Tured), Nuada, who took an active part in the fighting, was killed by Balar, king of the Fomorians (he of the evil eye). Llew himself was not active on the battlefield and served mostly behind the scenes, but after Nuada was felled, Llew killed Balar by hitting him right in his eye with a well aimed stone.

Nuada has possession of one of the four treasures of the Tautha De Danan – the "sword from which there was no escape". Nuada was associated with thunderstorms and lightening, and of course, the magic sword.

Nodens

Nodens was the god of sleep and dreams. The Celts believed that the sleeping state was a gateway to the "other world" and that dreams were mystical journeys into that world. Thus Nodens was associated with all that was possible in dreams and their interpretation. Nodens bore similarities to the Roman god Mars, who was admired by the Celts as a deity of sorrow.

Nwyvre

Astronomy and astrology were important to the Celts, and they accepted both disciplines as science. Nwyvre was the god of both as well as the god of the starry sky. He was the husband of Arianrhod and his symbole a nine-pointed star.

Nimue/Nimiane/Niniene/Nymenche

Nimue was the goddess of rivers and lakes, and was associated with the underground streams and sources of water. She was both student and teacher to Merlin the magician, and it was Nimue that fashioned and cared for the sword of Arthur – Excalibur.

Nechtan

Nechtan the water god was the husband of Boann, goddess of the river Boyne. Nechtan had a holy well of knowledge which only he and three water carriers had access to. Boann betrayed Nechtan with Dagda, father of the gods, and bore the god of love, Angus. When Boann tried to drink from the forbidden sanctified well, the earth rose up around her and formed banks, and she turned into a river.

Nemon/Neman/Nemain/Nemhain

Nemhain was an Irish war goddess. Like other goddesses of war, such as Morrigan, Nemhain did not take part in actual battle, but was a threatening presence, and an aggressive blood thirsty energy that infused the fighters with ability and bravery. At the same time, seeing her caused the enemy terror and panic. In the famous battle of Ulster against Conacht, Nemhain's blood-curdling howls caused one hundred Conacht soldiers simply to drop dead in their tracks.

Nemhain was the sister of Macha, goddess of the sun and fertility, who was also a war goddess. Like Macha, Nemhain was associated with ravens, but Nemhains additional symbol was the snake.

Nemed

According to the Book of Invasions, Nemed was the leader of the third race to invade Ireland, thirty years after the previous conquerors, under Parthalon, had taken over. He arrived in Ireland with four wives, and continued what Parthalon had started – the greening of Ireland by planting trees and forests and by developing successful agriculture. More lakes were created, and the landscape of Ireland took on a lush beauty.

Nemed was forced to battle the Fomorians and was successful

against them, until a cruel epidemic killed a large portion of his people. The Nemedians who survived lived under harsh Fomorian rule, and were forced to pay exorbitant taxes – two thirds of their crop, two thirds of their milk, and even two thirds of their children!

In the end, the Nemedians, led by Fergus, attacked the Fomorians, and Fergus killed their king – Conan. It was a hollow victory however, since only thirty Nemedians remained alive. These escaped into exile by sea. Some of the survivors settled in Britain, and others went to the "northern islands of the world". Others returned to their original homeland – Greece, where they were pressed into slavery. The offspring of these survivors the Fir Bolg (meaning sack people, denoting the sack cloth they were dressed in as slaves) returned to Ireland as the fourth race to invade and conquer her.

The survivors who settled in the northern islands later became the Tautha De Danan – the fifth group to invade Ireland.

Sadv

One of the most ancient Celtic deities, Sadv was considered a goddess of armies, forests, and nature. She was sometimes depicted as a woman from the "other world", and was able to change herself into a deer. Sadv's son was the poet-fighter Oisin (young deer), whom she raised wild in the forest. Sadv's was symbolized by the animals of the forest.

Sucellos

Sucellos was an aspect of the great father, and overseer of the dark months of the year. Sucellos was the twin brother of Dadga, god of the rivers, fertility, and death.

All over the Celtic world, and especially in Gallia, Sucellos was known as the very popular "hammer god". He was depicted as a bearded man carrying a very long handled hammer which he held high above his head. In his other hand he carried a pot.

Smertullos

Wearing a snake around his body as a belt, Smertullos was the lord of the unreachable deep, and of protection and guardianship. He was associated with the ram's head and the snake.

Cessair

The Book of Invasions tells us that Cessair was the woman who led the first wave of settlers of Ireland. According to myth, Noah's son came to Ireland forty days before the flood, and Cessair was his daughter. Cessair and her entire group were wiped out in the flood, with the exception of Cessair's husband, Fintan.

Parthalon

According to the Book of Invasions, Parthalon was the leader of the second race to conquer Ireland. Parthalon was the direct descendent of Noah and his son Japheth. Parthalon arrived in Ireland with five thousand people and four additional leaders, three hundred years after the flood. They ruled Ireland in an organized manner, and concentrated on bringing all the areas of the country under one cultural umbrella. They built new communities, raised cattle, and the populace became skilled in many crafts and occupations. Their enemies, the Fomorians, were the descendents of Ham, Noah's cursed son. In the end, an epidemic destroyed the Parthalon people, but not the Fomorians. Only one man was left alive from among the entire second invading race – Tuan Mac Starn.

Pwyll

Prince of Dyfed and later King of the "other world", Pwyll was always in the presence of dogs.

In the famous myth, Pwyll one day was out hunting, when he trapped a deer which had already been felled by some dogs which belonged to Arawn, king of the "other world", making it the king's property. Pwyll apologized for this encroachment and went into service to the king in payment. The two agreed to change places for a year. Arawn would be prince of Dyfed, and Pwyll would be monarch of the other world.

Pwyll had to quickly learn the customs of Annwn, the "other world". He succeeded in felling Arawn's arch enemy – Hafgan, and at the end of the year, Pwyll wanted to return to Dyfed and his own position as prince. When he returned however, he found that the people of Dyfed had grown used to the generous and agreeable rule of Arawn, and they did not wish to return to their previous situation. Pwyll promised to change in accordance to their wishes and to learn the generous ways of Arawn. The two exchanged many gifts, and Pwyll later began to be called Lord Arawn himself.

The love story about Pwyll and Rhiannon and the events the two shared, are a well known chapter in the Celtic tradition. One day, when Pwyll was riding his horse, he saw a lovely maiden on a white steed. He tried to chase her, but was too fast for him. When he stopped and called out to her, however, she turned and approached him. Then Pwyll realized – this was Rhiannon, daughter of Heveyth Hen. It turned out that Rhiannon was already in love with Pwyll and had been putting off a suitor of her parents' choosing named Gwawl. When Pwyll married Rhiannon, he approached Gwawl and offered him anything his heart desired. Gwawl declared that his only want was Rhiannon, and to make good on his promise, Pwyll sorrowfully gave up his wife to the man she had rejected. As Rhiannon left her husband, she handed him an enchanted sack which he later used to pry Rhiannon away from Gwawl once and for all.

Fomorian

The Fomorians were an evil monstrous race of robbers who, according to Celtic myth, were descendents of Ham, the accursed son of Noah. The Fomorians were sometimes depicted as people having only one hand and one foot. Bres, the king of the Formorians, had one giagantic eye which when it gazed upon a person, caused paralysis and death. The Fomorians were defeated in the second battle of the Mag Tured, by the Tuatha De Danan.

Findabair

A goddess of the underworld, the Celtics saw Findabair in a positive light having attributes of beauty, justice, and love. She was the daughter of the goddess-queen Maeve and a mortal father.

Finn mac Cumhal

Son of Cumhal, Finn mac Cumhal was the central figure in the Finian myths cycle. Finn was a military leader and head of the Fiana – an elite fighting group made up of the toughest soldiers and heroes. The Fiana were handsome, brave, and cold-blooded warriors who acted according to a strict code of rules and honor concerning women, war, and life. They had almost super-natural powers and outstanding intelligence. Their loyalty to Ireland was fierce.

Finn himself was a tall, blond, and of striking looks. He was a mighty fighter whose most burning desire was to avenge his father's death. Finn's own son was called Oisin.

Finn reorganized the Fiana and they fought many battles under his leadership. Men wishing to be accepted into the elite group had to undergo extremely rigorous tests. In one of these tests, the candidate dug a hole coming only to his knees, in which he stood with his shield and a stick. Then nine fighters, all armed with spears, attacked him from a short distance away. If he failed to deflect all nine spears, or if he came to any harm during the test, he was not considered Fiana material.

Finn lived in southern Ireland but he would hunt and fish in all of the uninhabited areas of the country, often going on trips during which he lived off his hunting prowess. He was not merely a military man, but also a prophet and a poet. He knew by heart the twelve Irish song books and was gifted with a special ability – when he bit his thumb he saw visions of the future and could read the thoughts of others.

One of the myths tells of the love of Cumhal, Finn's father and the previous leader of the Fiana, for the daughter of a Druid who forbade his daughter to see Cumhal and plotted to foil their love. Cumhal was killed by Goll, who had been sent by the Druid. The woman was already pregnant with Cumhal's child, and had a son who later became known as Finn. Finn learned the supernatural arts, and received the gift of prophecy after he burned his thumb on a cooked salmon of knowledge. He sucked on his thumb to ease the pain, and just that small taste of the magic salmon infused him with the special gift. Finn's teacher, then gave him his knew name, and from then on every time he bit his thumb he had access to any knowledge he desired.

Gaul had taken over the leadership of the Fiana after killing Cumhal, but when Finn came of age he overcame Goll and took the group into his own hands.

Many Celtic stories tell off the death of Finn. According to one of them, Finn was abandoned in his old age by the Fiana fighters and drowned in a river when he tried to prove he still had the strength of his youth. Another version holds that the hero simply went to sleep under the ground, and will someday return to Ireland, full of vigor and brawn when Ireland needs him most.

Fir Bolg

Fir Bolg was the name of the fourth race to overrun Ireland, according to the "Book of Invasions".

When the Fomorians conquered Ireland, some of the survivors went to Greece, their original homeland, where they were forced into slavery. They adopted the name Fir Bolg, which meant "sack people", denoting the sacks they wore and the type of work they did in the fields of Greece, covering boulders with earth they carried in sacks.

The Fir Bolg returned to Ireland and ruled there for thrity seven years during which their five leaders divided the country into five provinces: Ulster, Conacht, Lienster, Munster, and Meath. The Fir Bolg were beaten by the fifth race of invaders, the Tautha De Danan in the battle of the Mag Tured. In this battle, Eochaid, the ninth and last king of the Fir Bolg, was killed. The reign of the just and beloved Eochaid was thought of as the hayday of Ireland.

The Fir Bolg made peace with the new invaders and retired to the province of Conacht.

Fliodhas

Fliodhas, another goddess of the forests, was likely the earliest of all. Fliodhas protected the forested areas and the wild animals, and was associated with the underground springs and the fresh green fields and grass.

Fergus

The Irish hero, Fergus, was king of Ulster before Conchobar. He was a large man with superhuman strength and was famous for his military knowledge as well as his sexual prowess. One of Fergus' lovers was Ness, mother of Conchobar. Ness agreed to marry Fergus on one condition – that he allow her son Conchobar, who was at the time very young, to rule Ulster for one year. Out of his great desire for Ness, Fergus agreed to the condition.

Conchobar sat on the throne of Ulster, and at the end of the year had proven himself such a well-loved and respected young king, that the people were loathe to part with him. Fergus saw that it was best to allow Conchobar to remain in power and he made no trouble for him. In fact, he became his trusted helper and advisor. However, later Conchobar showed such callous treatment of his adopted daughter Deirdre – behavior that broke every rule of conduct by which Kings should abide. Fergus was so disappointed that he defected to Ulster's enemy – Conacht, and became the lover of Queen Madb. During the battle between Ulster and Conacht, Fergus and Conchobar were forced to fight hand to hand. Fergus was about to cut down his adversary when Conchobar's son, Cormak, intervened and begged Fergus to spare his father.

Fergus did not die a hero in battle. When the king of Conacht heard of his affair with the queen, he surprised the lovers as they bathed in a stream and killed Fergus on the spot.

Fer Diadh

Fer Diadh was an Irish mythological fighter, the adopted brother of Cuchulain. The two brothers were raised by the king of Ulster, Conchobar, and learned the military arts from a warrior witch, Scathach. Fer Diadh defected to the side of Ulster's enemy, and fought for Madb, the queen of Conacht.

The brothers tried not to have to fight one another directly, but in the end, Cuchulainnstood opposite Fer Diadh and killed him with one blow from his sword.

Cathbad

Cathbad was a fortunetelling Druid who figured strongly in the myths about Cuchulainnand Conchobar. Cathbad raised Conchobar, the legendary king of Ulster. It was Cathbad who nurtured him with stories of his impending glory, and taught him to wield his weapons to save Ulster in time of crisis.

Cuchulain

One of the best known of the mythological Irish heroes, Cuchulainn was only half-legendary. He seems to have actually lived during the first century. Cuchulainn was the son of Dechtere, sister of King Conchobar of Ulster. He was fathered by Llew, the supreme Celtic god, and leader of the Tautha De Danan. Llew often fought alongside his son, and even took his place when the going got the roughest in battle. Llew appeared in Dechtere's dreams, and informed her that he was planting a child in her womb. The infant was born with seven pupils in each eye, and seven fingers on each hand and foot.

Cuchulainn was raised by his aunt, Finchoem, but others assisted her in his education. Among them were Bly, Fergus, and Amargin. Cuchulainn was unusually handsome, tall and was full of joy. His pleasant qualities disappeared quickly however, when he took part in battle when rage took over his character.

Cuchulainn's heroic activities began when he was still quite young. At age five, the child went to the capital city of Ulster, and when he was seven, king Conchobar took him to a great celebration which was given by Colin the smith, and there the child was attacked by Colin's vicious watch dog. Without thinking twice, Cuchulainn killed the dog, but immediately apologized and offered to guard Colin himself until a replacement dog was found. (thus the name Cuchulainn – meaning "Colin's dog")

When he was still seven years old, Cuchulainn heard his tutor, Cathbad the Druid say that he was destined to live a short life but that his glory and fame would live after him. Learning this, Cuchulainn went to the king and asked for a weapon. This was at a time of great frustration for Ulster. Macha had placed a curse on the Ulster fighters which prevented them from taking part in battle. Since the young Cuchulainn was not included in the curse, he hurried to meet the enemies that were marching against Ulster in an effort to stop their advance. He called the sons of Madb who had destroyed a good portion of the Ulster army to battle, and managed to kill three of them.

In Cuchulainn's everyday life he behaved in a completely normal manner, but in battle, he was a crazed fighter full of fury. His body shook with violence, and one of his eyes sank into his forehead while the other strained forward, red and huge. His mouth could have swallowed the entire head of a man and his hair stood straight up on his head. When the battle ended, he had to rinse himself in three vats of cold water to revive from the insanity that had taken him over on the field. On one occasion it took one hundred naked women to distract him from his warrior rage. Each of the women held a bowl of cold water to cool the fighter's skin. Cuchulainn was embarrassed by the women's nakedness, and looked away. The first spray of water to hit his body turned to steam on contact, and the second boiled, and the third became very hot indeed. In this manner they managed to eventually calm and cool the hero.

In addition to his victories on the battle field, Cuchulainn was also talented in love. The legends about his adventures in romance are as many as those about his military rounds.

Queen Madb was the woman who finally did Cuchulainn in. She trapped him and forced him to eat the meat of a dog, food which he had absolutely forbidden himself. This transgression so weakened him that he was beaten by the son of one of his victims.

The cycle of legends about Cuchulainn greatly affected the development of the Arthurian tradition in Wales and England.

Conan

Conan was the son of Morna and the brother of Goll. Conan fought in the elite entourage of Finn. From Irish literature written in the twelfth century we learn that Conan had an impulsive and malicious character. Other writings describe him more as a comical figure – a glutton and a braggart.

In one of the legends Finn's fighters found themselves stuck to a floor in the "other world" as a result of an enchanted spell. After trying mightily to get free, they all succeed, save for Conan. His comrades finally free him, but the skin of his buttocks remains stuck to the floor.

Coventina

Goddess of the earth and the well, Coventina represents two aspects of motherhood and creativity. In accordance, she is also associated with the birth of infants, healing springs, and renewal.

Conchobar

Conchobar was the king of Ulster. He was the illegitimate son of Ness, Queen of Ulster. The Druid, Cathbad raised him. After Ness's husband died, his half brother, Fergus, inherited the throne. Ness became Fergus' lover on the condition that her young son Conchobar (who was only seven years old at the time) be given a chance to rule Ulster instead of Fergus for the period of one year. Fergus agreed, but after Conchobar ruled for a year, he had become so beloved by the people of Ulster that they would not allow Fergus to return to his reign. The people of Ulster so admired Conchobar that they began a new tradition whereby whenever any man took a wife Conchobar had the right to have sex with her even before the groom.

However, Conchobar's behavior toward his adoptive daughter, Deirdre, did not fit with the justice and reason the people had come to expect from him. When Deirdre ran away with her lover, Naoise to Scotland Conchobar promised the couple that no harm would befall them should they return to Ulster. When they arrived, however, he did not hesitate to murder Naoise and to put Deirdre in chains. Fergus was so disappointed and pained by Conchobar's behavior that he left Ulster and defected to Conacht where he had an affair with Queen Madb.

The ensuing war between the two provinces was won by Conchobar, mostly thanks to the bravery of the hero Cuchulainn. Conchobar died seven years after he was hit by a stone bullet launched from a slingshot. The stone lodged in Conchobar's brain and took seven years to kill him.

Conla

Conla was one of Finn's famous fighters. The most famous story involving Conla involved the "other world".

One day a woman seen only by Conla, appeared before him and begged him to join her in the happy land of the "other world" – an enchanted land of constant joy and satisfaction. The mysterious woman was sent away by Conla's father, who used his mystical Druid powers to expel her. As she left, however, she threw an apple to Conla. Conla ate the apple for a month, swallowing part of it day after day, but the apple was not consumed.

Conla wanted desperately to see the woman again, and when she finally did return he was susceptible to her invitation. Conla and the woman set sail in a glass boat and were never seen again.

Cordemanon

A god of knowledge, dynasty, and travel, Cordemanon was associated with the Circles of Stone, and with holy sites as well as with the great book of knowledge.

Cliodna

The young aspect of the goddess of the darkness, Cliodna was the goddess of birds, and was always accompanied by a flock of charmed winged creatures. Cliodna was extraordinarily beautiful, could change her form, and was associated with apple trees.

Camulus

A god of war who carried a giant sword on which was impaled the head of an enemy; Camulus was associated with clouds and storms.

Kerridwen

Kerridwen was the "mother of all" and considered "nine in one". She was the goddess of knowledge, wisdom, and inspiration. One of her strongest symbols was the potter's wheel. Kerridwen was another example of three aspects in one deity – or "three in one". In Kerridwen we see this multiplied by three, making her "nine in one".

The Celtic tradtion uses the three in one to describe the trinity of energy of the three worlds: The 'other world' of the fathers, this world, the earth and living creatures, and the heavens – home of the gods.

Kerridwen, the Mother goddess, had two moods, as does nature – the light and the dark. Each of these in turn had three aspects. Everything, whether it belonged to the light or the dark, had a beginning, middle, and end. In the case of humans this was reflected in youth, adulthood, and old age (or birth, life, and death). Positive, neutral, and negative were another expression of the three aspects.

The number three was the number consecrated to this goddess. She was worshipped in all three of her aspects – as mother, daughter, and grandmother, which were connected to the phases of the moon and the yearly calendar.

As a virgin or young maiden, Kerridwen gathered her powers, saving them and strengthening herself. As the mother, she spent her energies, and as an old woman she emptied her store of powers.

One of the famous myths about Kerridwen tells that she prepared a magic dish in her pot, a dish which took a year to cook. Anyone who partook of three drops of this, would immediately know all the secrets of the past, and be able to predict the future. By mistake, Gwion, the young cook's assistant, spilled three drops of the mixture on his hand and impulsively licked them off. He instantly attained all the knowledge of the world, and realizing what he had done, he ran off. Kerridwen followed him, but Gwion changed his form several times during the chase until finally he changed himself into a grain of wheat. Kerridwen then changed herself into a chicken and swallowed him!

Some consider this story a metaphor which tells of an innocent man, usually young, and in the formative years of his spirit and body, suddenly finds himself in possession of secret knowledge of the universe. Without thinking, he takes this knowledge on, and the hugeness of the knowledge itself destroys him. This is seen as a warning to those who would seek that which they are not ripe to know.

Creiddylad/Creudylad

Daughter of Llyr the sea god and the queen of the sea herself, Creiddylad later appeared in plays by Shakespeare as the Welsh goddess Cordelia.

Creidne

God of the braziers and of armor, Creidne was associated with metal working and other crafts. He was one of the three gods that worked with his hands.

Kernunnos

Described as an old man with the ears and horns of a deer, Kernunnos was the "horned one" and sometimes accompanied by a snake which had the horns of a ram. On the ruins of an ancient altar, Kernunnos is depicted holding a basket full of cakes and coins. On a silver bowl found in Denmark, he is shown sitting with crossed legs, surrounded by two bulls, a large deer, two lions, and two wolves. Next to him sits a child with a dolphin's back. From this bowl we get a clear idea of Kernunnos as the god of the animals.

Kernunnos was associated with life, fertility, wealth, abundance, and knowledge as well as the animal world. Many statues of this god with horns on his head have been found in sites from the ancient Celtic world – mostly what is today northern France (Gallia) and Britain. Kernunnos was a god of dead, as well, and had connections with the underworld. The ancient Celts would lay small stone wheels on the graves, symbolizing Kernunnos, in hopes that this would light the way of the dead in the underworld.

Kernunnos was sometimes associated with Mercury, the Roman god whose task it was to accompany the souls on their way to the land of the dead, and with Apollo, the Greek god of light.

Rosemerta

Rosemerta was the younger aspect of the mother goddess. She was the goddess of abundance and success. Her symbols were fresh green gardens, flowers, and horns of plenty.

Rhiannon

Sometimes called "Queen Mother", Rhiannon's original name was Rhigatona. She was the goddess of knowledge and power.

Rhiannon's parents promised her in marriage to Gwawl, but she was secretly in love with Pwyll. One day while each was out riding they chanced to meet, and Pwyll realized he was in love with Rhiannon. They hurried to wed, and at their wedding reception Pwyll promised Gwawl that he would compensate him by making any wish he had come true. Gwawl's one wish, however, was that Rhiannon be his, and Pwyll was bound by honor to keep his promise, so he sadly let Rhiannon go. As she parted from Pwyll, Rhiannon handed him a magic sack. One year later, Pwyll arrived at the home of Rhiannon and Gwawl disguised as a beggar, and in his hand was the magic sack. Using various tricks, he trapped Gwawl within the sack, and threatened not to let him out until he agreed to give up Rhiannon.

This was not the end of Rhiannon's story however. The next chapter was even more painful. Rhiannon gave birth to Pwyll's son and named him Pryderi. One day the child disappeared without a trace. Rhiannon was accused of the crime! She was sentenced to sitting at the gate to the palace, telling of her deed to every passer by and carrying them on her back. Soon, however, the child reappeared in the company of a robber who had been caught stealing calves in a nearby province. Rhiannon was restored to her rightful place on the throne next to her husband and she forgave her people for treating her so wrongfully.

Rhiannon's symbols were apples, horses (especially mares), and three birds.

contents

Gods of Greece and Rome

Gods of Ancient Egypt

Persian Mythology

Gods of Ancient Sumaria and Mesopotamia

The Great Celtic Epics